2

MORE WORDS YOU NEED

B Rudzka, J Channell, Y Putseys, P Ostyn

**MACMILLAN
PUBLISHERS**

First published 1985
Reprinted 1985, 1986

Published by *Macmillan Publishers Ltd*
London and Basingstoke
*Associated companies and representatives in Accra,
Auckland, Delhi, Dublin, Gaborone, Hamburg, Harare,
Hong Kong, Kuala Lumpur, Lagos, Manzini, Melbourne,
Mexico City, Nairobi, New York, Singapore, Tokyo*

Filmset by August Filmsetting,
Haydock, St. Helens.

Printed in Hong Kong

More words you need.
    1. Vocabulary———Problems, exercises, etc.
    2. English language———Text-books for foreigners
I. Rudzka, B.
428.1'076   PE1128

ISBN 0–333–36071–0

Contents

Preface

This book, like its companion *The Words You Need*, sets out to organise the acquisition of language skills within the context of a structured approach to language teaching. It is intended for late intermediate and advanced students who, having mastered the main grammatical structures and basic vocabulary of English, wish to extend their expressive and comprehension skills by increasing both the number of words they know, and their knowledge of how and when words are used. The book may be used equally well for self-study or as a course book. A full key to the exercises is provided in the Teacher's Book.

The approach is a completely new one, adapting insights from theoretical linguistics and psycholinguistics to the service of the language learner. Words are presented in sets whose members have similar meanings, which allows precise and detailed information about meaning and use to be given in an economical and thence learnable way. The techniques of vocabulary analysis used here have a wider application than just the material in this book, since once the analytical techniques are understood, they can be applied to any new vocabulary the student meets. Students using these materials not only learn new words, they also gain a greater sensitivity to vocabulary in general, relationships between words, and the important notion of appropriateness.

A teacher's book accompanies this student's book. In it we explain the teaching methods used and give practical guidance on the many and varied uses to which the material can be put.

Dictionaries consulted

The Barnhart Dictionary of New English 1963–72, London: Longman, 1973
Britannica World Language Dictionary, Edition of Funk and Wagnells Standard Dictionary, Volumes 1 and 2
Cassell's English Dictionary, London: Cassell, 1975
The Compact Edition of the Oxford English Dictionary, Volumes 1 and 2, London: Oxford University Press, 1971
A Dictionary of Slang and Unconventional English, Volumes 1 and 2, London: Routledge and Kegan, 1970
Oxford Advanced Learner's Dictionary of Current English, A S Hornby, E V Gatenby and H Wakefield, London: Oxford University Press 1975
Longman Dictionary of Contemporary English, London: Longman, 1978
Oxford Dictionary of Current Idiomatic English, Volume 1, London: Oxford University Press, 1975
The Oxford Illustrated Dictionary, Oxford: Clarendon Press, 1976
The Penguin English Dictionary, Harmondsworth: Penguin Books, 1973
Roget's Thesaurus, Harmondsworth: Penguin Books, 1973
Webster's New Students Dictionary, New York: American Book Company, 1964
Webster's New World Dictionary of the American Language, Cleveland and New York: The World Publishing Company, 1968
Webster's Third New International Dictionary of the English Language, Unabridged, Springfield, Mass.: GC Merriam Company, 1976

To the Student

How do you learn new words? If you have thought about this question, you may have decided that it is necessary to meet a new word several times, in different contexts, and to consult a dictionary, before you can be sure of it. In this book we save you time and effort by giving you all the information you need to use new words correctly. We show you how they are related to words you already know, and we teach you techniques which you can apply to any new vocabulary you come across on your own.

You may not have seen analyses of vocabulary like those in the Word Study sections before, but do not be discouraged! In Unit 1 you will find explanations of how to understand the grids and the terminology. Here are a few tips on how to use the book:

Once you have read the texts in any unit, go through the Word-Study section. You are not expected to learn the contents of the componential grids (analysis of meanings) by heart – rather you should start working through the exercises and keep going back to the Word-Study section or the texts when you find something you can't answer. You should aim to be able to give the answers to the exercises instantaneously when asked to do so in class, as this will be a similar situation to spontaneous speech. In this connection you are advised to pay special attention to the collocational grids (which words go with which) and example sentences. You will find the Word-Study slow at first but as you become more familiar with the method you will speed up.

Abbreviations

abbr	abbreviation	*of*	old-fashioned
Am	American	*sb*	somebody
Br	British	*sl*	slang
coll	colloquial	*sth*	something
esp	especially	*US*	United States of America
fig	figurative	usu	usually
lit	literally	*vulg*	vulgar

Symbols

★ indicates that the word or phrase used is considered incorrect

⇒ indicates the figurative sense of the word

{} used to enclose features which apply to more than one word

American and British English

This book teaches standard British English. Yet much written English is American, and you should be able to recognize and understand American English. Differences of spelling are noted below, with the unit number in which each word appears. The differences are not noted in the units. You will see that most of the differences are systematic.

AMERICAN	BRITISH
1 CONSONANT DOUBLING	
l → ll	
counseling (7)	counselling
fueled (10)	fuelled
grueling (6)	gruelling
labeled (1)	labelled
traveling (3)	travelling
others	
focusing (10)	focussing
program (6)	programme

(note that British English uses the American spelling for **program** when it refers to a **computer program** (8))

AMERICAN	BRITISH
2 . . . . . or → . . . . . our	
behavior (5)	behaviour
behavioral (9)	behavioural
favor (7)	favour
favored (5)	favoured
harbor (10)	harbour
humor (3)	humour
labor (6, 7)	labour
neighbors (8)	neighbours
neighborhood (1)	neighbourhood
3 . . . . . er → . . . . . re	
center (3, 7, 8, 10)	centre
fiber (2, 9)	fibre
meter (3)	metre
self-centered (3)	self-centred
4 s → c	
license (2)	licence
offense (8)	offence
5 others	
mold (3)	mould
cozy (4)	cosy

Stylistic distinctions

Where a word's use is limited to one particular style, we have pointed this out. We have also noted when a word should **not** be used in a certain style. The descriptions used in this connection should be understood in the following way:

slang   not accepted as correct English, not used in writing except personal letters. Used between close friends or members of a social group to express intimacy or sense of community eg criminals, students

colloquial   used between close friends, or people of equal age and social standing eg relations, work colleagues

informal   used between friends and acquaintances in informal settings eg parties, meals, classroom situations and in some publications eg popular newspapers

formal   used between people of unequal age or social standing, or people meeting for the first time. Also used, for example, in lectures, conferences, legal proceedings, academic writing, official documents and reports, and in business correspondence

literary   used in creative writing, novels, poetry, etc

These stylistic distinctions are intended as a general guide and are in no way definitive or exhaustive.

Acknowledgements

The inspiration for these books came directly from the work on semantic fields and lexical structure of Adrienne Lehrer from the University of Arizona, and we owe her a particular debt for her encouragement and continued interest.

We are most grateful to Sandra Colen, René Dirven, Roger Flavell, John Green, Adrienne Lehrer, Jacques van Roey, Emma Vorlat, and Don. Young, who read, reviewed and criticised sections of the manuscript. We would also like to express our thanks to the following people, who provided examples, comments, suggestions and the opportunity to discuss recalcitrant points: Alessandra Bini, the Channell family, Patrick Griffiths, Peter Kelly, Androulla Kyriacou, Mary Ann Martin, Maryam Mathis, Conny Templeman, Margie Thomas, Ludolph van Hasselt, June Wickboldt. The following people arranged or took part in tests and trials of the material: René Dirven and his seminar students at the University of Trier, Germany; students of English at the Katholieke Universiteit te Leuven, Belgium; and students at York Advanced English Summer School, summer 1978.

In preparing *More Words You Need*, we are fortunate in having had the benefit of comments from teachers and students who have used *The Words You Need*, and in this connection we would like to thank especially Ron Carter at the University of Nottingham for the constructive suggestions and feedback he has given us.

Unit 1   Live and learn

The Pygmalion Effect Lives

by ROBERT ROSENTHAL

Pygmalion created Galatea out of ivory and desire. In Ovid's account, Pygmalion fell in love with his own sculpture of the perfect woman, and Venus, who spent a lot of time granting requests in those days, gave life to Galatea.*

Psychologists have not yet learned how to produce Galatea or her male equivalent in the laboratory, but they have demonstrated that the power of expectation alone can influence the behavior of others. The phenomenon has come to be called self-fulfilling prophecy: people sometimes become what we prophesy for them.

Self-fulfilling prophecies even work for animals. Bertrand Russell, who had something to say about nearly everything, noticed that rats display the 'national characteristics of the observer. Animals studied by Americans rush about frantically, with an incredible display of hustle[1] and pep[2], and at last achieve the desired result by chance. Animals observed by Germans sit still and think, and at last evolve[3] the solution out of their inner consciousness.'

FONDLING[4] SMART RATS. Russell was not far off. We told a class of 12 students that one could produce a strain[5] of intelligent rats by inbreeding[6] them to increase their ability to run mazes[7] quickly. To demonstrate, we gave each student five rats, which had to learn to run to the darker of two arms of a T-maze. We told half of our student-experimenters that they had the 'maze-bright', intelligent rats and we told the rest that they had the stupid rats. Naturally, there was no real difference between any of the animals.

But they certainly differed in their performance. The rats believed to be bright[8] improved daily in running the maze – they ran faster and more accurately – while the supposedly dull[9] animals did poorly. The 'dumb[10] rats refused to budge from the starting point 29 per cent of the time, while the 'smart'[11] rats were recalcitrant[12] only 11 per cent of the time.

Then we asked our students to rate the rats and to describe their own attitudes toward them. Those who believed they were working with intelligent animals liked them better and found them more pleasant. Such students said they felt more relaxed with the animals; they treated them more gently and were more enthusiastic about the experiment than students who thought they had dull rats to work with.

If rats act 'smarter' because their experimenters think they are 'smarter', we reasoned, perhaps the same phenomenon was at work in the classroom. So in the mid-1960s a colleague and I launched what was to become a most controversial study.

INTELLECTUAL BLOOMERS[13]. We selected an elementary school in a lower-class neighborhood and gave all the children a nonverbal IQ test at the beginning of the school year. We disguised[14] the test as one that would predict 'intellectual blooming'. There were 18 classrooms in the school, three at each of the six grade levels. The three rooms for each grade consisted of children with above-average ability, average ability, and below-average ability.

After the test, we randomly[15] chose 20 per cent of the children in each room, and labeled[16] them 'intellectual bloomers'. We then gave each teacher the names of these children, who, we explained, could be expected to show remarkable gains during the coming year on the basis of their test scores. In fact, the difference between these experimental children and the control group was solely in the teacher's mind.

Our IQ measure required no speaking, reading, or writing. One part of it, a picture vocabulary, did require a greater comprehension of English, so we called it the verbal

* In Greek mythology, Pygmalion fell in love with a statue he had made of a beautiful girl, Galatea. She was brought to life by his prayers.

subtest. The second part required less ability to understand language but more ability to reason abstractly, so we called it the reasoning subtest.

We retested all the children eight months later. For the school as a whole, we found that the experimental children, those whose teachers had been led to expect 'blooming', showed an excess in overall IQ gain of four points over the IQ gain of the control children. Their excess in gain was smaller in verbal ability, two points only, but substantially greater in reasoning, where they gained seven points more than the controls. Moreover, it made no difference whether the child was in a high-ability or low-ability classroom. The teachers' expectations benefited children at all levels. The supposed bloomers **blossomed**[17], at least modestly.

EXPLAINING THE PYGMALION EFFECT. The current evidence leads me to propose a four-factor 'theory' of the influences that produce the Pygmalion effect. People who have been led to expect good things from their students, children, clients, etc. appear to:

— create a warmer social-emotional mood around their 'special' students (*climate*);

— give more **feedback**[18] to these students about their performance (*feedback*);

— teach more material and more difficult material to their special students (**input**[19]); and

— give their special students more opportunities to respond and question (**output**[20]).

We still do not know exactly how the Pygmalion effect works. But we know that often it does work, and that it has powers that can **hinder**[21] as well as help the development of others. Field and experimental studies are beginning to isolate the factors that will give some insight into the process. Such awareness may help some to create their Galateas, but it will also give the Galateas a chance to fight back.

Psychology Today

THE PYGMALION EFFECT LIVES

1 *coll* hurrying, doing things quickly and with energy, putting pressure on others so that they hurry
2 *Am sl* energy, go, activity
3 develop
4 touching, stroking and caressing lovingly
5 a breed, a line of ancestors and descendants
6 breeding from closely related animals
7 a construction of interconnecting passages without a direct route from one side to the other
8 clever
9 slow in understanding, stupid
10 *Am coll* stupid, foolish, *Br* thick, dim
11 *Am coll* clever, skilful
12 disobedient
13 people who have developed to be clever or beautiful, *lit* plants which produce many flowers
14 changed the appearance of in order to deceive
15 deliberately selected freely and irregularly, not according to any criteria or set pattern
16 put a label on, called
17 *lit* opened into flowers, had flowers
18 information which comes back to the originator of something about its effect
19 what is put in or fed into something, usually a process
20 what comes out, is produced
21 obstruct

DOWN WITH SCHOOL!

School is an institution built on the **axiom**[1] that learning is the result of teaching. And institutional wisdom continues to accept this axiom, despite overwhelming evidence to the contrary.

Most learning happens casually, and even most intentional learning is not the result of programmed instruction. Normal children learn their first language casually, although faster if their parents pay attention to them. Most people who learn a second language well do so as a result of odd circumstances and not of **sequential**[2] teaching. They go to live with their grandparents, they travel, or they fall in love with a foreigner. Fluency in reading is also more often than not a result of such **extra-curricular**[3] activities. Most people who read widely, and with pleasure, merely believe that they learned to do so in school; when challenged, they easily **discard**[4] this illusion.

Everyone learns how to live outside school. We learn to speak, to think, to love, to feel, to play, to **curse**[5], to **politick**[6] and to work without interference from a teacher. Even children who are under a teacher's care day and night are no exception to the rule. Orphans, idiots and schoolteachers' sons learn most of what they learn outside the 'educational' process planned for them. Teachers have made a poor showing in their attempt at increasing learning among the poor. Poor parents who want their children to go to school are less concerned about what they will learn than about the certificate and money they will earn. And middle-class parents **entrust**[7] their children to a teacher's care to keep them from learning what the poor learn on the streets. Increasingly, educational research demonstrates that children learn most of what teachers pretend to teach them from **peer**[8] groups, from comics, from chance observations, and above all from mere participation in the ritual of school. Teachers, more often than not, obstruct such learning of subject matters as goes on in school.

Half of the people in our world never set foot in school. They have no contact with teachers, and they are deprived of the privilege of becoming **dropouts**[9]. Yet they learn quite effectively the message which school teaches: that they should have school, and more and more of it. School instructs them in their own inferiority through the tax collector who makes them pay for it, or through the demagogue who raises their expectations of it, or through their children once the latter are **hooked on**[10] it. So the poor are robbed of their self-respect by subscribing to a **creed**[11] that grants salvation only through the school.

Ivan Illich, *Deschooling Society*

DOWN WITH SCHOOL

1 a principle or statement accepted as a basis for further research
2 following in order of time or place
3 not part of the curriculum but part of school or college life, eg athletics, fraternities, campus publications, etc
4 put aside
5 swear, use bad language
6 take part in political discussion or activity
7 give to another the responsibility for
8 equal in rank, age, etc
9 *coll* a student who leaves school or college before graduation, or a person who refuses to take a job and join society in the normal way
10 *coll* dependent on something to the extent of not being able to live normally without it, originally used for drugs, but now with wider use, *lit* caught with a hook
11 system of beliefs

A-level disillusionment

Anne Barrie's *Do We Over-educate Our Children?* reminded me that the German author Günter Grass once said failing his school leaving exams was a blessing without which he would never have achieved the position he now holds. I wonder how many other great men and women owe their success to having failed in their academic careers.

I was a schoolgirl in the 60s – the time when it was believed that the future wealth of the country depended on the education of the young: money was plentiful, new universities sprang up and great myths evolved to **lure**[1] young people into the academic life. And so I too became that magic person – a student.

Three years later, I obtained a first-class degree in mathematics. For some months there had been pressure to remain and try for a further degree – the more postgraduate students there are, the more financial benefits exist for the professor and for the department.

My fellow postgraduates and I knew nothing of the outside world, and happily believed that academic life for another three years would **enhance**[2] us in the eyes of future employers; and so I went to London and began work for a doctorate.

Here, for the first time, I came across 'mature students' – people who had left school at 16 and, years later, taken **A-levels**[3] at technical colleges and come to university. Having chosen their subject with great care, and being more mature, they found a joy in their courses unknown to most of us.

I have been working now for several years: life has been very different from what I had been led to expect. Many friends and colleagues have discovered that their chosen course of study has been a mistake and that they are unsuited to the work available. However, it is too late to change: the state understandably will not pay to re-educate people completely. As I think back, I regret that I did not fail my A-levels.
Dr M D B, London W6

Good Housekeeping

A-LEVEL DISILLUSIONMENT

1 attract, entice, tempt
2 add to the value of
3 *abbr* for General Certificate of Education, Advanced Level (school-leaving exams in GB, necessary for admission to University)

NIGHT SCHOOL

1 walking wearily and heavily or with an effort
2 crowding
3 *Am* fully-developed, *lit* of young birds having got their adult feathers, *Br* fully-fledged
4 with red cheeks denoting health
5 enrolled for
6 education for adults
7 number of students enrolled or written on the list of regular students
8 *Am* period of continuous teaching in university, usually about 12 weeks in length, *Br* term

Night School

Each weekday evening, a reverse rush hour takes place in Manhattan's Greenwich Village. While most New Yorkers are **trudging**[1] home from their jobs, a few thousand others are **piling**[2] into the three modern buildings that house the New School for Social Research. The 54-year-old institution is a **full-fledged**[3] university, but most of its students are not concerned with accumulating credits or earning degrees. Nor are they **apple-cheeked**[4] youngsters: a typical New School student is the wage-earning adult who has **signed up for**[5] a course in anything from sociology to computer programing to creative knitting in an effort to broaden his intellectual or occupational horizons. 'I don't want my mind to fall asleep while I have to work,' says a young banker who has signed up for a course in psychology.

The New School today remains the only degree-granting university in the nation devoted primarily to the education of adults. As such, it may well be riding the pedagogical wave of the future. Recently, the Educational Testing Service reported that nearly 80 million adult Americans want or need **continuing education**[6], but that less than half of them are getting it. Reflecting this thirst for learning, **enrollment**[7] at the New School has doubled in the past decade, and of the 13,000 students taking one or more of its 875 courses this **semester**[8], more than 80 per cent attend evening classes.

Newsweek

Aye, He's A Changed Man!!

When my No. 1 son was accepted for university, it seemed a good idea to me.

The fact he would no longer go through the **larder**[1] like a plague of **locusts**[2] every other night was bound to reduce housekeeping bills.

So, back in October, a tall, **clean-limbed**[3], innocent fresh-faced 17-year-old packed his **grip**[4] and headed into the unknown.

His mother **sobbed**[5] quietly into her **hankie**[6], I **relished**[7] the prospect of having the bathroom to myself of a morning.

I should add that, up till then, he had shown very little outside interest in anything but **Partick Thistle**[8] and the **exploits**[9] of that **sterling**[10] **bunch**[11] of musicians, The Who.

The change when he came home at the end of term was cataclysmic.

For a start, there was the minitache.

You couldn't call it a moustache. It was an under-nourished **seven-a-side**[12] that could have passed for a **streak**[13] of dirt at thirty paces.

I said as much, laughing heartily.

I was rewarded with a **scathing**[14] look and a comment to the effect that thin upperlip **adornment**[15] was the **in-thing**[16] among the **cognoscenti**[17].

It **transpired**[18] the **lad**[19] had broadened his interests by joining the debating society, the chess club, the **karate**[20] club, and music appreciation.

I wondered aloud how a former disciple of The Who could appreciate music of any kind.

The reply was another curl of the lip and the information that 'one's musical tastes cover a wide spectrum'. It was impossible to shut him up. **Weird**[21] and wonderful words literally sprayed out of him. Like **infrastructure**[22], **viability**[23], **through-put**[24].

When I mentioned I was sick of his nonsensical views about **devolution**[25] he **riposted**[26] with, 'I take your point, but—'

He took my point approximately 14 times over the following few days in a series of wide-ranging discussions – from whether Enoch Powell was adopting the correct attitude towards our coloured population, to whether Par-tick Thistle had sufficient depth of resources to stay in the Premier League.

Then he astounded his mother by producing what he described as 'a **frivolous**[27] little wine' to accompany her **mince and tatties**[28].

It added, he informed her, a 'touch of **je ne sais quoi**[29] to a rather pedestrian dish'.

At this point, his mother fetched him what I can only describe as a viable **clout**[30] around the infrastructure of his left earhole.

It must have brought him down to earth, because the following day he presented her with a half-pound box of chocolates, and invited me to be his guest at the Partick Thistle game.

Thistle lost. At time-up I asked him for his views.

'**Bunchamugs**[31],' he replied with feeling.

All is not yet lost, my son. – R.L.

The Sunday Post

A CHANGED MAN

1 pantry, room where foods and meat are stored
2 winged insects that migrate in great swarms, destroying vegetation and crops
3 having long slim legs and arms
4 a small travelling bag with two handles
5 wept, cried
6 *coll* handkerchief
7 enjoyed, appreciated
8 A Scottish professional football team
9 bold and adventurous acts
10 *fig* of good quality, pure, here ironical
11 band, group
12 *lit* a variety of the game of rugby football with teams half the size of the normal game, *here* a metaphor used to express smallness
13 smear
14 expressing contempt
15 ornament, decoration
16 *coll* the thing that was in fashion
17 insiders, specialists
18 became known
19 boy
20 kind of self-defence, originating in Japan
21 odd, strange
22 the essential elements of a structure or system
23 capability of being carried out, put into operation
24 the quantity of raw materials which may be processed in a given time
25 movement towards partial independence of regions of Great Britain, especially Scotland and Wales
26 replied
27 foolish, lacking in seriousness
28 dish consisting of very small pieces of beef with boiled potatoes (*sl* taties)
29 *French, lit* I know not what
30 blow, knock
31 *sl* bunch (collection) of mugs (idiots)

College Rags

Notice in a college canteen: 'Shoes are required to eat in the canteen.'

Someone has added: 'Socks can eat wherever they like.'   – *MS*

Two students in our class used to infuriate us by helping each other with set work in order to achieve better marks than anyone else. After a particularly **blatant**[1] piece of copying, however, their work was returned with a mark on only one paper. Underneath was the comment: 'Share this between you.'

– J F, Leeds

I was being shown some **digs**[2] by a **dour**[3] suspicious landlady. She **reeled off**[4] the usual restrictions: no male guests after dark, no loud music and no **clutter**[5].

'That's fine,' I replied, 'as long as there's room for my novels, grammars, anthologies, dictionaries .... and my **thesaurus**[6], of course.'

Disapprovingly, the woman shook her head. 'I forgot – no animals either.'

– *Theresa C. Nuneaton, Warwicks.*

COLLEGE RAGS

1 very obvious
2 *coll* lodgings
3 stern, severe, usually Scottish
4 tell fluently
5 untidiness
6 collection of words, phrases, selections from literature, etc

Discussion

1 'School has become the world religion of a modernized proletariat, and makes futile promises of salvation to the poor of the technological age' (Illich). What do you understand by this? Do you agree?

2 What is your opinion of teachers? Do we need them?

3 'Neither learning nor justice is promoted by schooling because educators insist on packaging instruction with certification.' (from 'Down with School' by Illich). What does this mean, exactly? What examples can you find among these articles or elsewhere to justify this view?

4 As a result of your studies, do you agree with Illich's assessment of how people learn foreign languages well?

5 Which is better, an educational institution which is strict and traditionally examination orientated, or one where those studying are free to choose how and when they study?

6 Was your education a good preparation for the job or studies you are now doing? Looking back, what would you have changed?

7 'Education today is faced with incredible challenges, different from, more serious than, it has ever met in its long history. To my mind, the question of whether it can meet these challenges will be one of the major factors in determining whether mankind moves forward, or whether man destroys himself on this planet, leaving this earth to those few living things which can withstand atomic destruction.'★

Do you agree that education is as important as this, and if so, what kind of new things does it have to try to do?

★ Rogers Carl L., *Freedom to Learn*, Charles E. Merrill Publishing Co., Columbus 1969, p. vi.

Word Study

This first Word Study contains guidance notes. All the other Word Study sections work in the same way as this one, and you will be able to study them by yourself. You can refer back to the notes in this unit when you need to.

A Semantic Field is a group of words which are similar in meaning. For example, the words printed in **heavy black type** in the COMPONENTIAL GRID below are all verbs which are used to describe someone passing on knowledge or skills to another person.

A Semantic Fields

1 Passing on knowledge or skills

	pass on knowledge or skill	develop intellectual abilities and	provide a good cultural background — or — send to school	usu in sth practical	in certain sports	through extra lessons	on a private basis	often implies the pupil is not up to standard	develop a particular skill or ability by giving practice	in a systematic way / in a particular subject
teach	+									
educate	+	+	+							
instruct	+			+						
coach	+				+	+		+		
tutor	+						+	+		
train	+								+	+

The differences and similarities between the words are shown by the *semantic features* at the top of the grid. If there is a + against a word this means that the feature is part of the meaning of the word, so here, both **coach** and **tutor** include in their meaning [+ often implies that the pupil is not up to standard]. (Note that when we write features outside a grid we put them in square brackets with a + sign.) If there is no +, either the feature is not part of the meaning of the word, or the feature does not help us to know the difference between this word and others in the field.

This grid shows features working in two different ways. All the words in the field are marked for [+ pass on knowledge or skill], so it is helping to distinguish one field from another. The other features distinguish the different words in the field from each other.

Or between two features can mean two things:
If a word is marked for both the features, then both of them are part of its meaning, although not necessarily at the same time. *Coach* is such a word – it describes passing on skills in certain sports, but in a different context it describes giving extra lessons in an academic subject to a student who is below the required standard.

If a word is marked for only one feature, the other one is not part of its meaning.

Educate, **coach**, **tutor** and **train** all collocate with the preposition **for**; **instruct**, **coach** and **tutor** take **in**, and **teach** and **train** occur in **to . . . . . sb to do sth**.

The next grid is a COLLOCATIONAL GRID. It gives examples of the most typical ways in which the words in the field are used. Of course it does not give all the possible uses, but if you know these examples, it will help you to decide whether the word is suitable in another situation. If there is a + against a word printed in heavy black type this means that the word collocates with the word or expression at the top of the grid. In this case **teach English** is a typical collocation, whereas **coach English** ⁎ is wrong. (+) means that the collocation does not seem correct to all speakers, although many would use it. Note that you can extend your knowledge of any word by making your own collocational grid and asking native speakers for their judgments of good and bad collocations.

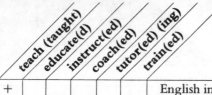

	teach (taught)	educate(d)	instruct(ed)	coach(ed)	tutor(ed)	train(ed) (ing)	
My sister	+						English in Africa for 3 years.
Mothers should	+						their children good manners.
I wish I could	+						my students more vocabulary.
Martin	+					+	his dog to fetch his newspaper.
He	+	+					himself in the evenings after work.
The Johnsons		+					all their children in private schools.
She was		+					in Belgium.
My father		+					my brother for the law.
Good schools don't just teach their pupils, they		+					them.
The ship's officers			+				us in life-saving techniques.
He used to			+				people in swimming.
He				+			the girl who won this year's Wimbledon tennis championships.
The headmaster himself				+			my brother because his Latin was so bad.
My older brother				+			me in exam techniques so I didn't have too much trouble.
The lecturer who is					+		me in psychology is really excellent.
An English lady				+	+		him for his English exam.
He used to				+		+	a football team.
She						+	as a nurse and then became a midwife.

2 Beginning or setting into motion

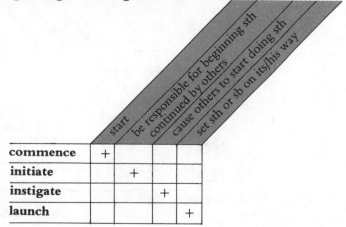

	start	be responsible for beginning sth continued by others	cause others to start doing sth	set sth or sb on its/his way
commence	+			
initiate		+		
instigate			+	
launch				+

Commence is used in formal style.

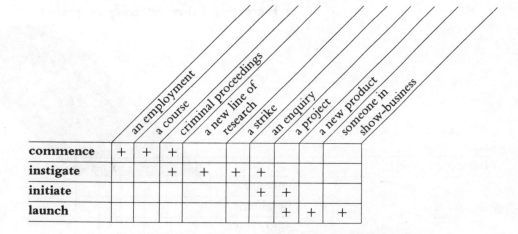

	an employment	a course	criminal proceedings	a new line of research	a strike	an enquiry	a project	a new product	someone in show-business
commence	+	+	+						
instigate			+	+	+	+			
initiate						+	+		
launch							+	+	+

3 Transferring to someone or somewhere else

	hand over or transfer				
	to the charge of another or to another place		usu private information often to sb with whom one is on intimate terms		based on trust and confidence
entrust	+				+
consign	+	+			
confide			+	+	

The verbs can occur in the following constructions:
to entrust sb/sth to sb; to entrust sb with sth
to consign sb/sth to sth
to confide sth to sb; to confide in sb

	entrust(ed)	consign(ed)	confide(d)	
I	+			you with my secret and you didn't keep it.
He has	+			me with the job of accompanying his wife to Brazil.
She	+			her diamonds to my care and they were stolen.
She has	+	+		her children to the tender care of her mother-in-law.
I had to		+		my old car to the scrap heap.
My sister			+	to me that she doesn't really get on with her husband.
Everyone likes to			+	in someone, but being responsible for other people's problems isn't always easy.

4 Increasing value, intensity or quality

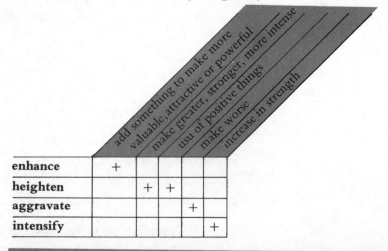

	add something to make more valuable, attractive or powerful	make greater, stronger, more intense	usu of positive things	make worse	increase in strength
enhance	+				
heighten		+	+		
aggravate				+	
intensify					+

Verbal classification   The categories *transitive* and *intransitive* are used differently in different books. We have adopted the following distinctions: If a verb can be used with no object of any kind, it is described as *intransitive*.

EXAMPLES

He is running   She goes out.
She cried.   We will go there tomorrow.

If it takes an object, noun, pronoun, participle, infinitive, object introduced by a preposition, sentential object, it is said to be *transitive*.

EXAMPLES

He bought a book.   I thought of my sister.
He said nothing.   I threw out all my old letters.
I like her.   He asked when we would come back.
I like swimming.   He said that he would come with us.
I like to swim.

In cases where the nature of the verbs is obvious, no comment is given.

All the verbs are transitive, and **heighten** and **intensify** are also intransitive.

EXAMPLES

The storm seemed to **heighten** and then subside.

As the sun rose higher in the sky, the heat **intensified**.

With only a week to go to the election the campaign is **intensifying** at all levels.

In colloquial style **aggravate** can also have the meaning of [+annoy], and in this sense, it often occurs as a present participle.

EXAMPLES

Both children seemed to be doing everything they could to **aggravate** me, when I was already in a bad mood before getting home.

I find his habit of opening windows all the time really most **aggravating**, particularly when the temperature is minus 10.

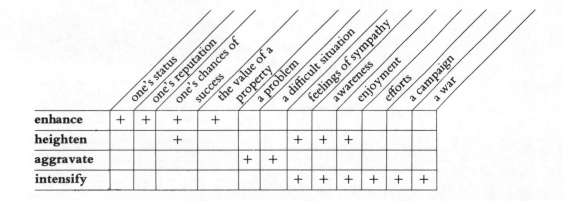

	one's status	one's reputation	one's chances of success	the value of a property	a problem	a difficult situation	feelings of sympathy	awareness	enjoyment	efforts	a campaign	a war
enhance	+	+	+	+								
heighten			+			+	+	+				
aggravate					+	+						
intensify							+	+	+	+	+	+

5 Receiving good from

Sometimes it is clearer to give an explanation of the differences between words. These three all share the feature in the heading [+ receiving good from].

benefit	profit	take advantage

Benefit and **profit** collocate with the prepositions **from** and **by**; **take advantage** always occurs with **of** and it differs from the other items in the feature [+ make use of to further one's own purposes]. **Benefit** can also take an object without a preposition and then it means [+ do good to].

EXAMPLE
I think it would **benefit** you a lot to take a physical fitness course.

	from a holiday	from a stay in England	from good advice	by a business association	by sb's death	from an experience of sb	of the opportunities open to one	of sb's bad English	of sb's stupidity	of someone's kindness	of sb's presence
benefit	+	+	+	+							
profit		+	+	+	+	+					
take advantage						+	+	+	+	+	+

6 Getting in the way of

	restrain freedom of movement or action	slow down progress or movement	make passage impossible	by placing obstacles in the way	by placing bars across	by interfering with normal action
hamper	+					
hinder		+				
obstruct		+		+		
impede		+				+
block			+	+		
bar			+	+	+	

Note that it is not necessary for all the words in a semantic field to share a single feature. In such cases, it is the similarity of features which brings the words together.

All the verbs are transitive and may be used in the expression
to . . . . .sb/sth in sth. They are frequently found in passive constructions.

	hamper(ed) (ing)	hinder(ed) (ing)	obstruct(ed) (ing)	impede(d) (ing)	block(ed) (ing)	bar(red) (ring)	
My movements are greatly	+						by having a broken arm.
Protests and objections from many people have	+	+		+			realisation of the Government's nuclear power programme.
Language problems often		+		+			children's progress in school.
Sally		+					me all the morning by insisting on confiding all her problems to me.
The opposition took action to		+	+		+		the Parliamentary Bill to reform the electoral system.
The way was			+		+	+	by a large tree which had fallen across the road.
Snow drifts had			+				the passage of the train.
If you refuse to answer a policeman's questions you are said to have			+				him in the course of his duty.
We tried to escape from the burning building but found the way was						+	by a locked door.

7 Hitting

strike			
	hit		
punch	clout	slap	smack

These words are related to each other in a way which can be explained by a diagram. The word at the top is more general. **Punch** and **hit** are kinds of striking, and **clout**, **slap** and **smack** are kinds of hitting.

	deal a blow	using a closed fist	not aiming carefully	hard	esp on the head	sharply	using the flat of the hand	producing a noise sometimes in fun	usu to a child in punishment
strike	+								
hit	+								
punch	+	+							
clout	+		+	+	+				
slap	+					+	+	+	
smack	+					+	+	+	+

Strike can be extended to mean [+ have a strong effect on the mind].

EXAMPLES

What **struck** me particularly about him was the direct way in which he answered our questions.

I was very **struck** by her gentleness in handling her patients.

Note the special expression **to strike a match** (to light a match by rubbing it sharply against a rough surface).

Scales can also show the relationship between words. This scale shows how formal these words are:

formal   colloquial

←——————————————————————————→

strike	**hit**	**clout**
	punch	**smack**
	slap	

Of course it is not exact, but it gives you an idea of when you can use these words. Try making your own scales of groups of related words, by asking native speakers when and how they would use them.

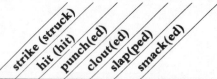

	strike (struck)	hit (hit)	punch(ed)	clout(ed)	slap(ped)	smack(ed)	
He	+	+			+		her sharply on the arm.
The man became angry and	+	+					the child with his stick.
Boys are taught that they should never		+					girls.
The farmer		+					the dog which had chased his sheep with a big stick.
The children		+					the branches with sticks to make the apples fall down.
One of the boys		+	+				the other and gave him a black eye.
The boxer			+				his opponent on the head and knocked him out.
Dad				+			Terry over the head when he came home drunk.
If you don't learn to behave, my girl, I'll				+			you over the head so that you won't forget it.
She					+		her fiancé in the face and threw her engagement ring on the ground.
He laughed loudly and					+		his companion on the knee.
If you children don't behave better, I will						+	you and send you to bed with no supper.
Mummy						+	me because I tore up one of her books.

B Synonymous Pairs

In this section, you will find pairs of words similar in meaning, with an explanation of the difference between them.

1 **to develop** [+move ahead or cause to move ahead] or [+begin to have]

   to evolve [+in a continuing process] [+usu gradually] [+usu gradually] [+over a long period of time] [+implies improvement]

EXAMPLES

Girls tend to **develop** earlier than boys.

He has { **developed** / **evolved** } a method of fertilising fruit trees artificially which guarantees success.

The day we were due to leave for the US all the children **developed** whooping-cough.

It took many thousands of years for man to **evolve** to the point where he could speak.

Language is constantly **evolving** so there can be no absolute criteria for correctness.

2 **to get rid of**
   to discard   [+after selection] [+usu of ideas or inanimate objects which can be handled]

When one member of a pair can be explained in terms of the other, we mention the features of the more specific word which make it different from the more general word. For example, here **discard** means 'get rid of, after selection'.

Get rid of is colloquial, whereas **discard** is formal.

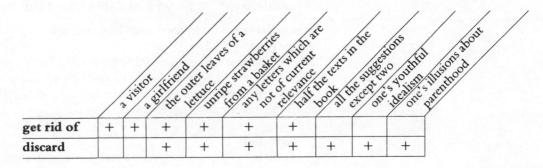

	a visitor	a girlfriend	the outer leaves of a lettuce	unripe strawberries from a basket	any letters which are not of current relevance	half the texts in the book	all the suggestions except two	one's youthful idealism	one's illusions about parenthood
get rid of	+	+	+	+	+	+			
discard			+	+	+	+	+	+	+

3   **to say**
    to reel off   │ [+without pause] [+sth quite long]

Reel off would not be used in formal circumstances.

to reel off {
a list of names
a speech from 'Romeo and Juliet'
the telephone numbers of all the members of one's
    family
the name of every station between London and
    Edinburgh one after the other
the names of all the presidents of the US

4   **to enjoy**
    to relish   [+often with excessive satisfaction]

EXAMPLES
I really relished the sight of my worst enemy's proposals being
demolished by the committee.
I do not much **relish** the idea of a three-hour wait at the airport.

5   **critical**
    scathing   [+contemptuous]

(a) **scathing** {
retort
reply
look
report
remarks
comments

Scathing is often used predicatively.
EXAMPLE
The professor was very **scathing** about my theory that
mathematics may be considered as a language.

6   **disobedient**
    recalcitrant   │ [+persistently] [+usu of children]

Recalcitrant is often used semi-humorously.
EXAMPLES
My **recalcitrant** daughter is doing no schoolwork at all, but
doesn't seem to know what she would like to do instead.
Our **recalcitrant** first year students refuse to do any further work
until the examination system is reformed.

7   **agitated**
    frantic   │ [+being very upset] [+suggests urgency]

EXAMPLES
She is **frantic** with worry, having just heard that her daughter was
probably on the plane which crashed this morning.
As we approached the area of the bushfire we saw **frantic** small
animals running anywhere to escape from the blaze.

8 **reliable**
sterling | [+admirable and moral]

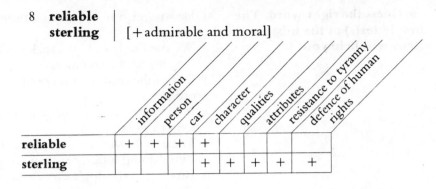

	information	person	car	character	qualities	attributes	resistance to tyranny	defence of human rights
reliable	+	+	+	+				
sterling				+	+	+	+	+

Exercises

1 Which nouns can be derived from the following?

1 hinder 2 aware 3 adorn 4 enroll 5 bloom 6 certify
7 accurate 8 own 9 fluent 10 prophesy 11 comprehend
12 press

2 Explain the meaning of each of the following in your own words:

1 orphan 2 pedestrian 3 sculpture 4 control group 5 maze
6 axiom 7 feedback 8 lure 9 come across 10 challenging
11 infuriating 12 rewarding 13 astounding 14 cataclysm
15 approximate 16 blatant

3 Replace the words in brackets with synonymous words or expressions from the texts.

1 People were (entering in a disorderly way) the building.
2 She (registered) for a course in computer programming.
3 Workers were (walking wearily, heavily) home from their jobs.
4 They wouldn't (make the slightest movement).
5 The child lovingly (caressed) his pet's long silky ears.
6 There was a warm social-emotional (atmosphere) around the bloomers.
7 How would you (evaluate) his performance?

4 In each case provide three or four nouns that can collocate with the following:

1 scathing 2 discard 3 benefit from 4 enhance 5 profit by
6 take advantage of 7 aggravate 8 intensify

5 Fill in the following grids:

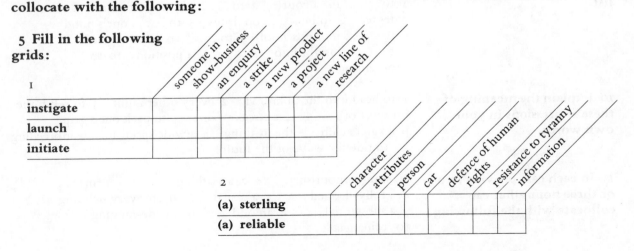

1

	someone in show-business	an enquiry	a strike	a new product	a project	a new line of research
instigate						
launch						
initiate						

2

	character	attributes	person	car	defence of human rights	resistance to tyranny	information
(a) sterling							
(a) reliable							

6 Guess the right word. The first letter(s) of the missing item will help you.

1 He struggled fr . . . . . to extricate himself from the overturned vehicle.
2 We tried to l . . . . . the snake from its hole by placing a dead frog just at the entrance.
3 Out of the confusion there slowly began to e . . . . . some sort of order.
4 It was a st . . . . . on such a small car to expect it to tow such a long caravan.
5 The people were h . . . . . out of the square by the soldiers, many complaining bitterly at their rough treatment.
6 He f . . . . . the dog's ears absentmindedly.
7 She was so convinced she was right that she wouldn't b . . . . . an inch and come to a compromise with us.
8 The r . . . . . schoolboy was finally expelled as being impossible to teach.
9 He d . . . . . himself of nothing during that holiday, buying himself just everything that took his fancy.
10 The fancy-dress party posed a problem for him for he had nothing with which to d . . . . . himself.

7 What differences and/or similarities are there between the following?

1 desire/expectation   2 creed/belief   3 input/output
4 a bright/a pretty girl   5 a verbal/a non-verbal test
6 a social class/the middle class   7 wisdom/intelligence
8 to run/to rush   9 to back/to help sb   10 to bloom/to blossom
11 conscious/conscientious   12 peer/equal

8 Sort the following words into those which can be used as compliments and those which cannot. What do they mean? Use each one with a suitable noun.

EXAMPLE: a **dull** teacher
weird   dull   sterling   suspicious   educated   recalcitrant
mature   devoted   frivolous   dim   coloured   accurate

9 Complete the expressions with words from the given list.

hold   earn   broaden   bring   raise   hook   sign up   set   show
launch
1 to . . . . . for a course   2 to . . . . . sb's expectations   3 to . . . . .
a degree   4 to be . . . . . on drugs   5 to . . . . . one's mind
6 to . . . . . foot in school   7 to . . . . . sb down to earth
8 to . . . . . insight into   9 to . . . . . a position   10 to . . . . . a
programme

10 Explain the meaning of these expressions in your own words.

1 to head into the unknown   2 every other night   3 to relish the
prospect of . . . . .   4 a streak of dirt   5 to pack one's grip
6 a karate club   7 the in-thing   8 a wide spectrum   9 inbreeding
10 to ride the wave of the future

11 In each case provide two or three nouns that can collocate with the following.

1 an undernourished . . .   2 a scathing . . .   3 a former . . .
4 a fully-fledged . . .   5 a casual . . .   6 an overwhelming . . .
7 a substantial . . .   8 an odd . . .   9 a wide-ranging . . .
10 a financial . . .

12 Find words to fit these descriptions/definitions.

1 that cannot be believed
2 a person who leaves school or higher education without completing the course or who refuses to take a job and join society in the normal way
3 a cool room or cupboard where meat and other kinds of food can be stored
4 the action of drawing in the breath sharply and irregularly from sorrow or pain, especially while crying
5 to change the appearance in order to deceive or hide the identity of
6 a game with thirty-two pieces (pawns, castles, knights, bishops) on a board with sixty-four squares
7 hours at which crowds of people travel to or from work
8 payment received (usu weekly) for work or services
9 to become a member of an institute or society
10 to do things quickly and with energy, or put pressure on another so that they hurry

13 What can one . . . . . ?

1 be hooked on   2 broaden (lit and fig)   3 achieve   4 be concerned with   5 come across   6 knit   7 reel off   8 share   9 spray   10 adopt

14 Describe the differences between the words within each group.

a   hinder, impede, hamper, bar
b   aggravate, heighten, enhance
c   punch, slap, smack

15 How would you explain the meaning of the following?

1 a behavioural science   2 a T-fork (of a road)   3 a random sample   4 an average IQ   5 test scores   6 an extra-curricular activity   7 one's peer group   8 a fully-fledged programme   9 to make a poor showing   10 continuing education

16 Fill in the blanks with appropriate prepositions.

1 There is evidence . . . the contrary   2 He was an exception . . . the rule   3 I think I'll subscribe . . . *Time Magazine*   4 Why do so many people fail . . . their academic careers?   5 He enjoys teaching English . . . Orientals   6 What does happiness depend . . .?   7 She obtained a first-class degree . . . philosophy   8 Her grandfather coached her . . . her Latin exam

17 Choose the word that best fits the context. Modify its form where necessary.

1 These modest blushes only . . . . . the girl's youthful appearance. (heighten, enhance, intensify)
2 The wound was . . . . . by the continual rubbing of his boot on his leg. (intensify, enhance, aggravate)
3 I . . . . . my cases to the hotel porter who disappeared into the lift with them. (consign, entrust, confide)
4 The scheme was . . . . . despite much scepticism from outsiders. (initiate, launch, instigate)
5 He was . . . . . in mathematics and passed the test easily. (train, teach, instruct, coach)
6 As it was a warm evening, the girl . . . . . her cardigan. (discard, get rid of)
7 The dog . . . . . us at every step by criss-crossing the path just in front of our feet. (bar, obstruct, hamper)

Unit 2   No place to hide

SO YOU THINK T.V. IS HOT STUFF?

Just you wait   by Erik Barnouw

Don't look now, but your television set is about to be replaced by something more up-to-date. As with many giant steps in technology, it will involve ideas that science-fiction people have been picturing for decades – in fact, for a century or so. Now, at last, in diverse laboratories and field tests, their visions are turning into practical **hardware**[1]. The **ingredients**[2] seem to be right at our hands.

Your television set, your stereo, your telephone are really quite primitive – **'tom-toms'**[3] compared to what is now possible and inevitable, according to Peter C Goldmark, the far-sighted retired chief of CBS Laboratories, responsible for many electronic **breakthroughs**[4].

A factor behind the **euphoria**[5] is a development relating to cable television. This system has long been able to deliver 20 channels or more – a **versatility**[6] impossible to over-the-air television – so far not at a sensational profit. Now it is about to be expanded further, in a fashion: it may soon offer a choice of hundreds of channels, along with another dramatic option – two-way communication, the chance to talk back.

The key to all this is a mysterious optical **fiber'**[7], now emerging from the laboratory. This glass fiber looks like a thin violin string. Laser **beams**[8] can travel through it and – incredibly – carry innumerable streams of communication simultaneously in both directions. Combine this virtuosity with various 'miracles' already familiar to us – computers, satellites, cassettes, **facsimile transmission**[9] – and what do you have? A 'telecommunications' revolution, it would seem.

This revolution might result in something like this. In one wall of your room will be a telescreen. It will be able to bring you a wide range of images and sounds and data, via push-button controls. In the first place, you can summon up current events, drama offerings, game shows,

TV IS HOT STUFF?

1 mechanical and electronic equipment used in the field of electronic data processing, opp: software (=programs)
2 components, items which make up the whole (usually used for cooking)
3 Indian drums used for signalling
4 advances, often in scientific knowledge, in which some major problem is solved
5 exaggerated sense of well-being
6 ability to do different kinds of work equally well
7 a single, slender thread (as eg in cotton, wool), a material made of such fibres
8 rays
9 exact copy or reproduction transmissions
10 a place in which things can be stored
11 called, sent for
12 method of dividing a television screen so that images coming from different sources may appear at the same time
13 people in control, *lit* persons responsible for checking all entries and exits to an institution, eg university, prison, factory
14 changing slowly from a simple to a more complex structure
15 scattered, sent in different directions
16 critical, very important, vital, essential

'HOW NICE THAT WE COULD HAVE DINNER TOGETHER LIKE THIS!'

athletic contests – not unlike your current television choices. But you may also decide to see a classic film which a computerized switching system can call forth from an archive. Or you may decide to take a university course, prepared and stored in an electronic **repository**[10]; each lesson, as and when you need it, can be **summoned**[11] by your push buttons. When ready, you can order the exam: question after question will appear on your telescreen, to be answered by push button, and the sequence will be climaxed by your grade, which will at once be recorded somewhere in a data bank. Some of the choices will be free, while others will involve payment but probably by as painless a method as possible. The act of tuning may simply deduct the fee electronically from your bank balance. People will be able to converse with data banks as easily as they do with one another.

Instead of conversing with a computer you may prefer to talk to a human being – your daughter in St Louis, for example. There seems no reason why the telephone function, including sight, should not be incorporated in the telecommunications system. Thus you and your daughter will be able to speak to each other while each appears on the other's screen. For conference calls, **split-screen arrangements**[12] can be used, so that face-to-face business conferences can involve representatives of widely scattered offices, even on several continents.

Almost everything will be possible at the touch of a button, so what will all those people do – those human beings who no longer need to stir from home, who will save endless hours of mass transport and be blessed with leisure? What will they do with their lives? What will their lives mean to them? Who will be the **gatekeepers**[13] of the **evolving**[14] system? Will authority be **dispersed**[15], or concentrated? Will the multiplicity of channels provide a rich diversity of choice, or only seem to? Who will decide what treasures are to be stored in the electronic archives available to your push buttons? Our whole history teaches us that these are **crucial**[16] questions. More recent history confronts us with still further questions. Will the right of privacy survive the telecommunications revolution and its network of data banks? For the moment such questions remain unanswered, and unanswerable.

Smithsonian

"NO PLACE TO HIDE"

In an interview last month, Frank Church, chairman of the Senate committee that is investigating the CIA, **issued**[1] an **oblique**[2] but **impassioned**[3] **warning**[1], that the technology of **eavesdropping**[4] had become so highly developed that Americans might soon be left with 'no place to hide'. That day may have arrived. *Newsweek* has learned that the country's most secret intelligence operation, the National Security Agency, already possesses the computerized equipment to **monitor**[5] nearly all overseas telephone calls and most domestic and international printed messages.

The agency's devices monitor thousands of telephone circuits, cable lines and the microwave transmissions that carry an increasing share of both spoken and written communications. Computers are programed to watch for '**trigger' words**[6] or phrases indicating that a message might interest **intelligence analysts**[7].

When the trigger is pulled, entire messages are tape-recorded or printed out.

That kind of eavesdropping is, however, relatively simple compared with the breakthroughs that lie ahead in the field of **snoopery**[8]. Already it is technically **feasible**[9] to '**bug**'[10] an electric typewriter by picking up its feeble electronic **emissions**[11] from a **remote**[12] location and then translating them into words. And some scientists believe that it may be possible in the future for remote electronic equipment to **intercept**[13] and 'read' human brain waves.

Where such capabilities exist, so too does the potential for abuse. It is the old story of technology rushing forward with some new wonder, before the men who supposedly control the machines have **figured out**[14] how to prevent the machines from controlling them.

Newsweek

NO PLACE TO HIDE

1 warned, cautioned against
2 indirect
3 showing deep emotion
4 listening secretly to a conversation one is not supposed to hear
5 receive and listen to
6 key words, words that trigger the computer and make it do certain things
7 people who study or analyse secret information gathered by the Intelligence Department of a government, which collects and studies information useful in war or defence
8 *coll* spying
9 that can be done, capable of being done
10 *coll* listen to by attaching a miniature electronic microphone
11 that which is sent out
12 far off

13 seize or catch between the starting point and the destination
14 *Br* more usually 'worked out'

THE COMPUTER & PRIVACY

1 becoming larger
2 needs
3 indications of the limits and scope of an undertaking
4 ways of approach
5 safe, prudent, reliable, dependable
6 the opportunity to get at or use
7 make alterations to
8 wrongly, in the wrong circumstances
9 one who has the care or custody of something
10 delicate
11 measures taken beforehand against possible danger, failure, etc
12 that can be relied on, trusted
13 promises solemnly

How much personal information about each of us is stored in computers?

The computer and privacy

In the last 20 years, the productivity of the computer has increased over 1000%.

With this kind of technological advance, the possibility of storing more and more information at a central point is growing at a phenomenal rate. But so is the possibility of gaining access to the stored information. And that raises serious questions regarding personal privacy.

For some time now, there has been a growing effort in many European countries to preserve the individual's privacy in the face of **expanding**[1] **requirements**[2] for information by business, government and other organizations.

In some countries, legislation has been enacted to protect the individual's privacy. In others, it is under study.

In searching for appropriate legislative **guidelines**[3], private and governmental groups have explored many **avenues**[4] and considered many aspects of the problem.

Four basic principles of privacy have emerged from these various studies, and appear to be the foundation for **sound**[5] public policy.

We at IBM believe:
1. Individuals should have **access**[6] to information about themselves in record-keeping systems. And there should be some procedure for individuals to find out how this information is used.
2. There should be a way for individuals to correct or **amend**[7] inaccurate records.
3. Information on individuals should not be **improperly**[8] disclosed or used for other than authorized purposes.
4. The **custodian**[9] of data files containing **sensitive**[10] information should take all reasonable **precautions**[11] to make sure that the data is **reliable**[12] and not misused.

Translating such broad principles into specific and uniform guidelines is not easy. It calls for thoughtful interpretation in terms of the widely varying purposes of information systems generally.

In particular, there must be a proper balance between limiting access to information for the protection of individual privacy on the one hand, and allowing freedom of information to fulfill the needs of society on the other.

Solutions must be found. And they will call for patient understanding and the best efforts of everyone concerned. In this search, IBM **pledges**[13] its full and whole-hearted cooperation.

International Herald Tribune

WHAT'S HAPPENING?

The wife of a **postman**[1] in a large city wrote to the local newspaper criticizing the school superintendent for reading *Playboy* magazine. She said a man who read such magazines should not have a position in the schools. The postman had approved her letter, the wife said, and it was as though he had sent it himself. It was he who had told his wife that he delivered *Playboy* to the home of the school superintendent every month.

The local postmaster ordered an investigation, saying that the postman had violated 'several sections' of the **mailmen's**[1] code of ethics that prohibit **mail carriers**[1] from telling anything about the mail they deliver. As a result of the investigation the mailman was barred from delivering mail and was

reassigned to the vehicle maintenance department.

The school superintendent said that he thought the real issue was not what he liked to read, but rather his right to privacy. He added that he felt sorry for people who must spy and **snoop**[2], but he did not intend to file legal charges.

1   What is the issue here? Does a mailman, or any person who has information about another, have a duty or a right to make the information known if he believes this will be in the public good? If a reporter stated in a newspaper story that the superintendent subscribed to *Playboy* magazine, would this constitute an invasion of privacy?

Freedom of thought

The idea of thought control is hateful to Americans, brought up as we have been with a tradition of freedom. The concept that we are not free to think what we like, even if we do not express our thoughts, has been the subject of many books (George Orwell's *1984*, for example), articles, and political arguments. No matter how many laws may **inhibit**[1] our speech and actions or how much our friends may influence our speaking out, we feel that one area is exclusively and completely ours – our thinking.

'Nobody can tell me what to think,' we say, secure that deep down inside we are free.

In reality, however, a great many people tell us what to think, and the idea that we are free-thinking persons becomes questionable when we consider the influences on our intrapersonal communication. Our values and attitudes often **stem from**[2] persons we admire. They probably shaped our opinions about dogs and cats, men with beards, tall people, fat people, black skin, white skin, yellow skin, brown skin, church ritual, and various kinds of food. Although we may change our minds as a result of personal experience – switch to mashed potatoes if **french fries**[3] give us indigestion, for example – we are influenced by the opinions of others in almost everything we do.

We usually borrow our beliefs from someone else – what we read and what we see others doing and hear them saying. Stereotypes develop when we assume that everyone or everything in a particular group is identical – that all Texans are rich and wear big hats, that all apples are red when they are ripe, and that all dogs are friendly, for example. You are rewarded by your friends if you believe the same things they do. You are probably more comfortable with yourself if you can depend on some ideas without having to think too much about every little item in your world. In many ways we become dependent on others for our ideas. It is very difficult to tell which ideas and attitudes you have developed for yourself and which you have simply borrowed from others you trust and admire.

WHAT'S HAPPENING?

1   mailman (US) = postman (UK)
2   *sl* spy, be inquisitive
3   damaging a person's reputation
4   the act of making known, of uncovering, of bringing to light

FREEDOM OF THOUGHT

1   restrain, hold back
2   come from, originate from
3   *Am* sliced fried potatoes, *Br* chips

2 Are there absolute rules governing what one citizen can make public about another? Generally speaking, libel is the act of **defaming**[3] with printed words, and slander is the act of defaming with spoken words. Would you have taken this case to court if you had been the superintendent?

3 Had you been the mailman, how would you have reacted to your wife's asking your help in making the **disclosure**[4] public? (She read the letter to him before sending it to the paper.) Would you expect the postmaster to take some action against you?

G E Myers and M Tolela Myers, *Communicating*

Discussion

1 How much personal information about you (your financial situation, age, health record, criminal record, educational history) is in the hands of different private or public organisations? Do you know how safe this information is? Have you ever thought that these organisations might exchange information about you? Would this be wrong?
2 Does the fact that the National Security Agency of the USA can monitor any overseas telephone call seem to you wrong, or is it justifiable for security reasons?
3 Suggest some answers to the questions about control of these new systems posed at the end of the television article on page 21.
4 What kind of effects would you envisage on 'these human beings who no longer need to stir from home'? (page 21)
5 Imagine learning English from a television course of the type described here. Compare it with the kind of lessons you are having now. Which do you think would be better and why?

Word Study

A Semantic Fields

1 Invading privacy

	listen secretly	to private conversation — or —	watch secretly — or —	try to obtain secret information	about — or — enquire into	look at	the affairs of others	especially personal affairs	suggests disapproval on the part of the speaker
eavesdrop	+	+							
spy			+	+					
snoop					+	+	+		+
pry					+	+	+	+	+

Eavesdrop is usually found in constructions denoting a continuous or repetitive action. **Snoop** and **pry** often collocate with the preposition **into**. **Snoop** may also be followed by **about**. **Spy** is quite common with **on**.

EXAMPLES

eavesdrop Two pupils who were **eavesdropping** outside the examiners' meeting were severely punished.
The safest place to have a private discussion is in the middle of a field because there no-one can **eavesdrop**.

spy   The children hid behind the hedge and **spied** on their sister and her boyfriend.

All the great powers **spy** on each other to try and find out what the others are doing.

snoop   A stranger has been **snooping** about, watching the house and asking questions about us in the village.

When will she stop **snooping** into our affairs!

pry   He's fascinated by other people's misfortune and is always **prying** into things which don't concern him.

I discovered my sister has been to see my doctor. I don't know why she is **prying** into my affairs behind my back.

2 Making known something hidden or secret

	act in a disloyal way	show or make known	sth that should have been kept secret or	sth normally expected to be kept secret	sth previously unseen or unknown	sth previously deliberately hidden or kept secret
betray	+	+	+	+		
divulge			+	+	+	
reveal		+	+		+	
disclose		+	+			+

	betray(ed)	divulge(d)	reveal(ed)	disclose(d)	
The enemy were waiting for us so someone had	+				us to them.
The Arab races very rarely	+				their real feelings.
Under pressure from his captors, the hostage		+	+		his secret.
Our long-held secret was		+			by a few careless words.
Someone has		+		+	the real value of the cargo to the customs authorities.
The authorities have now				+	the real facts about the economic situation.
The witness has now			+	+	that he was lying to protect his friend.
We stripped the paint off and			+		some beautiful old panelling behind.
The mysterious stranger			+		his true identity.

3 Acting contrary to

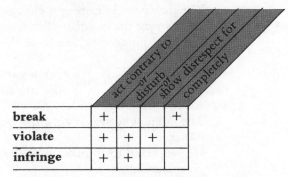

	act contrary to	disturb (or)	show disrespect for	completely
break	+			+
violate	+	+	+	
infringe	+	+		

Break is more colloquial than the other two words. **Infringe** collocates with the prepositions **on** or **upon**.

	a promise	a contract	an agreement	the rules	a law	sb's privacy	sb's right to freedom of expression	the charter of human rights	on sb's privacy
break	+	+	+	+	+				
violate		+	+	+		+	+	+	
infringe			+	+	+			+	+

4 Legal action

	cause official legal proceedings to begin	cause official legal proceedings to take place	to enforce payment of money owing from another — or	to obtain compensation for damage or loss	done by individuals or companies (civil proceedings)	be in charge of legal proceedings in a Criminal Court	done by the authorities (criminal proceedings)
bring a charge against	+					+	
sue		+	+	+	+		
take sb to court		+	+	+	+		
take legal action		+	+	+	+		
try					+	+	+
bring sb to trial		+				+	+

Take sb to court and **take legal action** are used by people outside the legal profession. **Take legal action** is the expression normally used by firms and individuals to threaten others with what they will do if they do not receive payment. The use of **sue** by non-specialists usually has the sense of [+ to obtain compensation].

EXAMPLES

The police are **bringing a charge of** drunken driving against him.

He is **suing** the company for damages amounting to £25,000 for loss of earnings, resulting from the accident he had while working for them.

The firm threaten to $\left\{\begin{array}{l}\textbf{take legal action}\\\textbf{take me to court}\end{array}\right\}$ if I do not pay their bill within two weeks.

The judge who was **trying** the case summed it up in a very impartial way.

He was **tried** for murder in the High Court and the case caused a great scandal.

He is **charged** with obstructing the course of justice but I don't think they will be able to **bring him to trial** for it because there really is not sufficient evidence.

Note also the expressions:

$\left.\begin{array}{l}\textbf{to be on trial}\\\textbf{to go on trial}\\\textbf{to stand trial}\end{array}\right\}$ to undergo legal proceedings in which one is accused of a serious infringement of the law.

EXAMPLE

He $\left\{\begin{array}{l}\textbf{is on trial}\\\textbf{will go on trial}\\\textbf{will stand trial}\end{array}\right\}$ for the murder of his sister.

5 Having as a source or cause

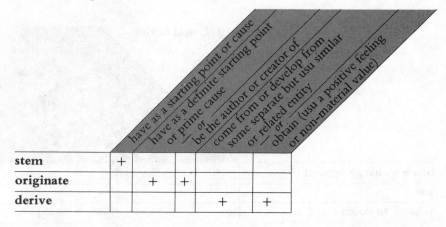

	have as a starting point or cause	have as a definite starting point or prime cause	be the author or creator of	come from or develop from some separate but usu similar or related entity	obtain (usu a positive feeling or non-material value)
stem	+				
originate		+	+		
derive				+	+

All the verbs are usually followed by **from**; **originate** may also (but less frequently) take **in** or **with**.

	stem(med)	originate(d)	derive(d)	
The problems we have now probably	+			from last year's very serious drought.
I would say the success of the book	+			from the fact that it filled an essential gap in theory.
She		+		from England, but now she lives in Canada.
This whole line of research		+		with/from one chance remark by a young research assistant.
He just sat in his office all day and		+		work for everyone else.
Clearly many English words are			+	from French.
I			+	a great deal of pleasure from the work I did with educationally subnormal children
My parents obviously			+	a lot of satisfaction from seeing their children succeed in life.
He			+	great benefit from his stay in America.

6 Sending out or throwing in different directions

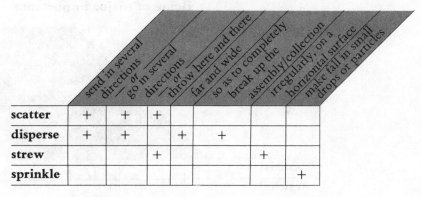

	send in several directions *or* go in several directions	throw here and there	far and wide	so as to completely break up the assembly/collection	irregularly, on a horizontal surface	make fall in small drops or particles
scatter	+	+	+			
disperse	+	+		+	+	
strew			+			+
sprinkle						+

Scatter and **disperse** can be either transitive or intransitive. **Strew** and **sprinkle** are transitive. **Scatter**, **strew** and **sprinkle** often collocate with the prepositions **on** and **with**.

	scatter(ed)	disperse(d)	strew(ed) (strewn)	sprinkle(d)	
The crowd	+				before the advancing soldiers.
He	+				grass seed over the area of land which had been prepared for it.
Pieces of paper were	+		+		about all over the room.
The crowd	+		+		flowers in the path of the victorious athlete.
Why do you have to	+		+		your possessions about all over the house.
I slept in a hut whose floor was			+		with leaves.
The crowd quickly		+			because the speaker was boring.
Sycamore seeds are		+			by wind.
The dish was				+	with cheese and grilled.
If you want houseplants to grow well				+	them regularly with water.

7 Being of major importance

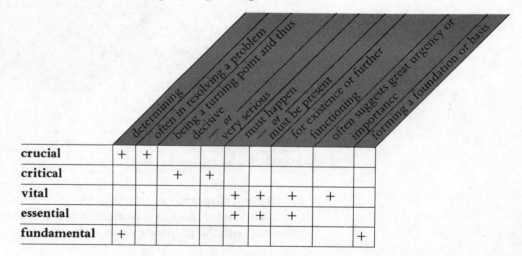

	determining	often in resolving a problem	being a turning point and thus decisive / or	very serious	must happen	or must be present	for existence or further functioning	often suggests great urgency or importance	forming a foundation or basis
crucial	+	+							
critical			+	+					
vital					+	+	+	+	
essential					+	+	+		
fundamental	+								+

In practice, these semantic distinctions are not respected and many speakers would use any of the words, except **fundamental**, to mean [+ very necessary]. All these adjectives collocate with the prepositions **to** and **for**.

	crucial	critical	vital	essential	fundamental	
New and	+				+	evidence about the causes of cancer has just been revealed.
Is it a(n)	+			+		requirement of the course that students should have previous knowledge of computing?
The success of this experiment is	+		+	+	+	to the whole project.
It's	+	+	+	+		for/to the success of the whole operation.
It's really	+		+	+		to get in touch with him before he leaves the country.
The		+				point in negotiations between the two countries has now been reached
Losses this year have made the company's financial situation extremely		+				
The injured girl is in St Mary's hospital where her condition is said to be		+				
The most			+	+		part of the machine has been broken.
In order to succeed in business it's now			+	+		to have good qualifications.
Flour is an				+		ingredient of most cakes and pies.
A good knowledge of grammar is				+	+	for language learning.

8 Having many characteristics, abilities or uses

	able to do many things	or able to be used for many purposes	having many aspects	or having many interests	denoting great quantity	or having or affecting many parts	of things differing widely from one another
versatile	+	+					
multi-purpose		+					
many-sided			+	+			
diverse			+				+
multiple					+	+	
multifarious					+		+

Notice that **multiple** cannot be used predicatively.

	artist	appliance	fibre	material	furniture	novel	student	person	attractions	achievements	talents	interests	duties	collection	sclerosis	fracture	choice
versatile	+	+		+		+	+	+									
multi-purpose		+	+	+	+												
many-sided					+	+	+										
diverse								+	+	+	+	+	+				
multiple								+	+	+	+			+	+	+	
multifarious								+	+	+	+						

B Synonymous Pairs

1 **to accuse** { [+say that sb is responsible for some wrongdoing] }
   to charge

[+officially] [+done by authorities] [+usu results in legal proceedings]

The most common constructions in which the verbs occur are:
to accuse sb of sth/of doing sth
to charge sb with sth/with doing sth

	accused	charge(d)	
The wife	+		her husband of cruelty during the time they lived together.
I have been	+		of cheating in the exam.
He is	+		of assaulting a policeman.
He was arrested after the fight but the police have decided not to		+	him.
After what happened at the demonstration she is being		+	with causing a breach of the peace (legal term for disorderly behaviour).

2 **to prevent**
   to bar   or [+exclude]

EXAMPLES
He has been **barred** from practising as a doctor.
The Department of Education has decided **to bar** all unqualified teachers from state schools.

3 **to stop**
to intercept [+ between starting-point and destination]

One can **intercept** { a letter
a telegram
a message
a radio signal
a messenger
someone making a journey.

4 **to investigate** [+ try to find out
more information
to explore about]

or [+ travel in little
known places] [+ to
know more about them]

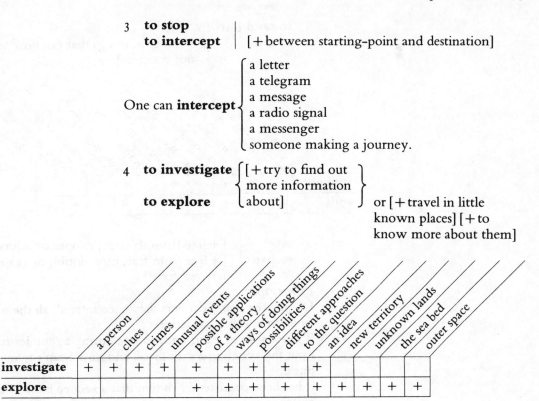

	a person	clues	crimes	unusual events	possible applications of a theory	ways of doing things	possibilities	different approaches to the question	an idea	new territory	unknown lands	the sea bed	outer space
investigate	+	+	+	+	+	+	+	+	+				
explore					+	+	+	+	+	+	+	+	+

5 **to malign**
to defame { [+ speak or write ill of sb] } [+ discredit sb's reputation]

Defame normally occurs in infinitive and participal constructions, and in its nominal form **defamation**.

EXAMPLES

The newspapers have all **maligned** this poor man who seems to me to have the best interests of his workers at heart.

I think you should not **malign** your teachers unless you are sure you could do better yourself.

I would say the television company deliberately set out to **defame** the reputation of the journalist who criticized it.

He is suing the paper for **defamation** of character because they printed an article saying he organised 'weekends of debauchery' at his country house.

6 **to send out**
   to emit   [+only of things that can flow or are not concrete]

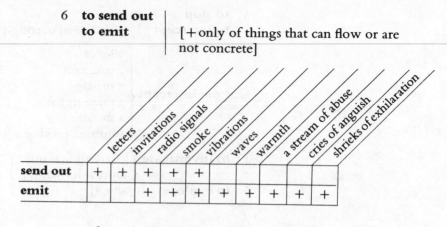

	letters	invitations	radio signals	smoke	vibrations	waves	warmth	a stream of abuse	cries of anguish	shrieks of exhilaration
send out	+	+	+	+	+					
emit			+	+	+	+	+	+	+	+

7 **safe**   [+free from damage, danger or injury]
   secure   [+free from fear, care, doubt, or anxiety] or [+well fixed]

EXAMPLES

Despite the many dangers they encountered, all the members of the expedition came home **safe**.

It is not **safe** to stand under a tree during a thunderstorm.

I put my watch in a **safe** place, and now I can't remember where I put it.

It has been consistently shown that a **secure** home life during childhood is very important for forming emotionally-balanced adults.

Having suffered a lot of unhappiness, she seems to find it hard to feel **secure** in any kind of emotional relationship.

The climber felt for his next **secure** foothold in the rock.

8 **possible**
   feasible   [+reasonable, given the circumstances]

EXAMPLES

Due to an air traffic controllers' strike, delays of up to two hours are **possible** today at London Airport.

It is **possible** to make fire by rubbing two sticks together.

Is it **feasible** to make the return trip from Brussels to London in one day?

The project seemed sound in theory but exploratory tests showed it was not **feasible.**

9 **dependable**
   sound   [+sensible or wise] or [+healthy] or [+sturdy]

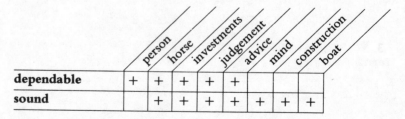

	person	horse	investments	judgement	advice	mind	construction	boat
dependable	+	+	+	+	+			
sound		+	+	+	+	+	+	+

10 **broad**
   wide   [+sometimes suggests that the thing qualified could be measured]

The difference between **broad** and **wide** is mainly collocational.

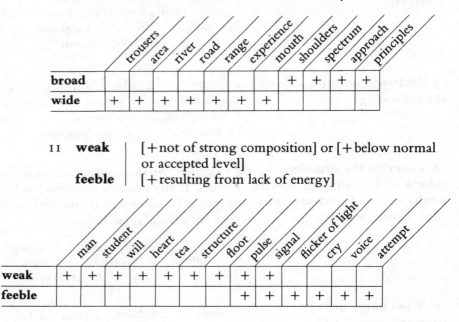

	trousers	area	river	road	range	experience	mouth	shoulders	spectrum	approach	principles
broad								+	+	+	+
wide	+	+	+	+	+	+	+				

11 **weak**   [+not of strong composition] or [+below normal or accepted level]
   feeble   [+resulting from lack of energy]

	man	student	will	heart	tea	structure	floor	pulse	signal	flicker of light	cry	voice	attempt
weak	+	+	+	+	+	+	+	+	+				
feeble								+	+	+	+	+	+

Exercises

1 Find words to fit the following definitions/ descriptions:

1 a major achievement in, for example, technology or negotiations
2 a small lever for releasing a spring, especially on a gun
3 exaggerated sense of well-being
4 a question or point that arises for discussion
5 an unvarying, often simplified, conventional expression, opinion, mental pattern
6 a folder, cover or case for keeping papers (documents) in order
7 a man-made object put into orbit around the earth
8 a ray or stream of light (eg from a light-house, laser)
9 components, items which make up the whole
10 person responsible for checking all entries to an institution

2 What can you . . . ?

1 grow   2 tape-record   3 sprinkle   4 disclose   5 misuse
6 prohibit   7 scatter   8 file   9 protect   10 store   11 shape
12 divulge

3 What do the following terms mean?

1 (violin) string   2 push-button control   3 archives   4 hardware
5 leisure   6 court (of justice)   7 screen   8 data bank   9 school
superintendent   10 laser   11 mashed potatoes   12 pledge
13 bug (eg sb's telephone)   14 inevitable

4 Fill in the blanks with appropriate words from the given list. Notice that one of the words will fit two contexts.

gain disclose explore bring monitor take pledge enact subscribe issue raise

1 to . . . . . legislation   2 to . . . . . to a magazine   3 to . . . . . legal action against   4 to . . . . . a warning   5 to . . . . . access to 6 to . . . . . all possibilities   7 to . . . . . telephone calls   8 to . . . . . precautions   9 to . . . . . questions   10 to . . . . . information 11 to . . . . one's cooperation   12 to . . . . . sb to trial

5 Add appropriate nouns to the following:

1 secure . . .   2 whole-hearted . . .   3 reliable . . . 4 expanding . . .   5 basic . . .   6 broad . . .   7 feasible . . . 8 far-sighted . . .   9 crucial . . .   10 giant . . . 11 multiple . . .   12 multifarious . . .

6 Describe the situations where the following words could be used and say why they would be used.

EXAMPLE: **smirk**: implies smiling for unpleasant or foolish reasons. If you describe somebody as smirking you express disapproval; moreover, if you say it to their face you are being very critical and quite rude.

1 to curse   2 to infuriate   3 to trudge   4 to blossom 5 to amend   6 to smack   7 mature   8 multiple   9 to intercept 10 wages   11 rags   12 stereotypes

7 What nouns are derivationally related to the following items?

1 approve   2 inhibit   3 store   4 rely   5 defame   6 private 7 maintain   8 proceed   9 snoop   10 disclose   11 emit 12 multiple   13 diverse

8 Fill in the missing prepositions.

1 That's the way it has been . . . centuries.
2 Everything is possible . . . the touch of a button.
3 He was prevented . . . leaving.
4 When was the issue brought . . .?
5 What are they suing them . . .?
6 I would never spy . . . anybody.
7 He was barred forever . . . delivering mail.
8 He disclosed their address . . . the police.
9 Will he go . . . trial?
10 She has been accused . . . theft.

9 Fill in the following grids.   1

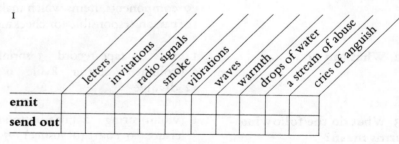

	letters	invitations	radio signals	smoke	vibrations	waves	warmth	drops of water	a stream of abuse	cries of anguish
emit										
send out										

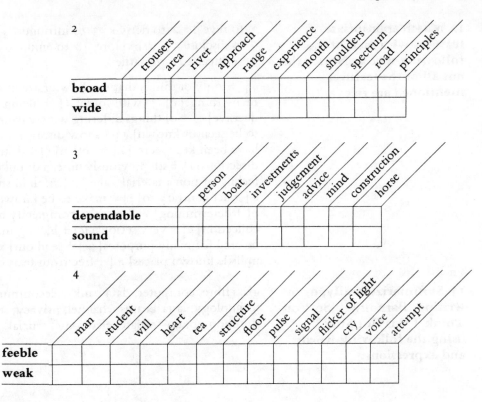

2

	trousers	area	river	approach	range	experience	mouth	shoulders	spectrum	road	principles
broad											
wide											

3

	person	boat	investments	judgement	advice	mind	construction	horse
dependable								
sound								

4

	man	student	will	heart	tea	structure	floor	pulse	signal	flicker of light	cry	voice	attempt
feeble													
weak													

10 Describe the differences and/or similarities between the following:

1 libel/slander   2 computer/brain   3 mashed potatoes/chips   4 spy/snoop   5 infringe/violate   6 stem/originate   7 accuse/charge   8 borrow/lend   9 correct/amend   10 bring up/breed   11 sensitive/sensible   12 many-sided/multi-purpose

11 Choose the word that best fits the context. Modify its form where necessary.

1 He was a typical village gossip, who loved nothing better than to . . . . . into the affairs of others. (spy, pry, snoop)
2 The proceedings of the conference were only . . . . . to the press after general agreement among its participants. (betray, reveal, divulge)
3 The young couple only . . . . . their recent engagement when all the guests had arrived. (reveal, disclose, divulge)
4 The crows . . . . . at the sound of the shotgun. (scatter, disperse, strew)
5 The crowd . . . . . quietly for once after the football match. (scatter, disperse, strew)
6 A national economic crisis was only averted by . . . . . last minute talks between employers and the unions. (critical, vital, crucial)
7 He was a . . . . . musician, changing from classical music to jazz with the greatest ease. (diverse, versatile, multiple)
8 There was a . . . . . spread of dishes for the guests to choose from. (multifarious, many-sided, versatile, multi-purpose)
9 She asked for a . . . . . cup of tea (weak, feeble).
10 The plan looked . . . . . to us. (possible, feasible, probable)

12 Match appropriate features with each of the following words. Notice that not all of the features mentioned are relevant.

1 to reveal   2 to derive   3 to infringe   4 to disperse   5 to bar   6 to disclose   7 to explore   8 to emit   9 diverse   10 secure   11 critical   12 versatile

a [+ only of things that can flow or are intangible] b [+ able to do many things] c [+ with force] d [+ being a turning point and thus decisive] e [+ of things differing widely from one another] f [+ make to be seen or known] g [+ show disrespect for] h [+ sth that should have been kept secret] i [+ obtain] j [+ disturb] k [+ go in several directions] l [+ sth previously unseen or unknown] m [+ usu positive feeling or non-material value] n [+ fall in small drops or particles] o [+ act contrary to] p[+ make to be known] q [+ far and wide] r [+ determining] s [+ so as to completely break up the assembly/collection] t [+ very serious] u [+ having many aspects] v [+ able to be used for many purposes] w [+ send out] x [+ exclude] y [+ travel in little known places] z [+ free from fear, care, doubt or anxiety]

13 Summarize orally, or in writing, Barnouw's 'So You Think TV is Hot Stuff?' using the following words and expressions:

glass fibre, computer, data bank, telecommunication, telescreen, technology, laser beams, channel, privacy, store, talk back, order, summon up, up-to-date, electronic, crucial

Revision Exercises

R1 Supply the words that best fit the following definitions/descriptions:

1 an equal in rank, age, etc
2 a student who leaves school or college before graduation
3 a construction of interconnecting passages without a direct route from one side to the other
4 information which comes back to the originator of something about its effect
5 breed, line of ancestors and descendants
6 to touch, stroke and caress lovingly
7 to walk wearily and heavily, or with effort
8 to attract, tempt

R2 List the most familiar collocations for the following:

1 to enroll in   2 to attend (a)   3 to subscribe to (a)   4 to grant
5 to be deprived of   6 to spray   7 to disapprove of   8 to accumulate   9 to curl   10 to owe sb

R3 What are the differences and/or similarities between the following items?

1 teach/instruct   2 initiate/instigate   3 enhance/intensify
4 benefit/take advantage of   5 obstruct/block   6 say/reel off
7 develop/evolve   8 critical/scathing   9 reliable/sterling

R4 Supply the missing prepositions.

1 to be frantic . . . worry   2 to be scathing . . . sth   3 to leave . . . England   4 to clout sb . . . the head   5 to coach sb . . .

mathematics   6 to hit sb . . . a stick   7 to take advantage . . . sb
8 to entrust sth . . . sb   9 to confide . . . sb   10 to slap sb . . . the
face   11 to profit . . . sb's death   12 to entrust sb . . . sth
13 to educate sb . . . the law   14 to punch sb . . . the head
15 to instruct sb . . . swimming

R5 What are the British English equivalents of these?

1 to mail   2 to figure out   3 dumb   4 pep (*sl*)   5 french fries
6 mailman

R6 Produce a logical and coherent story by filling in the blanks with appropriate words from the list below, modifying their form where necessary. Notice that not all of the words mentioned are relevant.

to launch, to initiate, to educate, to train, to coach, to commit,
to entrust, to consign, to summon up, to amend, to enhance,
to heighten, to aggravate, to benefit, to take advantage of, to
hinder, to impede, to evolve, to reel off, to eavesdrop, to abuse,
to intercept, to disclose, to display, to disperse, to dispel, to snoop,
to relegate, to investigate, breakthrough, strain, blatant, prudent,
remote, feasible, dour, versatile, crucial

The 1 . . . . . for the young writer came at last and his career was
2 . . . . . with the publication of his first book. It was a 3 . . . . .
moment for him and a 4 . . . . . . on his nerves, this waiting for the
critics' reactions. They were very cautious about the book, not
wanting to 5 . . . . . themselves too much. One 6 . . . . . journalist
7 . . . . . all the things that he didn't like about the book, 8 . . . . . ing
such 9 . . . . . prejudice against the author that his criticism in the
end only 10 . . . . . the young writer and 11 . . . . . his reputation as
one of Britain's controversial new novelists. The young man kept
a 12 . . . . . silence during this period of journalistic debate though
he 13 . . . . . afterwards that some of the misinterpretations about
the book had really 14 . . . . . him. Later, he 15 . . . . . a reception
held in his honour, 16 . . . . . his courage, and told his audience his
views on the matter. He was a 17 . . . . . speaker and showed that he
was capable of 18 . . . . . criticism and turning it to his own
advantage. He did not 19 . . . . . his position of importance by using
that as an argument in itself against his critics, but rather, 20 . . . . .,
with his audience, the basis of some of the criticism. In doing so he
21 . . . . . our fears about his being an arrogant young man, and
indeed, we were only too happy to 22 . . . . . our opinion of him.
He explained how he'd been 23 . . . . . in a small state school,
24 . . . . . to the back of the class as a slow learner and, having failed
his exams, had been 25 . . . . . by a private tutor. Our interest was
26 . . . . . when he explained how his own interest in writing had
27 . . . . . . The fact that he had learnt to read late in childhood had,
apparently, not 28 . . . . . his progress in adolescence. His story was
so 29 . . . . . from our own spoilt childhoods; and yet, explaining
his own rise to success, he made it all sound so 30 . . . . . . From the
moment he'd 31 . . . . . his manuscript to the hands of the
publishers his luck changed. At this, his chest swelled a little with
well-founded pride.

R7 Solve the crossword puzzle.

Across

1 person from Scotland (4)
4 make a sweater using wool and needles (4)
6 weep, cry (3)
8 takers (anagram) (6)
11 hams (anagram) (4)
13 touch, stroke, caress lovingly (6)
14 room where food is stored (6)
17 Bugging equipment can i . . . . . telephone calls automatically. (9)
18 vie in table (anagram), for 'difficult to avoid' (10)
19 libel or slander sb (6)
21 The Government's decision to tax refrigerators will t . . . . . off a storm of complaints. (7)
23 one who has the care or custody of sth (9)
27 install equipment for secret listening (3)
30 electronic wave which is sent out into the air (8)
31 a grave tag (anagram) makes things worse (9)
32 idiot (*sl*) (3)
33 I don't like people to p . . . . . into my affairs and try to find out what I am doing. (3)

Down

2 tell sb private information about oneself (7)
3 opposite of *short* (4)
5 Family difficulties often i . . . . . children's progress at school. (6)
6 sled ran (anagram), to speak badly of sb (7)
7 I hit bin (anagram), to prevent sth (7)
9 If players i . . . . . the rules, they are sent off the field. (8)
10 metal (4)
12 the act of doing things quickly and with energy (*coll*) (6)
15 quantity of things placed one on top of the other (4)
16 The rats had to run round a . . . . . . (4)
20 put two numbers together to make a total (3)
21 walk wearily and heavily (6)
22 opposite of *off* (2)
23 part of the face (5)
24 You must keep s . . . . . while I take your photograph! (5)
25 Elephants' tusks are made of i . . . . .. (5)
26 move from a fixed point (*coll*) (5)
28 ray of light (4)
29 small piece of cloth used, eg to wipe the floor (3)

Unit 3　The stream of time

Cultural concepts of time

The hustle and bustle of a British street.

The timelessness of an Indian town.

The **pace**[1] an individual keeps in work and recreation, his subjective sense of duration, and what he imagines he can accomplish within any specific interval are aspects of time that may be influenced by culture. Temporal attitudes **pervade**[2] a culture to such an extent that they are almost invisible, yet they are probably more influential than we imagine. In subtle but powerful ways, cultural concepts of time have helped to **mold**[3] the history of civilization.

CULTURAL CONCEPTS OF TIME

1 speed, rhythm
2 penetrate into every part
3 form into a certain shape
4 freedom from error
5 hurrying and wanting to hurry or push others into doing things
6 a part which shows what the whole is like
7 reprocessed so as to be used again
8 brief, lasting only a short time, not permanent
9 warnings, advice
10 hold fast to, stick to
11 penetrating into every part
12 people who walk while they are asleep
13 unaware, not mindful
14 pay attention to
15 boiling, moving rapidly, being excited, agitated, or disturbed
16 not harmonious
17 keeping to, not deviating from
18 rate of change increasing fast with time
19 quick and violent rise
20 throw with great force
21 increase of speed
22 push with force
23 desire greatly
24 great riches
25 arrangement in time
26 makes the most of
27 steadily changing according to a repeating pattern (usu biological)
28 difference
29 physical

Time concepts may help to explain the astonishing **accuracy**[4] of early Chinese histories. Not only did the Chinese document events from earliest antiquity, but they also expressed an orderly respect for family tradition and rules of human conduct, qualities that appear to have been generated by a philosophy embodying respect for time cycles of considerable magnitude. Naturalists and astronomers saw that the cycles of the sun and moon were reflected in life, and this in turn influenced their philosophy: 'The sun at noon is the sun declining; the creature born is the creature dying.' In cycle-oriented Taoism time was divided into seasons and eras, considered part of an infinite chain of duration – past, present, and future.

In the thirteenth century, the Chinese *Book of Changes* gave an estimate of phases in the evolution of life covering about 130,000 years. At that time the Chinese were calculating astronomical periods in millions of years. Western attitudes of that era were primitive by contrast. Judeo-Christian perception of time was linear. The flow of time was believed to begin with some specific point in space-time. In seventeenth-century Europe, people piously believed in Bishop Usher's calculation of the date of the Creation of the Universe – October 6, 4004 BC. Time, it was thought, had to begin with some significant event.

This simple linearity dictated much of Western thought, custom, and philosophical egotism. It encouraged a self-centered concept of our place in the universe, our **hustling**[5] individuality, and our philosophies of cause and effect. These notions have been instrumental in the development of Western science.

Westerners measure time by action and outstanding actions are recorded as history. In contrast, India has never produced a written history. The Hindustani never troubled to make detailed chronological records of their national development, for they lived in a time domain characterized by a changeless sense of ever-becoming. To Westerners, Indians may seem lacking in urgency. Their universe, world, and social order are eternal; personal life is only a **sample**[6] of a succession of lives, repeating themselves endlessly. Transmigration of souls and perpetual rebirth make meaningless any quantitative view of a particular period of time. Life, infinitely **recycled**[7], makes 'history less significant, and an individual's biography is merely a **transient**[8] moment in the process.

The Japanese Buddhist concept of the transience of the physical world has very different consequences: it has led to intuitive, sensitive **admonitions**[9] that if all things are transient, one must appreciate but not **cling**[10] to the moment. In Japanese sensibility, time is not an absolute nor an objective set of categories but a process. It is the change of nature. Man is part of that change and able to appreciate it, feeling transience to be part of the eternal loveliness of the universe rather than a threat to the ego (as Western man sees mortality).

Even the briefest statement is sufficient to indicate that cultural concepts of time have a **pervasive**[11] influence upon individuals and upon major social developments. One can see why ancient peoples might have accepted notions of biological rhythmicity, connecting human life with natural cycles, and why such ideas are almost nonexistent in our own society.

Most of us move from day to day in a measured circle of time. Slaves to the clock on the wall, we progress like **somnambulists**[12] in deep trance, unaware, out of contact, **oblivious**[13] to the clocks inside us. We **heed**[14] the gross demands of the flesh that our skeletons carry, but what principle gives order to the endless activity within this flesh? What force prevents utter anarchy?

Time structure gives this **seething**[15] life a shape. Yet nobody teaches us about our body's time. Body time is rarely mentioned by doctors and even more rarely considered by leaders of business and government who set the schedules by which we work and live. Time is the most-overlooked dimension in human nature.

As a result we now live at a pace that is **dissonant**[16] with our inner needs. We no longer act in harmony with natural cycles as did our ancestors throughout the millennia, working by day, resting by night, **abiding**[17] by the seasons, and traveling no faster than animal feet or sails could carry them. So man lived for perhaps 30,000 generations. Suddenly, only fifty years ago, the **exponential**[18] **surge**[19] of technology began to **fling**[20] us out of all former concepts of time and space. Today we travel at the speed of sound, and with media such as television it is possible to compress the information of several lifetimes into a month or two. It is an exciting time to be alive, but a disturbing one, for our bodies and brains have not changed so much from those of our primitive ancestors, yet we must adapt to constant change. **Acceleration**[21] is the **thrust**[22] of our technology. **Coveting**[23] the **affluence**[24] of technology we conform to the kind of social **scheduling**[25] that is economically efficient, and which **optimizes**[26] the use of machines. But it is not necessarily a beneficial pacing for human beings. In biological systems, time is represented in a **metabolic**[27] process that is cyclic, in which we eat and digest, inhale and exhale, absorbing and using energy in a rhythmic way. These time sequences in us are often dissonant with the social machine, and many victims of this **disparity**[28] suffer from emotional and **somatic**[29] illnesses.

Gay Gaer Luce, *Body Time*

A new lease of life

Once she had retired from her job as education inspector and **vocational guidance adviser**[1], Jeanne Lerot found the days **dragging**[2] **oppressively**[3]. Fortunately, she discovered Third Age College, and since she **enrolled**[4] last spring, her life has regained its former interest and activity.

Jeanne Lerot is one of nearly 1,000 students in their first year at Third Age College. This is a new section of the University of Toulouse and is intended exclusively for people who have reached retirement age.

The 'students' are not required to take entrance exams and the curriculum and pace are not as strenuous as for normal graduates. But the **fare**[5] is a rich and varied **mix**[6], including lectures, seminars, tutorials and study projects on a wide variety of topics, ranging from the theoretical to the very practical.

While at first there was a certain amount of **snickering**[7] on the part of the younger students, now the **denizens**[8] of the 'white hair college' are **taken for granted**[9].

This new College is the **brainchild**[10] of one of the University professors. So far he has run the college on a **shoe-string budget**[11] out of his own department's funds but now the French government is so impressed it has promised **substantial**[12] subsidies.

A NEW LEASE OF LIFE

1 somebody who advises young people about jobs
2 passing slowly
3 heavily
4 became a student
5 *lit* food and drink, menu, *here* courses
6 mixture
7 laughing a half-suppressed laugh, making fun of
8 inhabitants
9 accepted without question or special notice
10 invention
11 tight, small, barely sufficient budget
12 large

'Every day is a gift when you are over 100'

by Alexander Leaf, M.D.

VILLAGES WHERE TIME MOVES KINDLY

There are places in the world where people are **alleged**[1] to live much longer and remain more vigorous in old age than in most modern societies. I have visited the best known of these regions, all relatively **remote**[2] and mountainous: the Andean village of Vilcabamba in Ecuador, the land of Hunza in the Karakoram Range in Pakistani-controlled Kashmir, and Abkhazia in the Georgian Soviet Socialist Republic in the southern Soviet Union, where I met Khfaf Lasuria, oldest of the many centenarians I interviewed.

She is small – not five feet tall – white-haired, and full of humor. I visited her one spring morning and found her in her garden, surrounded by children, pigs, and chickens. I was greeted in warm Georgian fashion, and we **toasted**[3] each other first with vodka and then with wine as we talked.

She talked about her life, the present and the past, about things she remembered. She had a lot to tell because her memory was good – and she was more than 130 years old.

She told me about her first marriage at age 16; her husband died during an epidemic some twenty years later, and she married again when she was about 50. A son lives in the stone house next to hers. He is 82 years old.

She remembered as a recent event the big snowfall in 1910. 'My son was already an adult then, and I was about 70. The snow was more than two meters deep, and I helped him **shovel**[4] it from the roof.'

The present? She was just back from a visit to relatives in a distant village. She simply got on the bus alone and went visiting. She had worked on the local collective farm since it was formed some 40 years ago, retiring only in 1970; in the 1940's, when she was already more than 100 years old, she had held the record as the farm's fastest **tea-leaf picker**[5].

There is no baptismal record of Khfaf Lasuria. So as I talked to her, I kept doing mental arithmetic. I have said that she is more than 130; I should have said 'at least'. According to her **account**[6], her father lived to be 100 and her mother 101 or 102. She had seven sisters and three brothers, and is the only survivor. Her son, who was born when she was 52, is now 82 (arithmetic: $82+52=134$). She was married the second time at age 50, at the time of the Turkish war – which ended 94 years ago in 1878 ($50+94=144$). When she was 20, her first husband almost left home to fight in the Crimean War of 1853–56 ($118+20=138$). She started smoking in 1910 when her younger brother died at age 60; he was some ten years younger than she ($60+10+62=132$). Her second husband, who was two years younger than she, died 28 to 30 years ago, when he was more than 100 ($100+29+2=131$).

Khfaf Lasuriya with some younger friends.

My interview was conducted in such a way that it would have been difficult for each of these **assessments**[7] to come out in such **fair**[8] agreement unless a common **thread**[9] of reality linked them. Mrs Lasuria believes she is 141 years old; thus I would accept some age between 131 and 141.

INTEREST IN OPPOSITE SEX PERSISTS

In the Caucasus I asked the old people to what age they thought youth extends. Gabriel Chapnian of Gulripshi, age 117, gave a typical response, 'Youth normally extends up to the age of 80. I was still young then.' The youngest age cited was 60.

Quada Jonashian, aged 110, also of Gulripshi, was embarrassed at the question, since I was accompanied by a woman doctor from the regional health center. He thought 'youth' meant engaging in sexual activity and admitted that he had considered himself a youth until 'a dozen years ago'.

Professor Pitzkhelauri has collected some figures relating marital status to **longevity**[10]. He found from studies of 15,000 persons older than 80 that, with rare exceptions, only married people attain extreme age. Many **elderly**[11] couples had been married 70, 80, or even 100 years. He concludes that marriage and a regular, prolonged sex life are very important to longevity.

Women who have many children tend to live longer. His figures showed that among the centenarians only 2.5 percent of marriages were childless, whereas 44 percent of the women had four to six children, 23 percent had only two or three children, 19 percent had seven to nine children and 5 percent had ten to fifteen. Several women had more than twenty children!

USEFUL TO THE VERY END

A **striking**[12] feature common to all three cultures is the high social status of the aged. Each of the very elderly persons I saw lived with family and close relatives – often an **extensive**[13] household – and occupied a central and privileged position within this group. The sense of family continuity is strong.

There is also a sense of usefulness. Even those well over 100 for the most part continue to perform essential duties and contribute to the economy of the community. These duties included **weeding**[14] in the fields, feeding the poultry, **tending**[15] flocks, picking tea, washing the laundry, cleaning house, or caring for grandchildren, all on a regular daily basis.

In addition, the aged are **esteemed**[16] for the wisdom that is thought to derive from long experience, and their word in the family group is generally law.

In none of the three communities is there any forced retirement age, and the elderly are not **shelved**[17], as occurs in most of our industrialized societies. Khfaf Lasuria, the **former**[18] tea picker, had retired only two years before I met her. When I asked Seliac Butba, age 121, if he was helping in the construction of a new house springing up next to his own, he responded, 'Of course, they can't do without me.'

Many of the centenarians emphasized the importance of being independent and free to do the things they enjoyed and wanted to do, and of maintaining a **placid**[19] state of mind free from worry or emotional strain.

'Now everywhere people don't live so long because they don't live a free life,' commented Sonia Kvedzenia of Atara, age 109. 'They worry more and don't do what they want.' Gabriel Chapnian, 117, of Gulripshi expressed a similar thought when told that few Americans attain his age. His response: 'Hmm . . . too **literate**[20]!'

Expectation of longevity may also be important. In America the traditional **life-span**[21] is three **score**[22] and ten years. But when we asked the young people of Abkhazia how long they expected to live, they generally said, 'To a hundred'. Dr Georgi Kaprashvili of Gulripshi confirmed that the public has the notion that the normal life-span of man is 100 years. For exaggeration, when proposing toasts, they may say 300 years, but everyone expects to be 100.

National Geographic

'EVERY DAY IS A GIFT WHEN YOU ARE OVER 100'

1 supposed, it is claimed that
2 far away, distant, secluded
3 drink as a gesture of goodwill to somebody or something
4 to clear with a shovel
5 a person who picks or gathers leaves of the tea-plant
6 story, description, explanation
7 calculations, judgements
8 just, reasonable
9 chain, something which connects, *lit* a fine length of eg cotton, used for sewing two pieces of material together
10 long life, ability to live a long time
11 of advanced age
12 remarkable
13 large, *here* numerous
14 remove weeds, wild plants growing where they are not wanted
15 watching over, caring for
16 thought highly of, regarded as very valuable
17 no longer wanted, no longer used, *lit* put on a shelf, put aside
18 earlier
19 undisturbed, calm
20 educated, able to read and write
21 duration of life
22 twenty (only used in set expressions)

Retirees may overburden labor force

Caring for the elderly promises to pose increasing problems as senior citizens grow both in numbers and in average age.

Because of longer life expectancy and a decline in the birth rate, the number of people aged 75 and over in the US will grow at a rate two-and-a-half times that of the national average over the next two decades. Where there are now 4.6 workers for every retiree in the United States, by 1990 there will be only 3.5, according to the Ford Foundation, which is **funding**[1] a study to examine the need for new retirement policies. Many economists and policy analysts wonder whether the smaller pool of workers will be able to support future retirees. A trend toward early retirement aggravates the situation: the Social Security Administration reports that most applicants are now under 65. Many fear that the Social Security system will not stay **solvent**[2].

Part of the solution may lie in raising the retirement age. Robert N Butler, a psychiatrist and author of *Why Survive? Being Old in America*, cites Sweden, Japan, and the Soviet Union as countries who perceive the older worker as a valuable resource and provide **incentives**[3] to **delay**[4] his retirement. In 1972, 53% of Soviet men **eligible**[5] for retirement were still working, including almost three per cent of the 80-year-olds, according to Butler.

The Futurist

RETIREES MAY OVERBURDEN LABOUR FORCE

1 paying for
2 able to pay its debts
3 that which incites a person to action, stimulus
4 postpone
5 fit to be chosen, having the right qualifications

NOT EYE!

1 clinic which provides advice and help with contraception

Not eye!

My sixty-eight year old uncle walked into a hospital clinic and said to the receptionist: 'I need my eyes tested'.

'You certainly do, Sir', she answered. 'This is the **Family Planning Clinic**[1]'.

Miss P.R., Yorkshire

'Senior Power'

Members of the British Pensioners Trade Union Action Association prepare to present a petition to the Prime Minister.

Just as blacks exposed racism and women uncovered sexism, so the nation's elderly citizens have now discovered the demon of 'ageism', by which they mean the systematic discrimination against people on grounds of age.

Responding to slogans like 'Don't Agonize – Organize', the elderly are **pooling**[1] their power through such organizations as the National Council of Senior Citizens (which claims 3.5 million members in 3,500 clubs), the Gray Panthers (a smaller, more **boisterous**[2] confederation **boasting**[3] 6,000 members) and hundreds of state- and city-sponsored groups that champion the rights of senior citizens.

The fight against ageism will be won only when the young discover that they are the ones who suffer when the old are segregated. This realization, says Sharon Curtin, author of a **touching**[4] book on the elderly entitled 'Nobody Ever Died of Old Age', appears **to be dawning on the children**[5] of 'nuclear' **families**[6]. 'Children need their grandparents as much as the grandparents need them,' she observes, 'because children need more than one or two adults who love them regardless of what they do.' At the same time, she argues, mobile middle-class neighborhoods need old people who can add stability, variety and character to the community.

Newsweek

SENIOR POWER

1 putting together
2 rough, noisy, *here* politically aggressive
3 having the advantage of possessing
4 emotionally moving
5 the children are beginning to realize
6 group living together consisting only of two parents and their children

A tip for readers living alone

For years my Great Aunt Maud lived alone in a **remote**[1] cottage beside a road in the Welsh hills. Yet she was never afraid of being attacked or **robbed**[2] because she had **devised**[3] a unique way of protecting herself. Hanging in the **lobby**[4] of her house, and visible from the front door, was a policeman's hat. Naturally anyone calling at the house immediately noticed the hat and **assumed**[5] that there was a policeman living there.

Aunt Maud never had any trouble from doorstep **dodgers**[6] or people calling at the house to try and find out if it was worth **burgling**[7]. She felt quite safe.

After her death, her cottage was cleared out, and the policeman's hat was packed away in a suitcase and forgotten. Just the other day I came across it, and remembering Aunt Maud's idea, I hung it on a **peg**[8] in the hall for any caller to see as soon as the door opens. I really feel safe and **snug**[9] now it's there!

– *Miss A S, Devon*

A TIP FOR READERS LIVING ALONE

1 far away from populated areas
2 having possessions taken from one by a criminal
3 thought out, planned, invented
4 small entrance hall
5 accepted as a fact without definite evidence
6 dishonest people who call at houses trying to sell things or obtain money falsely
7 the house is entered and property illegally removed
8 a hook on the wall to hold clothes
9 cosy, comfortable, warm

Discussion

1 What is the attitude to time in your country? How do *you* feel about it?
2 Are you afraid of growing old? If so, why?
3 In your experience, is it true that older people are discriminated against and forced into a secondary role in society? What reasons can you find for this?
4 What can the younger generation learn from older people?
5 What do you think of the idea of the 'Third Age' college?
6 Do you want to live a very long time? Why? Will you try to make sure you do by adopting a healthy life style?

Word Study

A   Semantic Fields

1 Rate at which things happen

	rate	at which sth moves — or at which sth	progresses or develops	maintained over a period of time	often implies fast rate
pace	+	+	+	+	
speed	+	+	+		+
tempo	+		+		

All the nouns collocate with the preposition **of**. **Speed** can also take **with**. **Tempo** originally applied only to music, but now refers to life or existence.

	pace	speed(s)	tempo	
You can walk much further if you maintain a steady	+			
Work on the project is proceeding at a very slow	+			because of a shortage of funds.
The rapid	+		+	of present-day life would astound our ancestors.
He walks at such a tremendous	+	+		that I cannot keep up with him.
The		+		with which one event followed another left me quite breathless.
The car was travelling at high		+		, could not turn the corner and crashed into the fence.
They usually take months to answer letters so the		+		of their reply is really remarkable.
He maintained a terrifying		+		throughout the whole journey.
My new tape recorder can run at three different		+		.
The music is marked by its many changes in			+	in just a few bars.

2 Areas of activity or interest

Originally these words were used only to delimit physical areas or
objects. All are now used in a figurative sense as well.

domain   [+ area of land] [+ owned or controlled by one person,
or a group of people]

field   [+ piece of land] [+ divided off from other land, often by a
fence]

province   [+ administrative territorial area] [+ forming part of a
larger political entity]

sphere   [+ globe] [+ usu planet or star]

realm   [+ country] [+ ruled over by a king or queen]

territory   [+ area of land] [+ ruled by one individual or
government] or [+ area or district] [+ in which sb does his work]

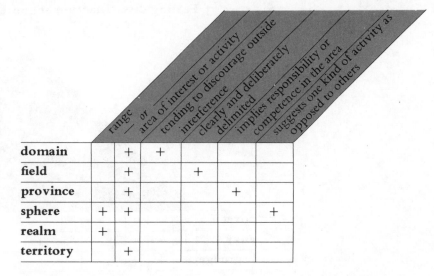

	range — or	area of interest or activity	tending to discourage outside interference	clearly and deliberately delimited	implies responsibility or competence in the area	suggests one kind of activity as opposed to others
domain		+	+			
field		+		+		
province		+			+	
sphere	+	+				+
realm	+					
territory		+				

Realm only occurs in a few set expressions, the most common of which are:

realm of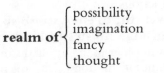
possibility
imagination
fancy
thought

The figurative use of **territory** is colloquial.
Notice that the verbs which collocate with these nouns in their physical sense may also be used figuratively.

EXAMPLES

domain Most research into animals' ability to acquire speech has so far been carried out in the **domain** of psychology, though one might feel it belongs properly in the province of linguistics.
This article on talking dogs is good, but I fear we shall be accused of trespassing in the **domain** of psychology if we print it.

field While I find industrial relations very interesting, it is really outside my **field**.
Candidates are asked to name their **field** of research, and describe what they intend to do within it.

province The **province** of a bank is to deal with my money, not to make judgements about the social acceptability of the job I choose to do.

sphere While we found your article on talking dogs very worthwhile, we feel it is really outside the **sphere** of interest of the *Journal of Modern Languages*.
She is as talented in the **sphere** of the creative arts as she is in her scientific work.

realm It is within the **realm** of possibility for us to finish the work tonight, but I think it would be better if we did not.

territory I am the Sales Manager here and I regard your instructions to the salesmen as a deliberate attempt to encroach on my **territory**.

3 Feeling dissatisfaction at another's advantages

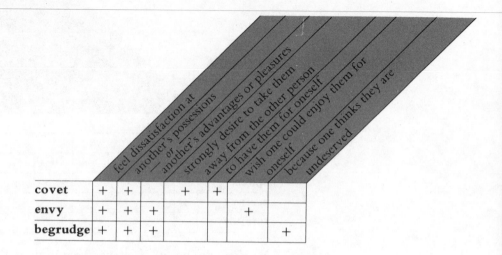

	feel dissatisfaction at another's possessions — or	another's advantages or pleasures	strongly desire to take them away from the other person	to have them for oneself	wish one could enjoy them for oneself	because one thinks they are undeserved
covet	+	+		+	+	
envy	+	+	+			+	
begrudge	+	+	+				+

These verbs are all transitive and occur in the following constructions:

to covet sth; to envy sth/sb/sb sth
to begrudge sth/sb sth/sb's doing sth

Covet in older usage implied something very wicked (and sometimes it still does). But it is now often used colloquially to express approval and liking. For example, 'I **covet** your new sheepskin rug' does not mean 'I want to take it away from you' but rather 'I like it very much'.

Note that informally **envy** is often used in the negative to mean 'be glad that one does not have to do sth', for example:
I certainly don't **envy** you having to teach grammar to that difficult first-year class.

EXAMPLES
It is wrong to **covet** another's possessions.
It is natural for the poorer classes in society to **covet** the wealth they see in the hands of a few rich people.
Julia seems to **envy** everything her brother says and does, even though she has the same advantages herself.
I can't help **envying** you your good knowledge of English.
I certainly don't **begrudge** my sister her wealth and fame, but sometimes I **envy** her just a little.
John really **begrudges** Arthur his success in winning a scholarship to the United States.
I do **begrudge** Mary's winning the first prize, when she had done so little work.

4 Caring for

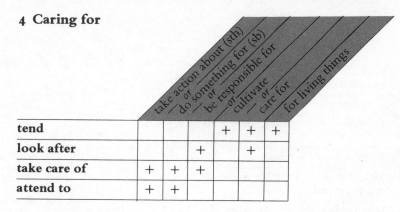

	take action about (sth)	or do something for (sb)	or be responsible for	or cultivate	or care for	for living things
tend				+	+	+
look after			+		+	
take care of	+	+	+			
attend to	+	+				

Tend and **attend to** are formal, **tend** is slightly old-fashioned.
Notice that **look after** may suggest caring for something that is
not one's own.

EXAMPLES

Could you **look after** my dog when I go away for the weekend?
I am **looking after** a friend's children while she takes a week's
holiday.

	a flock of sheep	a fire	a garden	animals	children	an ill person	the elderly	oneself	a part of a business	one's house	a client	a problem	a customer	some business	a complaint
tend	+	+	+	+	+										
look after		+	+	+	+	+	+	+	+	+		+			
take care of			+	+	+		+	+	+	+	+	+	+	+	
attend to											+	+	+	+	+
care for				+	+	+	+								

5 Being peaceful

	peaceful and undisturbed	or not of an excitable nature	or of untroubled disposition	often clear headed	apparently not threatened	preferring a peaceful existence
calm	+	+		+		
tranquil	+	+				
serene	+		+		+	
placid		+				+

	calm	tranquil	serene	placid	peaceful	
The best drivers are those who are very	+					.
In an emergency, one should try to keep as	+					as possible.
After two days of storm we were glad to find the sea	+					again.
Life in the country is more		+		+		than in the city.
The family at home together in the evening presented a		+		+		scene.
The new bride's face was a picture of			+			happiness.
The sky over the lake was			+	+		and cloudless.
Peter won't be upset, he has a most				+		nature.
He is a very				+		baby and hardly ever cries.

6 Being comfortable

	providing ease or material comfort	suggesting a place of shelter	from unpleasant things (eg bad weather, physical hardship)	usually quite small	usually warm	aiding relaxation, rest
comfortable	+					
cosy	+	+	+			
snug	+	+	+	+		
restful						+

Cosy and **snug** are very colloquial.

	shoes	car	hotel	woollen jacket	flat	little cottage	little room	corner	atmosphere	day	holiday	view	colour
comfortable	+	+	+	+	+	+	+	+					
cosy			+	+	+	+	+	+					
snug			+	+	+	+	+						
restful					+				+	+	+	+	+

When **comfortable**, **cosy** and **snug** are used predicatively and with a [+ animate] subject, their features change to read [+ having ease or material comfort] and/or [+ being in a place of shelter].

EXAMPLES

comfortable   I can see you've made yourself very **comfortable** in your new house.

I'm not very **comfortable** sitting on this hard stool.

cosy   Well, you look very **cosy** here by the fire!

snug   We're very nice and **snug** in here out of the rain.

7 Recurring, continuing or never-ending

	unchanging	repeating itself or being repeated many times	extending without interruption	in time	in place	often regularly	for an indefinite length of time / forever
continual		+					
continuous			+	+	+		
constant	+	+				+	
perpetual		+	+	+		+	
incessant			+	+		+	
eternal			+	+			+

In colloquial style, **eternal** is often used with the sense of **continual** or **incessant**.

EXAMPLE

This **eternal** bickering has really got to stop!

It may also be used metaphorically.

EXAMPLE

My love for you is **eternal**.

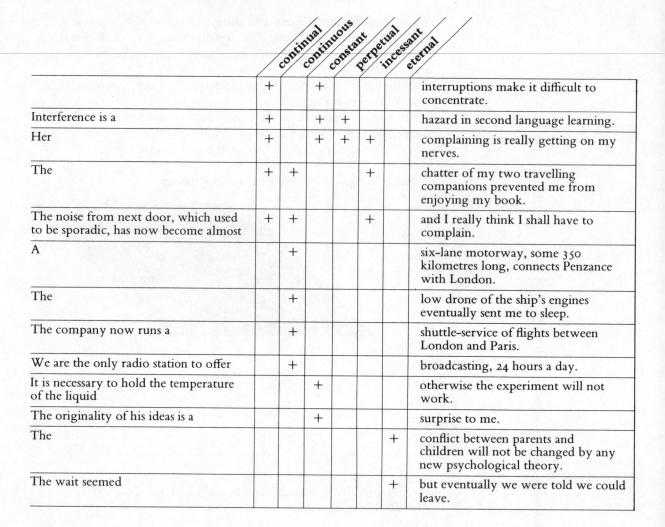

	continual	continuous	constant	perpetual	incessant	eternal	
	+		+				interruptions make it difficult to concentrate.
Interference is a	+		+	+			hazard in second language learning.
Her	+		+	+	+		complaining is really getting on my nerves.
The	+	+		+			chatter of my two travelling companions prevented me from enjoying my book.
The noise from next door, which used to be sporadic, has now become almost	+	+		+			and I really think I shall have to complain.
A		+					six-lane motorway, some 350 kilometres long, connects Penzance with London.
The		+					low drone of the ship's engines eventually sent me to sleep.
The company now runs a		+					shuttle-service of flights between London and Paris.
We are the only radio station to offer		+					broadcasting, 24 hours a day.
It is necessary to hold the temperature of the liquid			+				otherwise the experiment will not work.
The originality of his ideas is a			+				surprise to me.
The						+	conflict between parents and children will not be changed by any new psychological theory.
The wait seemed						+	but eventually we were told we could leave.

B   Synonymous Pairs

1   **to decline** / **to wane** [+ decrease]

[+ in quantity, quality or value]

[+ in power, importance, extent or intensity]

[+ implies the subject has previously reached a peak of force, excellence or intensity]

Note the use of **decline** in the expresssion **one's declining years**.

	wane(d) (ing)	decline(d) (ing)	
After a rapid rise to stardom at only 17, his popularity now seems to be	+	+	fast.
The power of the Roman Empire slowly	+	+	over a long period.
The influence of the Church has tended to		+	in Western Europe in recent years.
After her return to England her health		+	rapidly.
The value of the dollar has		+	rather than increased.

2 **to extend** $\left\{ \vphantom{xx} \right.$ [+in length, width or amount of time] or [+reach as far as]

to expand [+increase] [+in size, area, volume] or [+open, unfold] or ⇒ [+give more detail]

⇒ indicates the figurative sense. For example, the literal sense of **expand** is 'to increase in size, area or volume' as in:
Grains of rice **expand** as they are cooked.
Used figuratively, it means 'to give more detail' as in:
Could you **expand** a little on the research proposal you have put forward?

EXAMPLES
The road **extended** in an unbroken grey line as far as the eye could see.
We are **extending** our house and creating two new bedrooms and a study.
Is it possible to **extend** the time allowed for writing a dissertation?
The firm is **expanding** and taking on more personnel to produce a greater range of products.

3 **to stick to** [act according to] or [+follow] or [+keep to]

to abide by [+carefully or exactly]

Stick to is not used in formal style.

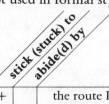

	stick (stuck) to	abide(d) by	
They did not	+		the route I had given them, so they got lost.
Don't talk about anything too difficult, just	+		what you know.
If people would	+	+	the rules there wouldn't be any trouble.
Many firms have not	+	+	the pay guidelines issued by the Government.
I am very angry that you have not	+	+	the agreement we came to.

4   **to hold**
     to cling │ [+tightly] [+by embracing, grasping] or
                  │ [+be or stay near]

Like **hold**, **cling** may be used figuratively.

EXAMPLES

The climber **clung** desperately to the cliff as the wind suddenly increased in strength.

People tend to **cling** to old habits and customs.

The child **clung** to his mother's arm and screamed when she tried to leave the hospital.

5   **to take notice of**
     to heed │ [+closely or attentively] [+usu of advice
                 │ or warnings or forecasts of the future]

EXAMPLES

I told you it would be impossible to travel by plane in this weather, but you didn't **heed** my warning.

If I had **heeded** the good advice I was given 3 years ago, I would have studied harder and passed my exams.

6   **to help**
     to sponsor │ [+make possible an undertaking by giving or
                    │ guaranteeing financial support]

EXAMPLES

He has persuaded a large engineering firm to **sponsor** his attempt to sail around the world alone.

The University's leukaemia research scheme is **sponsored** by a group of pharmaceutical companies.

7   **to postpone**   ⎰ [+put off until later] ⎱
     to delay   ⎱   ⎰ or [+make or be slow]

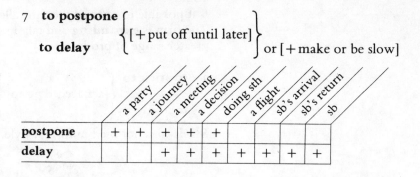

	a party	a journey	a meeting	a decision	doing sth	a flight	sb's arrival	sb's return	sb
postpone	+	+	+	+	+				
delay			+	+	+	+	+	+	+

EXAMPLE

I **delayed** as long as possible to try to see you, but eventually I had to leave.

8   **old**   ⎰   ⎱ or [+previous, former]
                      ⎱ [+of advanced age]   ⎰
     elderly   ⎱   ⎰ [+of people only]

Elderly is more polite than **old** and is normally used attributively.

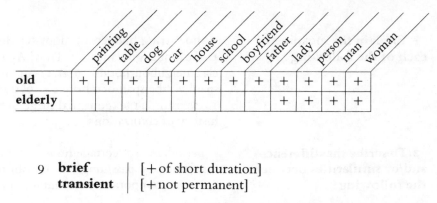

	painting	table	dog	car	house	school	boyfriend	father	lady	person	man	woman
old	+	+	+	+	+	+	+	+	+	+	+	+
elderly								+	+	+	+	

9 **brief**   [+ of short duration]
    transient   [+ not permanent]

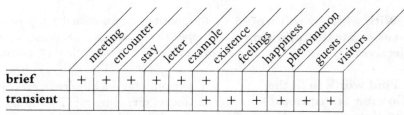

	meeting	encounter	stay	letter	example	existence	feelings	happiness	phenomenon	guests	visitors
brief	+	+	+	+	+	+					
transient					+	+	+	+	+	+	

10 **unmindful** { [+ not noticing] or } or [+ forgetting]
    oblivious { [+ deliberately ignoring] }

Both adjectives collocate with **of**. **Oblivious** can also take **to**.
EXAMPLES
Unmindful of everything she had meant to do, she rushed to the airport to meet her long-lost friend.
Unmindful of his own safety, the boy plunged into the freezing river after the struggling child.
He goes through life completely **unmindful** of the needs or feelings of others.
Once I start concentrating on my work, I'm quite **oblivious** to any nearby noise.
He's completely **oblivious** to criticism and refuses to believe there is anything wrong with his behaviour.

11 **difference**
    disparity   [+ usu in rank, amount, size or quality]

EXAMPLES
The **disparity** of age between the different participants is likely to affect the results of the tests.
University lecturers are complaining about the **disparity** between their salaries and those paid to teachers in Polytechnics and Colleges of Education.

Exercises

1 Explain the meaning of each of the following:

1 shoe-string budget   2 doorstep dodger   3 nuclear family   4 vocational guidance   5 Third Age College   6 mobile middle-class neighbourhoods   7 state- or city-sponsored groups   8 'life span' v. 'the span of a bridge'   9 transient physical world   10 sexism   11 exponential surge of technology   12 to mould the history of civilization

2 Describe the differences and/or similarities between the following:

1 period/era   2 cottage/house   3 burglar/intruder   4 alleged thief/thief   5 pass/drag on   6 rob/steal   7 remember/remind   8 eternal/temporal   9 mountainous/hilly   10 eligible/fit

3 With which words would you associate the following adjectives?

1 opposite   2 emotional   3 privileged   4 boisterous   5 proud   6 specific   7 infinite   8 outstanding   9 endless   10 intuitive   11 efficient   12 somatic   13 constant   14 seething

4 Find words to fit the following descriptions/ definitions:

1 person who is a hundred years old
2 disease spreading rapidly among many people in the same place
3 non-material part of a human being
4 list of times of recurring events, projected operations
5 long life, ability to live a long time
6 wish sb happiness, success while raising a glass of wine
7 enlist or register as a member of an institute or society
8 laugh a half-suppressed laugh, make fun of
9 give up one's work or position mainly because of one's age
10 load too heavily
11 able to pay one's debts

5 What can you . . . ?

1 abide by   2 calculate   3 cling to   4 attend to   5 mould   6 claim   7 sponsor   8 compress

6 Give as many synonyms and antonyms of each word as you can.

1 touching   2 rigorous   3 subtle   4 extensive   5 distant   6 ancient   7 exciting   8 self-centered   9 brief   10 pious   11 eternal   12 mental   13 brutal   14 outstanding   15 utter (adj)   16 major

7 Guess the right word.

1 She tried to find someone who would be prepared to sp . . . . . her application for a loan from the bank.
2 Despite opposition from her parents, the girl p . . . . . in going out with the young man.
3 He s . . . . . earth out of the hole and into the wheelbarrow with great energy.
4 Delighted with their financial project, the two businessmen t . . . . . each other's health with two large whiskies.
5 The pretentiousness of the man before him ag . . . . . the doctor.
6 He was of a b . . . . . nature, always shouting and singing, and generally waking up the household.
7 He sewed the material together using a strong t . . . . . .
8 The mission a . . . . . ed, the soldiers returned back to base.

8 Provide a few collocations in each set can appear.

EXAMPLE: dry, dull: dry ⎫ lecture/subject/book
dull ⎭

1 old, elderly   2 continuous, continual   3 serene, peaceful
4 snug, cosy   5 perpetual, incessant, eternal   6 to postpone,
to delay   7 to hold, to cling on to   8 to care for, to look after,
to take care of

9 What differences and/or similarities are there between the following pairs?

1 survive/live   2 fling/throw   3 pervade/spread   4 confirm/
establish   5 sponsor/be responsible   6 ancestor/descendant
7 sample/part, one of a number   8 admonition/warning
9 subsidy/money   10 affluent/rich

10 Describe the contexts in which the following would have negative connotations.

1 decline   2 begrudge   3 drag on   4 overlook   5 boisterous
6 oblivious   7 incessant   8 illiterate   9 dissonant   10 jostle

11 Fill in the following componential grids.

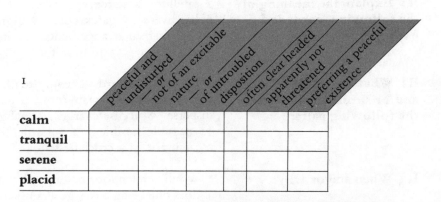

	peaceful and undisturbed	not of an excitable nature	of untroubled disposition	often clear headed	apparently not threatened	preferring a peaceful existence
calm						
tranquil						
serene						
placid						

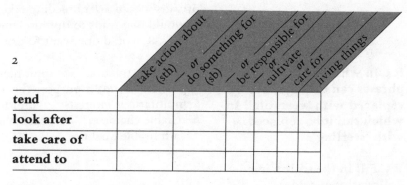

	take action about (sth)	do something for (sb)	be responsible for	cultivate	care for living things
tend					
look after					
take care of					
attend to					

12 Choose the word that best fits the context. Modify its form where necessary.

1 If one doesn't . . . . . the doctor's advice, one only finds oneself really ill later on. (take notice of, heed, pay attention to)
2 With an impetuous gesture she . . . . . the knife across the room in the direction of her employer. (fling, throw)
3 He secretly . . . . . his brother's farm. (envy, covet, begrudge)
4 The girl was too strong-willed to let herself be . . . . . by the evil influences now at work around her. (form, shape, mould)
5 He . . . . . with contempt, sending a shiver up my spine. (snicker, giggle, laugh)

6 Heavy traffic . . . . . us and we were a little late for the meeting.
(postpone, put off, delay)

7 The child looked very . . . . ., tucked up at last in a warm bed.
(restful, snug, cosy)

8 There was nothing he could say to ruffle her . . . . . countenance
(face, its appearance and expression). (placid, calm, peaceful)

9 Now that sleep had overcome her, her face took on a . . . . .
expression. (placid, serene, calm)

10 All their children looked well . . . . .. (tend, attend to, care for)

Revision Exercises

R1 Explain the meaning of the following words and expressions.

1 satellite   2 stereotype   3 laser   4 breakthrough   5 trigger
6 hardware   7 gatekeeper   8 ingredients   9 precaution
10 split screen arrangements   11 intelligence analysts
12 to pledge   13 to monitor

R2 What are the differences and/or similarities between the following pairs?

1 get rid of/discard   2 enjoy/relish   3 instigate/commence
4 stem/originate   5 spy/pry   6 disclose/divulge   7 scatter/
disperse   8 accuse/charge   9 malign/defame   10 agitated/frantic
11 possible/feasible   12 versatile/diverse   13 disobedient/
recalcitrant   14 crucial/essential

R3 When and/or why:

1 would a telephone be bugged?   2 would a letter be intercepted?
3 does one bring a charge against sb?   4 does one infringe on sb's
privacy?   5 does inbreeding take place in a community?
6 would one-want to disguise oneself?   7 can sb be barred from a
club?   8 would one want to pry into other people's affairs?

R4 In which of the given phrases can the adjective be replaced with 'versatile'? In which can it be replaced with 'sterling'?

1 diverse attractions   2 multiple achievements   3 multi-purpose
appliance   4 multi-purpose furniture   5 many-sided student
6 multifarious interests   7 multiple choice   8 diverse duties
9 reliable character   10 reliable information   11 reliable car
12 admirable qualities

R5 Fill in the following collocational grids:

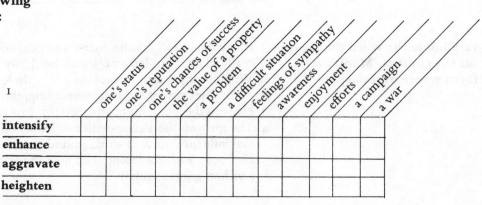

	one's status	one's reputation	one's chances of success	the value of a property	a problem	a difficult situation	feelings of sympathy	awareness	enjoyment	efforts	a campaign	a war
intensify												
enhance												
aggravate												
heighten												

2

	an employment	a course	criminal proceedings	a new line of research	a strike	an enquiry	a project	a new product	someone in show-business
launch									
instigate									
commence									
initiate									

R6 The words mentioned below can be used in several (literal or extended) senses. Identify these senses by giving distinctive semantic features (without looking back at our analyses!).

1 to benefit   2 to educate   3 to coach   4 to aggravate
5 to strike   6 to betray   7 to violate   8 to derive   9 multiple

R7 In each case give a less precise synonym of the given word.

EXAMPLE: hustle: push
1 covet   2 trudge   3 clout   4 wane   5 pledge   6 fling
7 blatant   8 crucial   9 perpetual   10 impassioned   11 euphoria
12 thrust   13 surge

R8 Choose the word that best fits the context. Modify its form where necessary.

1 Having lost her dog, the girl was . . . . . to find him before he got onto the road. (frantic, agitated)
2 It's amazing that no other mammal . . . . . in the direction man took, towards enhancing his intellectual capabilities. (develop, evolve)
3 The tennis player . . . . . the ball before it touched the ground on her side of the court. (stop, intercept)
4 A major . . . . . in medicine was when penicillin was discovered. (discovery, breakthrough, finding)
5 The . . . . . by Gallileo that the world was round altered man's vision of himself and the world. (discovery, breakthrough, finding)
6 She . . . . . her earlier statement that she'd never seen the accused before. (maintain, keep up)
7 He lived in the world of . . . . . business and high finance. (large, great, big)
8 Being generous, they gave . . . . . amounts of money to charities. (large, great, big)
9 The situation has . . . . . rapidly in your absence. (develop, evolve)

R9 Solve the crossword puzzle.

Across

1 admit onion (anagram) for 'telling off' (10)
5 process food which has been eaten (6)
8 He'll r . . . . . the prospect of no work for two weeks! (6)
10 produce flowers (of a plant) (5)
15 Tell me . . . . . results, please. (2)
16 defames in writing (6)
18 scatter here and there over a horizontal surface (5)
20 belief (5)
21 What goes up must come . . . . . (4)
22 Fruit must be r . . . . . before you eat it. (4)
23 The test consists of m . . . . . choice questions. (8)
25 be responsible for beginning sth continued by others (8)
28 This report certainly e . . . . . the student's chances of success for the scholarship. (8)
29 metal used to make cans (3)
30 dye mob (anagram) (6)

Down

2 postpone, make sth/sb late (5)
3 opposite of *bottom* (3)
4 No, it's . . . . . as easy as it looks! (3)
6 the self, as perceived in relation to the rest of the world (3)
7 ear (anagram) for 'period' (3)
9 to hit sharply with the flat of the hand (5)
11 past of *light* (3)
12 woe (anagram) (3)
13 very obvious (7)
14 Equals in rank or age are known as a p . . . . . group. (4)
15 to speak or write sth bad about sb, which is not true (6)
17 His s . . . . . qualities have made him admired by everyone. (8)
19 decrease in power, importance or intensity (4)
21 D . . . . . your hands in the river to cool them off! (3)
24 used to tie a shoe (4)
26 in GB (*of*) place where travellers stay (3)
27 The hand is joined to the . . . . .. (3)

Unit 4   To ban or not to ban

Curb that filth!

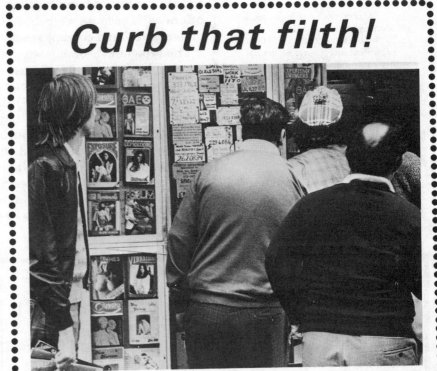

CURB THAT FILTH

1 official prevention of the publication of a book, play, film etc, because it might offend the public or have a bad influence
2 *fig* and *coll* morally offensive, usu in a sexual way
3 convincing
4 believing one is doing sth which will benefit others
5 able to express thoughts and feelings clearly
6 people who write letters, take part in demonstrations and are generally active in support of a certain cause
7 was widespread
8 something which interrupts the action of something else, the act of doing so
9 being prevented from doing something one wants to do
10 plainly, directly, without tact
11 filled up with sth, *lit* when an area of land normally dry, is covered with water
12 prevented from being known or seen
13 made less strict, lessened, *lit* loosened
14 strange to say
15 voluntary sexual intercourse (between unmarried persons)
16 the act of one male forcing sexual intercourse upon an unwilling male partner
17 shown, exhibited
18 flooded with, full of
19 morally offensive words and pictures, *lit* dirt
20 rushes to in large numbers

Censorship[1] is becoming more and more of a **dirty**[2] word. So **persuasive**[3] have been the arguments against it, put forward by intelligent, **well-meaning**[4] and above all **articulate**[5] **campaigners**[6], that nowadays censorship is hardly found in any State of the US. These people argued that the censorship which had **prevailed**[7] throughout most of history had resulted in needless **interference**[8] with, and **frustration**[9] of, the creative talent of artists and writers.

So now we have the opposite situation. But are the effects of this change as beneficial as expected? To put it **bluntly**[10], has the literary market been **flooded**[11] with hitherto **suppressed**[12] masterpieces since censorship was **eased**[13]? **Oddly enough**[14], rather the opposite is the case, and moreover we now have a situation in which **fornication**[15] and **homosexual rape**[16] can be **displayed**[17] on stage in the name of entertainment. The book and magazine market is **awash**[18] with printed **filth**[19] and the public **flocks**[20] to buy it.

21 anxiety, troubled condition
22 *informal* a habit or attitude which remains after the conditions which caused it have disappeared
23 cause sb to lose sense of what is right and good
24 the sport of inciting dogs to attack a chained bear
25 fights between gamecocks for public entertainment
26 crimes against the law of a country
27 make morally bad
28 to follow or discover by observing evidence
29 not allow sth to happen
30 control systematically, in accordance with a rule or standard
31 forcibly imposing rules
32 explicit reference to, or depiction of, sexual intercourse or genital organs in book, film or picture
33 (*Am*) people who campaign for the rights and liberties of ordinary people
34 increasingly large amount of, *lit* rising and falling of the sea, attracted by the force of the moon's gravity
35 kept under control
36 not able to be repaired or put right

But perhaps I am wrong to be worried by this – maybe my **disquiet**[21], and that of others like me, is just a **hangover**[22] from the former more restrictive situation. Many people would argue against us that books, plays and films do not have the power to **corrupt**[23].

Yet it's clear that society does have some conscience about what its members do in the name of entertainment. We would not, for example, allow someone to take his own life as part of a television show (although a recent Hollywood movie was frighteningly realistic in its depiction of TV producers promoting just this event to enhance their audience ratings). We have made such entertainments as **bear-baiting**[24], and **cockfighting**[25], **criminal offences**[26], because we believe that watching such things tends to **deprave**[27] and corrupt spectators.

The type of censorship we need is, in my view, similar to the laws we have governing the use of alcohol and tobacco. Although we can **trace**[28] the bad effects of smoking and drinking, we have not **prohibited**[29] them, but introduced laws which **regulate**[30] their use, rather than **repressing**[31] it altogether. In the case of **pornography**[32], such legislation would not run contrary to liberal principles and should therefore be acceptable to even the most ardent **civil libertarians**[33]. The **rising tide**[34] of pornography must be **curbed**[35], before it does **irreparable**[36] damage to the quality of life in our country.

Responses after observation of movie violence

Mayra L Buvinic and Leonard Berkowitz

It is now widely agreed that **witnessed**[1] violence **heightens**[2] the chances that its observers will act **aggressively**[3] themselves, particularly if they are already in an aggressive mood for other reasons.

People's reactions to observed violence undoubtedly depend upon what they learn from the scene *and* their level of excitement *and* the degree to which the scene stimulates aggressive responses *or* lowers their **restraints**[4] against such behavior.

If all these processes explain the immediate effects of movie violence, there is greater uncertainty as to how long (and why) these effects last.

The present experiment asks whether filmed violence will have an aggression **enhancing**[5] effect an hour after the movie is viewed as well as immediately afterwards.

A violent scene from the film Shane.

The Book Banners

Book **banning**[1] is not as much a thing of the past as most Americans might like to believe. The American Library Association reports more than 100 attempts last year to ban books from school libraries or curriculums. 'The general situation today is much worse than just five years ago,' says ALA official Judith F Krug.

'People are worrying about things like drugs and crime. They are looking for easy solutions, and they think that if we can just get rid of this "dirty" book or that "**subversive**[2]" book, our problems will go away.'

Books are banned for nearly as many reasons as they are written. The most suppressed book in the country is JD Salinger's 'Catcher in the Rye', a favorite of high-school English teachers that has been attacked for twenty years because of its **four-letter words**[3] and disrespect of parental authority. Right behind 'Catcher' on last year's censorship list was 'The Inner City Mother Goose,' which retells nursery rhymes in a bitter urban **vernacular**[4]. Conservative whites have sought to ban Eldridge Cleaver's 'Soul on Ice', while black activists have **set out after**[5] 'Huckleberry Finn'. Other books frequently **assailed**[6] include '1984', 'Grapes of Wrath' and even 'Gulliver's Travels'.

Newsweek

THE BOOK BANNERS

1 forbidding, excluding
2 tending to overthrow existing beliefs
3 words considered very rude or shocking
4 local popular language
5 attacked, *lit* chased
6 attacked

MOVIE VIOLENCE

1 watched, seen
2 increases
3 wanting to fight
4 selfcontrol
5 heightening
6 something (or somebody) set up to be attacked, *lit* circular object for practising shooting
7 one who torments, tortures, teases, annoys
8 went down, became less violent
9 made stronger
10 incited, motivated
11 probably
12 caused to suffer

Perhaps more important, it also inquires whether a preliminary attack upon an available **target**[6] right after the film is seen helps maintain the heightened aggressive tendency that had been initially produced by the movie.

The subjects were university men who first received either an insulting or neutral evaluation of themselves from their supposed partner and then watched either a prize fight or an exciting but nonaggressive scene. After this, they either had an opportunity to evaluate their partner right away or they had to wait an hour before evaluating him.

We found that (a) the fight movie enhanced the aggressive tendencies in the angered viewers, (b) the angered subjects' initial attack on their **tormentor**[7] immediately after the conclusion of the violent film strengthened the movie-produced reactions so that the effect of the aggressive movie could still be seen one hour later, and (c) the aggressive inclinations stimulated by the violent movie **subsided**[8] within the hour if these hadn't been acted upon soon after the film was viewed.

We cannot be certain why the 'practice trial' led to this more persistent aggression but we believe the persistence of the aggressive tendency over time can best be explained if we assume that the observation of the fight film had somehow interacted with the aggressive responses performed in the course of the initial aggression measurement. The insulted men in our aggressive film condition might have also **reinforced**[9] their relatively intense, movie-enhanced attacks on their tormentor by imagining their victim's pained reaction to what they were saying about him.

Another possibility is that the initial evaluation of the partner was reinforcing for the provoked subjects who had seen the aggressive film because it enabled them to carry out an action they were strongly **instigated**[10] to perform. The first opportunity to evaluate the tormentor was therefore a relatively gratifying chance to aggress against him. Carrying out this activity thus enhanced the inclination to further aggression (**presumably**[11] until the subjects thought they had **inflicted**[12] a sufficient degree of injury).

condensed from *Journal of Experimental Social Psychology*

A Frightening Catalogue

A Glasgow **tenement flat**[1] was broken into recently. It was **wrecked**[2], and a puppy **hacked**[3] to death.

Police say it was the work of **hooligans**[4] imitating a scene in an X film.

An isolated incident? Sadly not.

Look at these examples of recent crimes up and down the country.

● 16-year-old boy tried his hand at a **bomb hoax**[5] by phoning Heathrow Airport and demanding £250 from Pan American.

● 14-year-old boy, said to be **obsessed**[6] with horror films, **plunged**[7] a five-inch knife into a woman's back while he rode along the pavement on his bike.

● 15-year-old boy was found guilty of demanding money with menaces. He tried to copy a story of **extortion**[8] he saw on TV.

● 16-year-old boy dressed like a character in A Clockwork Orange — described by the Judge as an evil film — caused **grievous**[9] bodily harm to a 15-year-old boy by kicking him.

● Two boys, aged 12 and 14, tried to **derail**[10] trains by placing metal **bars**[11] on the track.

● After watching a TV programme a 15-year-old boy made a petrol bomb and threw it towards two teachers.

A frightening catalogue.

The Sunday Post

A FRIGHTENING CATALOGUE

1 flat in a large building divided into many cheap low standard flats
2 destroyed, ruined
3 chopped with an axe, cut roughly and clumsily
4 members of a gang, usually of young men, which causes disturbances in the streets and other public places
5 false bomb alarm
6 excessively interested in, thinking of nothing else
7 thrust forcibly
8 obtaining money from others by threats
9 severe
10 cause to go off the rails
11 long, stiff pieces of some solid material, such as iron, etc

SILENT TOO LONG

1 able to speak about anything
2 *coll* shout or cry loudly
3 said in a low voice
4 the name or idea is appropriate; cap, *lit* kind of flat hat
5 saying what one does not believe
6 from now
7 hit hard and often
8 rawest, roughest, most unpleasant, unrefined
9 result
10 morally offensive spoken words
11 abnormal, twisted, corrupt
12 up to now
13 liable to be brought to court
14 tendency
15 official person who examines books, films, etc to see that nothing in them might offend or have a bad influence on the general public
16 protected, looked after, *lit* having soft things placed around for protection
17 not being given what is needed
18 on defining the limits, on stating how far one can go
19 ability to be disgusted, scandalized, outraged

Silent Too Long

by JOSEPH McCULLOUGH

Talking about what adjective, other than 'permissive', would describe our society today, someone suggested it should be called 'the **unreticent**[1] age'. If that is taken to mean an age in which people do not know when to keep their mouths shut and **bawl**[2] what should not even be **whispered**[3], the **cap**[4] certainly **fits**[4].

The Victorians are accused of being **hypocritical**[5] because they regarded so many subjects as 'unmentionable'. What, I wonder, will be the verdict a century **hence**[6] on us, who have gone to the opposite extreme and even in our own homes allow our ears and eyes to be **battered**[7] with the **crudest**[8] explicitness? 'Not in front of the children' has ceased to be anything but a comic idea from a previous age. Could there be anything more hypocritical than our shocked surprise at the **outcome**[9]? We take immense care nowadays to protect bodies from infection but precious little to protect minds.

You may do yourself and your children irreparable damage by propagating lies, half-truths, and **foul-mouthed indecencies**[10] as well as **perverted**[11] ideas of the most intimate and (**hitherto**[12]) sacred things in human experience without being **indictable**[13] before any earthly judge. There is nothing to stop you, except your own sense of decency and values, and your own awareness of the feelings and sensibilities of other people.

I suspect that an opinion poll would reveal an increasing majority against this ugly **trend**[14] of our times. The most effective **censor**[15] in any society is educated public opinion. By educated I mean all whom the school of experience has taught to think and act responsibly, with common sense, especially in regard to their children. Who in his senses wants the kind of society in which nothing is held sacred, and where children, as like as not, will grow up without manners, morals or faith, materially **cushioned**[16] but spiritually **deprived**[17]?

We have certainly been silent too long on this subject. For the sake of our children it is time we became our own censors and made plain where we insist **that the line is drawn**[18]. 'A society' said an eminent judge 'is to be measured by the level of its **disgustability**[19]'. We must admit our level looks remarkably low at present.

She

Discussion

1 How do the censorship laws in your country compare with the 'liberal censorship' proposed in the first article? If you were in charge of censorship, what would you want to control, and why?
2 Discuss the validity of the statement 'Books, plays and films do not have the power to corrupt'.
3 In the face of the evidence about the bad effects of film and TV violence, should depiction of violence be restricted? What objections would be raised to this restriction, and by whom?
4 How can censorship be carried out? Who, in your opinion, is qualified to decide which things are bad for people, and which are not?
5 Which have the strongest effect on people, things they read, things they hear or things they can see? Why? What effect does this have on censorship laws?

Word Study

A Semantic Fields

1 Not allowing

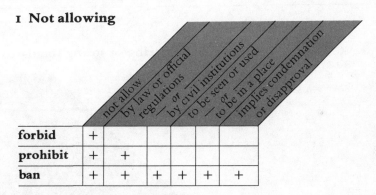

	not allow	by law or official regulations	or by civil institutions	to be seen or used	or to be in a place	implies condemnation or disapproval
forbid	+					
prohibit	+	+				
ban	+	+	+	+	+	+

The verbs are all transitive and pattern in the constructions:
to forbid sth/sb to do sth; to prohibit sth/sb from doing sth; to ban sth/sb from doing sth; to ban sth/sb from
Prohibit is quite formal.

	forbid (forbade) (forbidden)	prohibit(ed)	ban(ned)	
The farmer has	+			the children to play in the barn.
I	+			you to use those swearwords to me.
It is	+			to spit on the floor.
Smoking in cinemas is		+	+	by law in many States of the US.
The Government has		+	+	all further sales of the drug pending an enquiry.
The controversial film about race relations has been			+	in many countries.
Many quite harmless books are being			+	by prejudiced heads of school.
The University has			+	him from doing any further teaching.
He has been			+	from entering Britain because of his political activities.

2 Lowering or losing standards

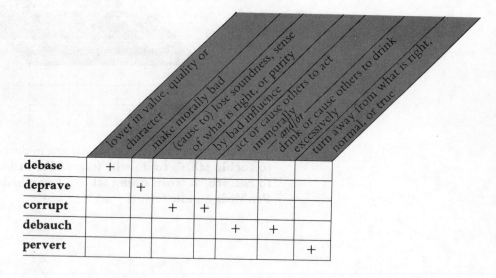

	lower in value, quality or character	make morally bad	(cause to) lose soundness, sense of what is right, or purity	by bad influence act or cause others to act immorally *and/or* drink or cause others to drink excessively	turn away from what is right, normal, or true
debase	+				
deprave		+			
corrupt			+	+	
debauch				+	+
pervert					+

All the verbs are transitive and **corrupt** is also intransitive. All, except **debase**, occur frequently as past participles and in passive constructions.

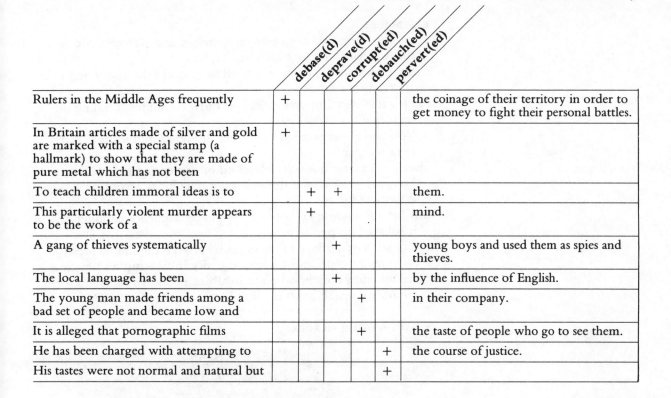

	debase(d)	deprave(d)	corrupt(ed)	debauch(ed)	pervert(ed)	
Rulers in the Middle Ages frequently	+					the coinage of their territory in order to get money to fight their personal battles.
In Britain articles made of silver and gold are marked with a special stamp (a hallmark) to show that they are made of pure metal which has not been	+					
To teach children immoral ideas is to		+	+			them.
This particularly violent murder appears to be the work of a		+				mind.
A gang of thieves systematically			+			young boys and used them as spies and thieves.
The local language has been			+			by the influence of English.
The young man made friends among a bad set of people and became low and				+		in their company.
It is alleged that pornographic films				+		the taste of people who go to see them.
He has been charged with attempting to					+	the course of justice.
His tastes were not normal and natural but					+	

3 Controlling and stopping

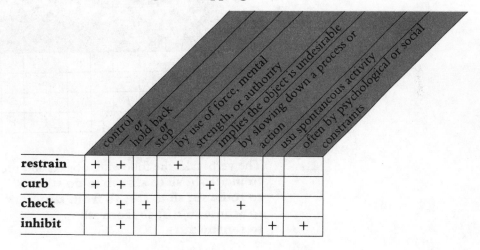

	control	or hold back	or stop	by use of force, mental strength, or authority	implies the object is undesirable	by slowing down a process or action	usu spontaneous activity	often by psychological or social constraints
restrain	+	+		+				
curb	+	+			+			
check		+	+			+		
inhibit		+					+	+

The verbs are transitive and take the following types of objects and prepositional adjuncts:
to restrain sb/sth; sb/sth from sth; sb/sth from doing sth
to curb sth; to check sth
to inhibit sb/sth; sb/sth from doing sth

EXAMPLES

restrain   He could not **restrain** his anger and was very rude to the driver of the car which had hit his.

Six men with ropes were needed to **restrain** the angry bull from attacking the farmer.

curb   It is very important that we **curb** consumer spending on imported luxuries.

You will never succeed in business if you cannot learn to **curb** your temper.

check   Adverse publicity **checked** his meteoric rise to fame.

Struggle as he would, he could not **check** the aeroplane's downward dive.

inhibit   Knowing his parents were in the audience definitely **inhibited** his performance.

The student's failure to distinguish between the simple present and present continuous is undoubtedly **inhibiting** his progress.
An unhappy childhood often **inhibits** a person's ability to form emotional attachments in adult life.

4 Stimulating to action

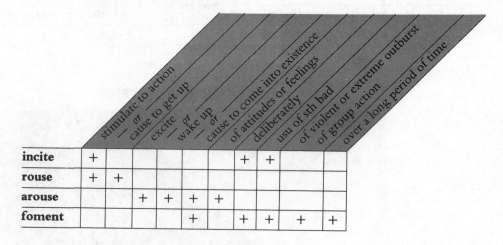

	stimulate to action	or cause to get up	excite	or wake up	cause to come into existence	of attitudes or feelings deliberately	usu of sth bad	of violent or extreme outburst	of group action	over a long period of time
incite	+							+	+	
rouse	+	+								
arouse			+	+	+	+				
foment					+		+	+	+	+

The verbs take the following objects and prepositional adjuncts:
to incite sb; sb to sth; sb to do sth
to rouse sb; sb to sth; sb from sth
to arouse sb/sth; sb from sth
to foment sth

	incite(d)	rouse(d)	arouse(d)	foment(ed)(ing)	
Political agitators deliberately	+				the crowd to violent action.
He was	+				to dislike his mother by the attitude of his step-mother.
At 3 a.m. a tremendous storm		+			everybody from their beds.
His flagrant disrespect for the rules has		+			everybody to action.
The shortage of food			+		deep feelings of discontent among the people.
Seeing injustice tends to			+		all my aggressive feelings.
Militant students are				+	some kind of direct action against the authorities.
The revolt was in fact				+	by a small group of people within the Government.

5 Spreading and multiplying

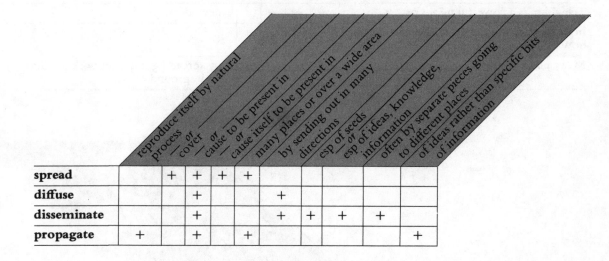

	reproduce itself by natural process	or cover	or cause to be present in	or cause itself to be present in many places or over a wide area	by sending out in many directions	esp of seeds	esp of ideas, knowledge, information	often by separate pieces going to different places	of ideas rather than specific bits of information
spread		+	+	+	+				
diffuse		+			+				
disseminate		+			+	+	+	+	
propagate	+	+		+					+

All the verbs are transitive and **spread** and **propagate** are also intransitive. All, except **spread**, are more usual in formal style.

	spread (spread) (spread) (ing)	diffuse(d) (ing)	disseminate(d) (ing)	propagate(d) (ing)	
The disease was brought into the country in contaminated food and has	+				rapidly throughout the South of England.
He	+				his bread with a thick layer of fresh butter.
The invention of the printing press meant that new ideas	+				much more quickly than before.
The sunlight was		+			through a thin layer of clouds.
Information bulletins on the progress of war were		+	+		to the troops.
The new doctrine has been widely		+	+		by its followers.
Sycamore seeds are			+		by the wind.
Animals may also help to			+		seeds by carrying them on their feet or bodies.
Television is a powerful means of	+	+	+		new ideas.
In the 19th century little was known about how diseases	+			+	
Many plants				+	by spreading out a network of roots underground.

6 Coming in great numbers

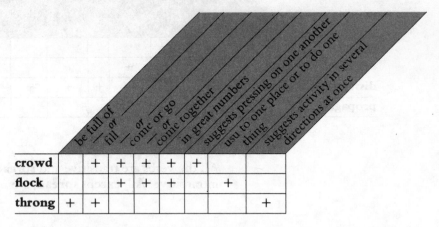

The verbs are usually only used with animate agents and objects/ adjuncts denoting place or direction. Colloquially, however, **crowd** may be extended to other objects when it means [+ make closer together].

EXAMPLE
Crowd the potatoes up a bit or they won't all fit in the pan.
The verbs collocate with the following prepositions:
to crowd together/round/through/in/into
to flock together/round
to throng round/with (people)
EXAMPLES
crowd Thousands **crowded** into the hall to hear the Queen
speak.
  Everyone **crowded** into my little room for tea and cakes.
  The restaurant was so **crowded** that we couldn't find a place to
sit.
  People waiting to see the star **crowded** the airport lounge and
spilled out into the street.
  When I opened the cage all the rats **crowded** together in one
corner in fright.
flock Everyone **flocked** around her to congratulate her on her
success.
  People are **flocking** to see the new film about space exploration.
throng The narrow street was **thronged** with shoppers as it was
Saturday morning.
  People were **thronging** the streets, all eager to celebrate the
news of the end of the war.

7 Being well known

	well known	to the general public	to a limited group of people or	repeatedly named for a particular quality or achievement	for intellectual or aesthetic achievement	for great achievement	usu in academic disciplines or public life	suggests respect
famous	+	+						
renowned	+	+	+	+				
celebrated	+	+			+			
distinguished	+		+			+	+	
eminent	+		+			+	+	+

The difference between **distinguished** and **eminent** is mainly
collocational.

	ski resort	robbery	crime	athlete	racing driver	actress	opera singer	artist	scholar	surgeon	authority on grass diseases	public figure	writer	linguist	nuclear physicist	philosopher	judge
famous	+	+	+	+	+	+	+	+	+	+							
renowned										+	+	+	+				
celebrated						+	+	+	+			+	+				
distinguished									+	+	+	+		+	+		
eminent									+	+	+		(+)	+	+	+	+

Famous, renowned and **celebrated** can be used in the following constructions:
to be famous/renowned/celebrated as (eg) **a painter**
to be famous/renowned/celebrated for (eg) **one's knowledge/skill**

B   Synonymous Pairs

1   **trick**
    hoax   [+ deliberate deception] [+ for gain] or [+ for fun]

EXAMPLES
The people who bought tickets for a trip to the moon realised they were the victims of a **hoax** when they discovered the rocket in which they had been loaded had no engine and no pilot.
The telephone call we had telling us we had to go to the station urgently was a **hoax** to get us out of the house.

2   **to lessen**
    to ease   [+ make less tight] ⇒ { [+ diminish] } [+ mental or physical anguish]

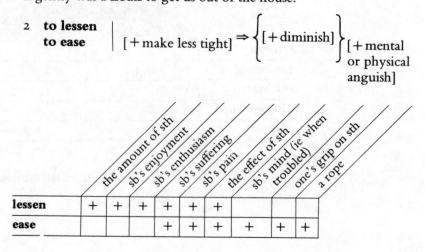

	the amount of sth	sb's enjoyment	sb's enthusiasm	sb's suffering	sb's pain	the effect of sth	sb's mind (ie when troubled)	one's grip on sth	a rope
lessen	+	+	+	+	+	+			
ease				+	+	+	+	+	+

	lessen(ed)	ease(d)
The rain	+	+
The number of applicants	+	
The storm	+	+
The pain	+	+
The situation		+

3 **to strike**
  to batter | [+hard] [+repeatedly]

	strike (struck)	batter(ed)	
He	+		her on the side of the face.
The brick	+		the window with a tremendous force and broke it.
Her jealous husband	+	+	her on the head with a stick.
The thieves		+	the door down to get in.
The waves threw the boat on the rocks and		+	it to pieces.

4 **to control**
  to repress | [+ to the extent of taking away all freedom of expression or action]

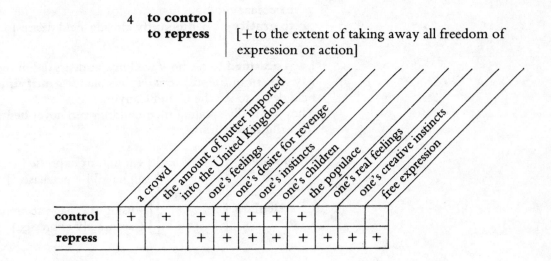

	a crowd	the amount of butter imported into the United Kingdom	one's feelings	one's desire for revenge	one's instincts	one's children	the populace	one's real feelings	one's creative instincts	free expression
control	+	+	+	+	+	+	+			
repress			+	+	+	+	+	+	+	+

5   **to wane** $\left.\begin{array}{l} \\ \\ \end{array}\right\{$ [+become less] $\left.\begin{array}{l} \\ \\ \end{array}\right\}$ [+having reached a peak of force or excellence]

to subside [+of violent activity or disturbance]

	wane(d)	subside(d)	
The moon has	+		without the weather improving.
The influence of antigovernment agitation has	+		in recent months.
After a rapid rise to fame the star's career	+		equally quickly.
The storm finally		+	after causing considerable damage.
After causing a noisy scene, the girl suddenly		+	into tears.
The volume of traffic should		+	later in the evening.

6   **to attack**
to assail | [+violently] ⇒ [+pester]

Assail often occurs in the construction **to assail (sb) with sth.**
EXAMPLES
Although I have decided to leave, I am constantly **assailed** with doubts about whether I am doing the right thing.
Everyone wanted to hear all about England, and they **assailed** me with questions every time I appeared in public.
Two toughs **assailed** him in the street, hit him on the head, and stole his wallet.

7   **to please**
to gratify | [+to satisfy already-held desires]

EXAMPLES
I was **gratified** to see how well my students did in their exams.
My American friends were responsible for **gratifying** my long-held desire to see the Grand Canyon.
They are really spoiling their children and never hesitate to **gratify** their slightest whims.

8   **eloquent** $\left.\begin{array}{l} \\ \\ \end{array}\right\{$ [+using, or expressed in, elegant language] [+persuasive]

[+fluent]

articulate [+using language accurately] or [+accurately expressed]

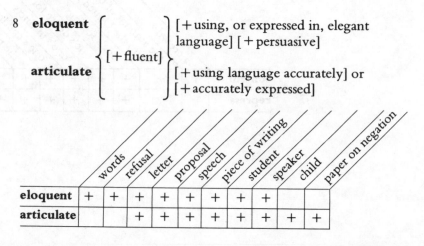

	words	refusal	letter	proposal	speech	piece of writing	student	speaker	child	paper on negation
eloquent	+	+	+	+	+	+	+			
articulate			+	+	+	+	+	+	+	+

Exercises

1 What differences and/or similarities are there between these pairs?

1 flock/throng   2 curb/check   3 debase/deprave   4 diffuse/spread   5 attack/assail   6 please/gratify   7 wane/subside   8 corrupt/debauch   9 control/repress   10 celebrated/eminent

2 Provide synonyms which are more intense than the given words.

EXAMPLE: dirty → filthy
1 ugly   2 tactless   3 pleased   4 to destroy   5 to thrust   6 to shout   7 to strike

3 Fill in the missing words.

1 The emergency services call turned out to be a . . . . . .
2 They tried to . . . . . the train by placing metal bars on the
   . . . . . .
3 He . . . . . his hand into the hole and, to his great surprise, took out a purse full of old coins.
4 You'd better keep your . . . . . shut!
5 His anger . . . . . when he realised that it wasn't their fault.
6 He was found . . . . . of murder.
7 What's the name of the main . . . . . in that film?
8 It is not clear where we should . . . . . the line.
9 How are they going to protect themselves . . . . . the cold?

4 What are/were the functions of the following?

1 a gladiator   2 a mechanic   3 a plumber   4 a censor   5 a physician   6 an electrician   7 an activist   8 a parent

5 Fill in the following collocational grids.

1

	ski resort	robbery	crime	judge	racing driver	actress	opera singer	artist	scholar	surgeon	authority on grass diseases	public figure	writer	philosopher	nuclear physicist
eminent															
renowned															
celebrated															
distinguished															
famous															

2

	the amount of sth	sb's enjoyment	sb's enthusiasm	sb's suffering	a rope	the effect of sth	sb's mind (ie when troubled)	one's grip on sth	sb's pain
lessen									
ease									

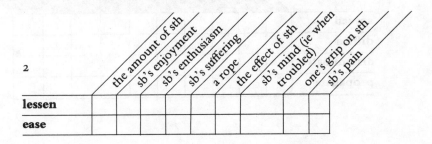

3

	speaker	speech	letter	proposal	child	piece of writing	student	words	refusal
eloquent									
articulate									

6 Describe the differences and/or similarities between:

1 show/display   2 batter/strike   3 hack/cut   4 target/goal   5 drug/medication   6 library/bookstore   7 survey/opinion poll   8 curriculum/schedule   9 liar/hypocrite   10 bruises/injuries   11 articulate/eloquent   12 reticent/reserved

7 What nouns can collocate with the following:

1 permissive   2 subversive   3 bitter   4 conservative   5 crude   6 hypocritical   7 intimate   8 ugly   9 triumphant   10 utter   11 familiar   12 grievous

8 Explain the meaning of the following words and expressions:

1 witness   2 liberal   3 civil-libertarian   4 fornication   5 hangover   6 tenement flat   7 bomb hoax   8 fine   9 common sense   10 railway track   11 absurdity   12 bearbaiting   13 vernacular   14 suicide   15 in all sincerity   16 oddly enough   17 irrelevant   18 reticent   19 foul-mouthed   20 sacred

9 What kinds of things can one . . . ?

1 curb   2 produce   3 disseminate   4 enhance   5 wreck   6 repress   7 work out   8 ban   9 witness   10 be obsessed with   11 regulate   12 subdue   13 display   14 restrain   15 inflict

10 Fill in the following grids:

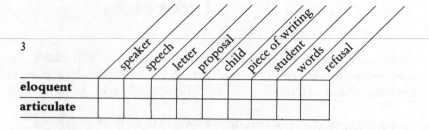

1

	reproduce itself by natural process or cover	cause to be present in or cause itself to be present in	many places or over a wide area	by sending out in many directions esp of seeds	esp of ideas, knowledge, information	often by separate pieces going to different places	of ideas rather than specific bits of information
spread							
diffuse							
disseminate							
propagate							

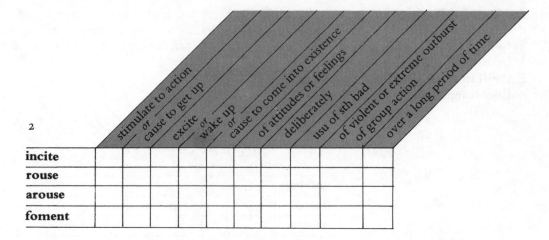

2	stimulate to action *or* cause to get up	excite *or* wake up *or* cause to come into existence	of attitudes or feelings	deliberately	usu of sth bad	of violent or extreme outburst of group action	over a long period of time
incite							
rouse							
arouse							
foment							

11 Choose the word that best fits the given context and modify its form where necessary.

1 For a child of eight, she was astonishingly . . . . .. (fluent, eloquent, articulate)

2 Once we had been able to . . . . . her fits of hysteria, we could begin to find out what had happened. (repress, subdue, calm down)

3 We found their solicitude (concern, help) very . . . . . ing. (gratify, satisfy, please)

4 The number of children . . . . . to death every year is increasing. (strike, hit, batter)

5 Britain's most . . . . . poet, the Poet Laureate, died yesterday. (eminent, renowned, distinguished, celebrated)

6 The early Protestants . . . . . their new religion with an ardour rarely seen among established Catholics. (propagate, diffuse, spread)

7 'That boy really is one for . . . . . ing trouble,' sighed the despairing teacher. (incite, arouse, rouse, foment)

8 Because her parents were there, the girl felt a little . . . . . about showing her feelings towards her fiancé. (inhibit, restrain, curb, check)

9 The longer he knew the girl, the more . . . . . ed his values became. (deprave, debase, debauch)

10 Dutch Elm disease has . . . . . to many countries and wiped out their most beautiful trees. (diffuse, spread, disseminate)

Revision Exercises

R1 In what style (formal, informal, colloquial, slang) are the following words most likely to be used?

1 commence   2 cosy   3 discard   4 aggravate (=[+irritate])
5 clout   6 serene   7 smack   8 ban   9 the in-thing   10 infringe
11 tranquil   12 hankie   13 get rid of   14 attend to   15 snoop
16 snug   17 perpetual (=[+too long])

R2 What differences and/or similarities are there between the following pairs?   1 coach/instruct   2 develop/evolve   3 say/reel off   4 entrust/confide   5 slap/smack   6 stop/intercept   7 send out/emit   8 hinder/obstruct   9 safe/secure   10 crucial/critical

R3 Fill in the following collocational grids:

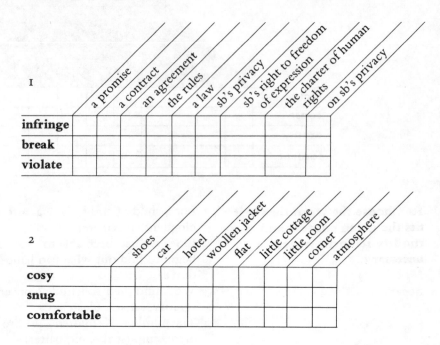

1

	a promise	a contract	an agreement	the rules	a law	sb's privacy	sb's right to freedom of expression	the charter of human rights	on sb's privacy
infringe									
break									
violate									

2

	shoes	car	hotel	woollen jacket	flat	little cottage	little room	corner	atmosphere
cosy									
snug									
comfortable									

R4 What are the British English equivalents of the following expressions?   1 elementary school   2 pep (*sl*)   3 dumb (*coll*)   4 french fries   5 mailman   6 movie   7 prize fight   8 sidewalk   9 to figure out   10 to sign up (for a course)

R5 Fill in the following collocational grids:

1

	disclose(d)	reveal(ed)	divulge(d)	betray(ed)	
The enemy were waiting for us so someone had					us to them.
The Arab races very rarely					their real feelings.
Under pressure from his captors, the hostage					his secret.
Our long-held secret was					by a few careless words.
Someone has					the real value of the cargo to the customs authorities.
The authorities have now					the real facts about the economic situation.
The witness has now					that he was lying to protect his friend.
We stripped the paint off and					some beautiful old panelling behind.
The mysterious stranger					his true identity.

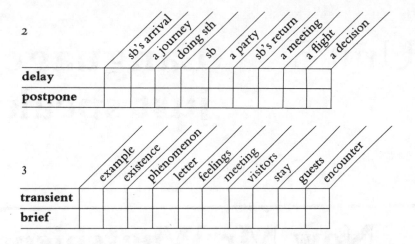

2

	sb's arrival	a journey	doing sth	sb	a party	sb's return	a meeting	a flight	a decision
delay									
postpone									

3

	example	existence	phenomenon	letter	feelings	meeting	visitors	stay	guests	encounter
transient										
brief										

R6 Produce a logical and coherent story by filling in the blanks with appropriate words from the given list. Modify their form where necessary.

eminent, distinguished, gratified, incited, snug, subversive, striking, elderly, placid, serene, boisterous, substantial, eligible, bluntly, hangover, expedient, outcome, hoax, longevity, centenarians, to enroll, to pose, to persist, to sponsor, to esteem, to curb, to ban, to debase, to pervert, to restrain, to inhibit, to arouse, to propagate, to attack, to subside, to step in, to bawl

Mr Jones was an 1 . . . . . young man with a 2 . . . . . bank balance and a 3 . . . . . laugh. He was the proud owner of a 4 . . . . . little flat and in short, 5 . . . . . that any young lady should be only too 6 . . . . . were he to offer her his hand in marriage. He had 7 . . . . . blue eyes that had already 8 . . . . . the sleeping heart of many a young woman. He had a 9 . . . . . nature but one which, when 10 . . . . ., there was no 11 . . . . .ing. He had been known to 12 . . . . . at his 13 . . . . . parents when he'd drunk a glass too many but in the morning, suffering from a 14 . . . . ., would have resumed his air of reserve.

Some years ago he 15 . . . . . for evening classes which were 16 . . . . . by a local political party, but was 17 . . . . . from them because of a chance remark he had 18 . . . . . let fall about its 19 . . . . . chairman. The 20 . . . . . of this last incident was that he had begun to be thought of as rather a 21 . . . . . element in the community, some people even going so far as to 22 . . . . . libellous stories about his private life. At this point though he 23 . . . . . and made a public declaration; the rumours soon 24 . . . . . . That is, among all but the 25 . . . . . who, anyway, could not hear what was said, and thus 26 . . . . . in dragging his name through the mud. The only 27 . . . . . then, he realised, was to publish his declaration, which 28 . . . . . no problem as his uncle was a printer. He was not 29 . . . . . about 30 . . . . . his critics with a verbal force of which the villagers had not seen the like. Some people took the pamphlet for a 31 . . . . . . Others complained that he was 32 . . . . . the tone of the village by publishing such things . . .

Unit 5 Language isn't just speaking

Now Mr Whatshisname will say a few words

To the unintiated, making a speech carries with it a certain glamour.

After hearing an expert, you may think, 'That's as easy as falling off a **log**[1]'.

With the result that when a **wily**[2] secretary of a golf club, &c., phones to ask if you'll say a few words at some **function**[3], you may be filled with a warm glow of pride.

You make some modest reference to your inexperience, &c., whereupon he **gives vent to**[4] a hearty laugh of disbelief, and says, 'Well, that's settled, Friday the 13th at 7.30 p.m.' And the phone goes click.

You don't know, of course, that he has already tried half a dozen other **suckers**[5] and received an emphatic refusal in each case.

In your mind's eye you see an audience, hanging on your every word, laughing **uproariously**[6] at your jokes, and giving you a standing ovation.

A thought may **intrude**[7]. You don't know any jokes!

So you go out and buy 'A thousand and one jokes for after-dinner speakers'.

You spend a happy hour **browsing**[8] over this wealth of material, and finally decide on number 563: –

1st gent – 'Who was that lady I saw you with last night?'

2nd gent – 'That was no lady, that was my wife!' That'll **bowl them over**[9]!

For the next fortnight, you go about **glassy-eyed**[10]. You lose a stone in weight. Your best friend hints there is no disgrace in seeing a mental specialist.

At last the dreaded evening arrives.

Not all the **meat cubes**[11] in the world will give that dinner any flavour.

The speakers are listed on the menu. You are second last.

You listen, dry-mouthed and trembling as the other speakers **ramble on**[12] to the point the audience is bored to tears and you've still to face them!

To your horror, the speaker immediately before you seems to be saying exactly what you had so laboriously **rehearsed**[13].

The chairman rises. 'Mr . . . will now say a few words,' and he looks **pointedly**[14] at you as he stresses the word 'few'.

You **stagger to your feet**[15]. 'Mr Chairman, ladies and gentlemen.'

Your mind goes blank.

In desperation, you try to save the situation with number 563 from the joke book.

'Ha, ha, ha,' you **babble**[16]. 'That woman the chairman was out with last night was certainly no lady!'

Have YOU ever tried to explain a joke to a sea of hostile faces, or, for that matter, explain a joke to anyone?

What happens for the rest of the evening would be a blessing if it could be called **amnesia**[17]. But you will remember only too well the horrible details.

Within the next day or two, you will receive a letter from the chairman's lawyers, **suing**[18] you for **slander**[19].

You will have to resign from a position which had a promising future, and the only place left for you is darkest Africa.

My advice therefore is, when you are asked to 'Say a few words', **don't**. – M L

The Sunday Post

LANGUAGE AND SEX DISCRIMINATION

Language differences often betray discrimination in social relationships. In her book *Male/Female Language*, **Mary Ritchie Key describes how** labels[1] **and descriptors can imply unequal status:**

A study of the *descriptions* of females who are in public or professional positions provides examples of the actual values put on females in society. The following are illustrations I have collected from magazines and newspapers. The women described are not women who won the lottery, but are women who have positions **entailing**[2] a good deal of training and expertise. The women were variously described as: 'a serene, delicately formed woman' (referring to an executive chairperson); 'a brown-eyed **cutie**'[3] (referring to an athlete); '(she) speaks softly . . . **blushes**[4] and laughs . . .' (referring to a commanding officer); 'a very feminine woman' (referring to a chief of a Flight Service Station). A pilot was headlined as 'Woman flier . . .' A member of a commission was designated a 'mother'. A book which received considerable attention was written by a 'housewife with an Oxford degree in English'. Apparently an attempt is being made to assure women they can still remain sexually attractive even if professionally competent.

Unreal and cruel **dichotomizing**[5] in language behavior inevitably leads to double standards in the treatment of male and female in every aspect of language use.

Job titles and classifications are different depending upon whether male or female fills the position. A male is an 'assistant manager'; a female is an 'administrative assistant'. A female professor will be 'Mrs Doe' while her husband (on the same campus!) is 'Prof Doe'. Descriptions of male and female have a different ring to them: an older woman has '**wrinkles**'[6] but an older man has 'deep **crevices**'[7].

The matter of description of people and the interpretation of human qualities is based for instance on this double standard. A **bold**[8] man is 'courageous' but a bold woman is 'aggressive'. A student pointed out to me that one can say of a woman who is easy to **seduce**[9], 'She's easy' but one cannot say 'He's easy'. A person who is innovative is '**pushy**'[10] if female, but 'original' if male. If **insistent**[11], a female is 'hysterical', but a male is 'persistent'. If politically involved, a female is 'over-emotional', a male is '**committed**'[12].

Mary Ritchie Key, *Male/Female Language*

LANGUAGE AND SEX DISCRIMINATION

1 word or short phrase associated with a person or thing to describe and identify it
2 making necessary
3 *Am coll* a cute, attractive, pretty, and charming girl
4 becomes pink in the face (because of embarrassment)
5 making dichotomies, divisions into two parts
6 small folds or ridges in the skin especially on the face
7 cracks or openings (*lit* in walls, rocks, etc)
8 without fear or pushing oneself forward
9 persuade to engage in sexual intercourse
10 *coll* trying to attract too much attention to oneself
11 commanding and compelling attention
12 devoted to a cause

A FEW WORDS

1 a rough mass or length of wood as it comes from the tree
2 crafty, cunning
3 a social meeting (of an important kind)
4 expresses
5 *coll* a person who is easily deceived
6 very noisily
7 force or push (itself) in without permission or invitation
8 reading here and there for enjoyment
9 *coll* idiom, really amaze them
10 lifeless and without expression
11 blocks of compressed foodstuff designed to add flavour to meat dishes in cooking
12 talk on without much purpose
13 repeated, recited in order to practise
14 emphatically, directly
15 stand up unsteadily
16 utter a stream of words which make little or no sense
17 loss or impairment of memory
18 take legal action, make a claim in a court of law
19 the offence of uttering a false statement which is intended to damage a person's reputation

Standard, non-standard, or both?

If non-standard-English-speaking children suffer educationally because standard English is not their native language, what steps can be taken to solve this problem?

So far it is possible to distinguish three different approaches. The first approach has been described as '**elimination**[1] of non-standard speech'. In this approach, every attempt is made in the schools to prevent the child from speaking his native non-standard variety, and each non-standard feature of which the teacher is aware is commented on and corrected. For example, the child will be told that it is 'wrong' (and perhaps even bad or a **disgrace**[2]) to say *I done it, I ain't got it*, or *He a good guy*. Standard English, on the other hand, is presented as 'correct' and 'good' – the model to be aimed at.

Linguists, and many others, believe this approach to be wrong, for several reasons. First, it is wrong *psychologically*. Language is not simply a means of communicating messages. It is also very important as a symbol of identity and group membership. To suggest to a child that his language, and that of those with whom he identifies, is inferior in some way is to **imply**[3] that *he* is inferior. This, in turn, is likely to lead either to **alienation**[4] from the school and school values, or to a rejection of the group to which he belongs. It is also *socially* wrong in that it may appear to imply that particular social groups are less valuable than others.

Finally, and perhaps most importantly, it is *practically* wrong: it is wrong because it does not and will not work. To learn a new language is a very difficult task, as many people know, and in many ways it is even more difficult to learn a different dialect of one's own language – because they are so similar, it is difficult to keep them apart. The fact must also be faced that, in very many cases, speakers will not *want* to change their language – even if it were possible. First, there are no communication advantages to be gained (as there would be in learning French, for example) since the child was already able to communicate with standard English speakers. Second, the pressures of group identification and **peer-group**[5] solidarity are very strong. Linguistic research has shown that the **adolescent**[6] peer-group is in many cases the most important linguistic influence.

The second approach has been called 'bidialectalism', and has received the **overt**[7] support of many linguists. This approach teaches that the individual has a right to continue using a non-standard dialect at home, with friends, and in certain circumstances at school. But it also advocates that children should be taught standard English as a school language, and as the language of reading and writing. The two varieties, standard and non-standard, are discussed and treated as **distinct**[8] **entities**[9], and the differences between them are illustrated and pointed out as an interesting fact. The aims are to encourage the child's interest in language by study of his own dialect as a **legitimate**[10] and interesting form of language, and to help the child to develop an ability in *code*-**switching**[11] – switching from one language variety to another when the situation demands.

However, children will learn to speak standard English, which is a dialect associated with and symbolic of a particular social group in our society, only if they both want to become a member of that group *and* have a reasonable expectation that it will be possible, economically and socially, for them to do so.

The third approach, which appears to be obtaining growing (but still minority) support in America, has been called 'appreciation of dialect differences'. This view states that if children suffer because of their non-standard language, this is due to the attitudes society as a whole, and perhaps teachers in particular, have to language of this type. If this is the case, then it is the attitudes that should be changed, and not the language. In other words, the problem is not really a linguistic one at all. We should, according to this approach, teach children the ability to read standard English, but, beyond that, we should simply attempt to educate our society to an understanding, appreciation and tolerance of non-standard dialects as complex, valid and adequate linguistic systems. Critics of this approach have called it hopelessly **utopian**[12]. Given time, however, it might prove to be simpler than the other two approaches, since it may be easier to change attitudes than to alter the native speech patterns of the majority of the population.

From the point of view of the linguist, therefore, the most satisfactory solution to the problem of non-standard speakers in a standard-English-dominated culture is the adoption in schools of a combination of the two approaches, bidialectalism and appreciation of dialect differences, **bearing in mind**[13] that bidialectalism is likely to be only partially successful (and then probably only in the case of writing) and may be dangerous, particularly if **insensitively**[14] handled, from the point of view of **fostering**[15] linguistic insecurity.

P Trudgill, *Sociolinguistics: An Introduction*

Watch it!

Have you ever noticed that in most conversations the person who is being spoken to watches the face of the speaker, until it is his turn to speak, when he alternately watches the other and looks away. And the direction in which that person looks away is very revealing. Researchers have found – and this can be tested literally anywhere – that when people look to the left they are remembering, and when they look to the right they are thinking. Like all scientific discoveries, this one could be dangerous. Next time your boyfriend has been away and you ask him where he has been, watch his eyes. If, as he replies, they look up to the left, you know that he is trying to remember, but if they slide down to the right you know something imaginative is coming.
JEROME BURNE

Honey

Personal Space

How much space does a man need?

I had lunch not too long ago with a psychiatrist friend. We sat in a pleasant restaurant at a **stylishly**[1] small table. At one point he took out a **pack**[2] of cigarettes, lit one and put the pack down three-quarters of the way across the table in front of my plate.

He kept talking and I kept listening, but I was troubled in some way that I couldn't quite define, and more troubled as he moved his **tableware**[3] about, **lining it up with**[4] his cigarettes, closer and closer to my side of the table. Then leaning across the table himself he attempted to make a point. It was a point I could hardly appreciate because of my growing uneasiness.

Finally he took pity on me and said, 'I have just favored you with a demonstration of a very basic step in body language, in non verbal communication.'

Puzzled, I asked, 'What was that?'

'I aggressively **threatened**[5] you and **challenged**[6] you. I put you in a position of having to **assert yourself**[7], and that bothered you.'

Still uncomprehending, I asked, 'But how? What did you do?'

'I moved my cigarettes to start with,' he explained. 'By unspoken rule we have divided the table in half, half for you and half for me.'

'I wasn't conscious of any such division.'

'Of course not. The rule remains though. We both **staked out a territory**[8] in our minds. Ordinarily we would have shared the table by some unspoken and civilized command. However, I deliberately moved my cigarettes into your area in a **breach**[9] of taste. Unaware of what I had done, you still felt yourself threatened, felt uneasy, and when I aggressively followed up my first breach of your territory with another, moving my plate and silverware and then **intruding myself**[10], you became more and more uneasy and still were not aware of why.'

It was my first demonstration of the fact that we each possess zones of territory. We carry these zones with us and we react in different ways to the breaking of these zones.

How different cultures handle space

Westerners see space as the distance between objects. To us, space is empty. The Japanese see the shape and arrangement of space as having a **tangible**[11] meaning. This is apparent not only in their flower arrangements and art, but in their gardens as well, where units of space **blend**[12] harmoniously to form an integrated whole.

Like the Japanese, the Arabs tend to **cling**[13] close to one another. But while in public they are invariably crowded together, in private, in their own houses, the Arabs have almost too much space. Arab houses are, if possible, large and empty, with the people **clustered**[14] together in one small area. Partitions between rooms are usually avoided, because in spite of the desire for space, the Arabs, **paradoxically**[15], do not like to be alone and even in their spacious houses will **huddle together**[16].

The difference between the Arab huddling and the Japanese **proximity**[17] is a deep thing. The Arab likes to touch his companion, to feel and to smell him. To deny a friend his breath is to be ashamed.

The Japanese, in their closeness, preserve a formality and an **aloofness**[18]. They manage to touch and still keep rigid boundaries. The Arab pushes these boundaries aside.

PERSONAL SPACE

1 smartly, fashionably
2 *Br* prefers packet
3 dishes, knives, forks, spoons, etc used at meals
4 arranging it in line with
5 communicated an intention to punish or hurt
6 communicated an invitation to compete (*lit* deliver an official invitation to fight)
7 insist on your rights, put yourself forward and try to be important
8 to mark the limits of a territory
9 violation (of a law, a promise, taste, etc)
10 forcing myself upon you
11 capable of being touched, definite, clear, not vague
12 mix together or become mixed
13 hold fast to, stick to
14 gathered in a group
15 apparently in disagreement with the facts
16 crowd or press together
17 closeness
18 distance (of people)
19 pushing vigorously
20 forcing sexual intercourse on an unwilling partner
21 squeezing a small amount of flesh between the thumb and the finger
22 *lit* a very thin ball of liquid filled with air or gas
23 attack

Along with this closeness, there is a pushing and a **shoving**[19] in the Arab world that Americans find distasteful. To an American there are boundaries in a public place. When he is waiting in line he believes that his place there is inviolate. The Arab has no concept of privacy in a public place, and if he can push his way into a line, he feels perfectly within his rights to do so.

As the Japanese lack of a word for privacy indicates a certain attitude toward other people, so the Arab lack of a word for **rape**[20] indicates a certain attitude toward the body. To an American the body is sacred. To the Arab, who thinks nothing of shoving and pushing and even **pinching**[21] women in public, violation of the body is a minor thing. However, violation of the ego by insult is a major problem.

The Arab at times needs to be alone, no matter how close he wishes to be to his fellow man. To be alone, he simply cuts off the lines of communication. He withdraws, and this withdrawal is respected by his fellows. His withdrawal is interpreted in body language as 'I need privacy. Even though I'm among you, touching you and living with you, I must withdraw into my shell.'

Were the American to experience this withdrawal, he would tend to think it insulting. The withdrawal would be interpreted in his body language as 'silent treatment'. And it would be further interpreted as an insult.

When two Arabs talk to each other, they look each other in the eyes with great intensity. The same intensity of glance in our American culture is rarely exhibited between men. In fact, such intensity can be interpreted as a challenge to a man's masculinity. 'I didn't like the way he looked at me, as if he wanted something personal, to sort of be too intimate,' is a typical response by an American to an Arab look.

So far we have considered body language in terms of spatial differences in widely disparate cultures, the East and Near East as opposed to the West. However, even among the Western nations, there are broad differences. There is a distinct difference between the way a German, for instance, handles his living space, and the way an American does. The American carries his two-foot **bubble**[22] of privacy around with him, and if a friend talks to him about intimate matters they will close enough for their special bubbles to merge. To a German, an entire room in his own house can be a bubble of privacy. If someone else engages in an intimate conversation in that room without including him he may be insulted.

These are all elements of nonverbal communication. This guarding of zones is one of the first basic principles. How we guard our zones and how we **aggress to**[23] other zones is an integral part of how we relate to other people.

Julius Fast, *Body Language*

Body Language

Feature   **Kirsty McLeod**

How to decide whether people **warm to**[1] you or not? Are enjoying themselves or are bored? Are pleasant or **nasty**[2]? Are responding irresistibly to your sexual power or are just being friendly? . . . such questions as these are fundamental to organising our lives properly and not making **appalling**[3] misjudgements. We tend to think that what people say is of most significance; but it is only in telephone conversations that words are the only, or even the best, **clue**[4]. Most of the time we have whole people to watch and (much in the same way of our ape forefathers) the appearance, **posture**[5], **expressions**[6] and **twitches**[7] of human beings tell you quite a lot of what's going on in their heads.

First Impressions

THE STUDENT AND THE BANKER
By wearing the exact uniforms their **peer**[1] groups expect of them, these two communicate their age, class, occupation and probable **IQ**[2]. Moreover, by telling us just this and no more, they both reveal a whole lot more about themselves. A person frightened of being an individual, of giving anything away about himself, is likely to lack confidence and ambition, be unimaginative and over-anxious.

LUSCIOUS[3] LATIN LOVERS
Such is the reputation of the hot-blooded Latin that any dark-skinned man is in danger of being mistaken for one, and expected to be quick-tempered, **sly**[4] and **conceited**[5] – the assumptions we generally make about Mediterranean males.

BODY LANGUAGE

1   become interested in, like
2   unpleasant
3   serious, *lit* horrific, disgusting
4   something that helps to solve a problem or a mystery
5   the carriage or attitude of the body
6   peculiarities of speech, behaviour, gesture, style, etc
7   jerky, usually uncontrolled movements of some part of the body

FIRST IMPRESSIONS

1   equal in rank, merit or quality
2   *abbr* for intelligence quotient (measurable amount of intelligence)
3   suggesting rich sensual delights
4   not frank; deceitful, untrustworthy
5   vain, having too high an opinion of oneself
6   identifying mark, *lit* code of letters and numbers assigned to an operator, activity or station for use in radio communication
7   Laura Ashley is a British clothing firm specialising in long, frilly, flowery, romantic dresses
8   *coll* takes advantage of
9   a venomous female spider, so called from its colour and its habit of eating its mate
10 free from roughness, even, soft
11 display proudly, show off
12 intelligence, quickness of mind, ability to be verbally amusing

RICH AND SUCCESSFUL
Generally those who have it **flaunt**[11] success, however subtly. It's about the most potent physical signal of all, especially in a man. Women are less attracted by looks than they are by things like ability, achievement, **wit**[12], a strong personality. Think of the men, ugly but rich and successful, who are married to beautiful women. Then think of it the other way round.

Honey

THE PROFESSIONAL ROMANTIC
Recognisable by her **call-sign**[6] (the **Laura Ashley**[7] look), she **trades on**[8] her apparent helplessness and the male instinct to protect. In fact she's about as helpless as a **Black Widow spider**[9]. Adult love, psychologists tell us, is a replay of our first experience of love in childhood: the male playing parent, the female as child. Women use make-up to emphasise their childish qualities – **smooth**[10] skin, soft hair, large, round eyes.

Discussion

1 What do you think is meant by 'personal space'? In what way is it handled in your culture as compared to those mentioned here?

2 The notions of 'body language' and 'personal space' may explain some traditional racial type–castings and prejudices which encourage or discourage relations between certain racial or cultural groups, eg 'Luscious Latin Lovers'. Cite as many examples of this type-casting as you can, and try to say which characteristics are responsible for them.

3 'The Student' and 'The Banker' are said to be hiding behind their outward appearance. Does this seem to you true, and can you cite other examples of types of people who do the same thing? Or do we perhaps all do it?

4 Are you conscious of distinguishing people socially by the way they speak? If so, does this distinction seem to you useful, or unjust and likely to lead to prejudice and resentment?

5 What is the social effect of the existence of a standard or 'correct' version of any language? What happens to people who cannot speak it?

6 Compare the situation in Britain and America outlined by Peter Trudgill, with that in your own country. If your country uses several languages, what difference does this make?

7 'Just be yourself' is an old axiom. But isn't it impossible once you are aware of how others are judging you by your appearance and speech? How much do you think you 'act a role' to achieve a certain reaction in others?

Word Study

A   Semantic Fields   1 Speaking in different ways†

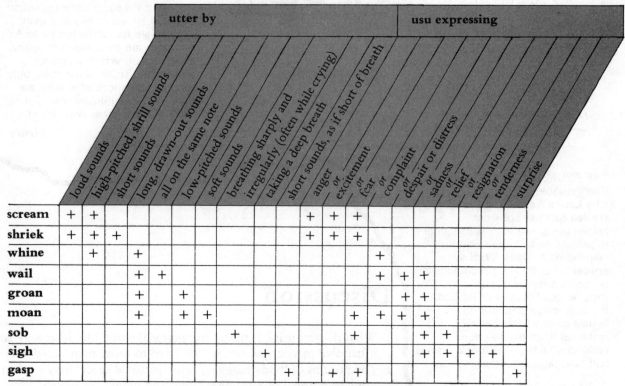

	utter by										usu expressing									
	loud sounds	high-pitched, shrill sounds	short sounds	long, drawn-out sounds	all on the same note	low-pitched sounds	soft sounds	breathing sharply and irregularly (often while crying)	taking a deep breath	short sounds, as if short of breath	anger or	excitement or	fear or	complaint or	despair or distress or	sadness or	relief or	resignation or	tenderness	surprise
scream	+	+									+	+	+							
shriek	+	+	+								+	+	+							
whine		+		+										+						
wail				+	+									+	+	+				
groan				+		+									+	+				
moan				+		+	+						+	+	+	+				
sob								+							+	+	+			
sigh									+							+	+	+	+	
gasp										+		+	+							+

All these verbs can follow a direct quotation and may precede it if they occur in conjunction with another verb. All take direct objects which name the type of message (eg 'a story', 'orders', 'a few words') and all, except **sigh** and **gasp**, collocate with **about**.
Scream and **wail** can also be followed by a **that**-clause.
Obviously, all these verbs can also denote sounds not accompanied by words.

EXAMPLES

scream   'Let me go!' she **screamed**.
  What is that child **screaming** about now?

shriek   The children **shrieked** with excitement when we told them about their holiday.

whine   She came **whining** to me with some story about unfair reports from her supervisor.

wail   'I'll never see him again,' she **wailed**.
  Margot **wailed** that everyone had gone out and left her by herself and she was lonely.

groan   He **groaned** when he saw the mess which had been made by the cars on the grass.

moan   'It's my arm, it hurts,' she **moaned**.
  He's always **moaning** and **groaning** about something.

sob   'He hit me,' **sobbed** the small boy.
  She clung to me and **sobbed** convulsively.

Based partly on G. Miller and P. Johnson Laird (1976), p 627.

sigh Everyone **sighed** with relief when they saw the rescue boat approaching.

'Don't ever leave me,' he **sighed**.

gasp The messenger was so out of breath that he could hardly gasp out his news.

'Water,' she **gasped**.

2 Talking informally

talk	in a friendly manner	usu about non-serious matters	foolishly	in high-pitched voices	rapidly	almost without interruption	pass on personal information about others *or*	make incoherent sounds *or*	reveal secret or confidential facts	implies negative opinion (on the part of the user of the word)
chat	+	+								
chatter		+	+	+	+	+				
prattle		+	+			+				+
babble							+	+		+
blab			+				+		+	+
gossip		+					+			

The use of all these words is restricted to colloquial speech or writing.

EXAMPLES

chat I've been next door **chatting** to the neighbours and catching up on the news.

Once you invite him in he sits and **chats** for hours on end.

chatter The little girls **chattered** incessantly instead of going to sleep.

I waited 15 minutes to telephone while this girl **chattered** on to her boyfriend about the most trivial incidents.

prattle Once she gets started she **prattles** on endlessly about nothing.

'What are you **prattling** about? I wasn't listening.'

babble With everyone **babbling** at once I can't understand a word.

She's **babbled** our secrets all over the village.

blab Someone has **blabbed** – the police know of our plan to raid the bank.

He's **blabbed** to everyone that we have serious financial problems.

gossip I despise people who **gossip** about their friends behind their backs.

I must admit I enjoy **gossiping** as long as it is not harmful to anyone.

3 Suggesting

	suggest	indicate	without saying openly or directly	intentionally *or* unintentionally		of sth disagreeable
imply	+		+	+	+	
intimate	+		+	+		
hint		+	+	+		
insinuate		+	+	+		+

The verbs are all transitive and take a **that**-clause as direct object. **Imply** may also take a nominal object. **Hint** may be followed by the preposition **at**. **Intimate** is the least common of these words.

	imply (ies) (ied) (ing)	intimate (s) (d)	hint (s) (ed)	insinuate (s) (d) (ing)	
I think the letter	+				that you will be offered the money.
His behaviour seems to	+				that he intends to leave.
He	+	+			a lot of things without being explicit.
He seemed to	+	+			that I would get the job.
He	+	+	+		to me that he was willing to help.
The report			+		at corruption in high places.
I felt he			+		at things which he didn't feel able to say directly.
Worse things have been	+	+		+	than have actually been said.
Are you	+			+	that I am dishonest?
If you want to accuse me, why not do so directly rather than				+	vaguely?

4 Getting close together

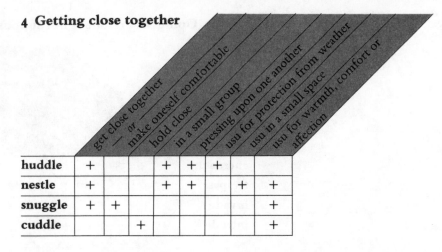

	get close together — or — make oneself comfortable	hold close	in a small group	pressing upon one another	usu for protection from weather	usu in a small space	usu for warmth, comfort or affection
huddle	+		+	+	+		
nestle	+		+	+		+	+
snuggle	+	+					+
cuddle			+				+

The verbs are all intransitive and **cuddle** may also be transitive.
They occur in the following prepositional constructions:
to huddle together/up against/under
to nestle together/up against/up to
to snuggle/up (together)/up to/into sth/down in
to cuddle up (together)/up to
Huddle and **nestle** may be used figuratively for inanimate objects
(usu buildings). **Snuggle** and **cuddle** are colloquial.

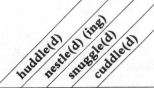

	huddle(d)	nestle(d) (ing)	snuggle(d)	cuddle(d)	
The sheep	+				together for warmth behind a hedge.
Four of us tried to	+				under one umbrella but the rain was so heavy that we all got wet.
A few cottages	+				up against an old grey church formed the village.
The child slept		+			in her father's arms.
The chicks		+			under the mother hen's wings to sleep.
The farm		+			at the foot of the mountain in a sheltered valley.
The puppies			+		together for warmth.
The sleeping child		+	+		up to his mother.
The puppy		+	+		up to his young owner.
The mother				+	the little girl after she had a nightmare.
My brother thinks it's babyish to let our mother				+	him, now he is eleven.

5 Going where one is not supposed to

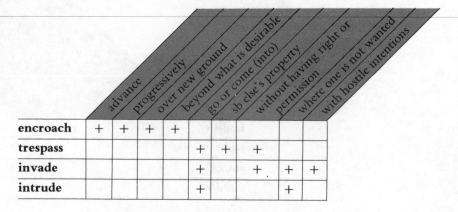

	advance	progressively	over new ground	beyond what is desirable	go or come (into)	sb else's property	without having right or permission	where one is not wanted	with hostile intentions
encroach	+	+	+	+					
trespass					+	+	+		
invade					+		+	+	+
intrude					+			+	

The verbs occur in the following constructions:
to encroach (up)on sth/over sth
to trespass upon/on/over sth
to invade sth
to intrude (up)on sth
Notice that only **invade** can take a direct object. The use of all these verbs can be extended to personal space, psychological freedom or sphere of influence.

	encroach(ed)	trespass(ed) (ing)	invade(d)	intrude(d) (ing)	
The sea gradually	+				over the low-lying land.
The green fields are being	+				on faster and faster by new housing development.
While I don't want to	+				on your territory, I do feel my experience in this matter may be of some value.
Although this section of coastline is private, people		+			over it all the time.
We have put up high fences but it is impossible to stop people		+			in our woods and picking all the spring flowers.
I hope I have not		+			too much on your time.
England was			+		by the Normans in 1066.
At holiday times London is			+		by foreign tourists.
Some people seem quite unaware that they are				+	on one's privacy.
Please excuse me – I see I have				+	on a private conversation.

6 Moving unsteadily

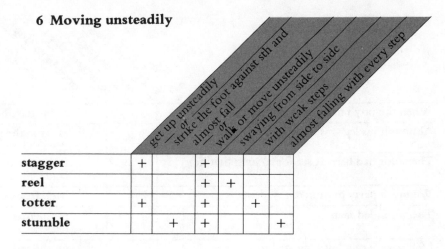

	get up unsteadily or strike the foot against sth and almost fall	or	walk or move unsteadily swaying from side to side	with weak steps	almost falling with every step
stagger	+		+		
reel			+	+	
totter	+		+		+
stumble		+	+			+

All the verbs are intransitive and usually collocate with the following prepositional adjuncts:

to stagger {
along sth
across sth
from side to side
to one's feet
}

to reel {
from sth
like sb
like sth
}

to totter **to one's feet**

to stumble {
along sth
across sth
on sth
over sth
into sth
}

Stagger, **reel** and **stumble across/on** may be used figuratively, in which case **stagger** and **stumble across/on** are transitive.

In their figurative uses, which are informal, **stagger** has the features [+shock deeply] or [+cause worry or confusion to], **reel** has the feature [+be shaken] and **stumble across/on** means [+find by accident].

EXAMPLES

What **staggered** me was the barefaced lies he told.
I was **staggered** by the news of my daughter's elopement.
The idea that my own daughter would do such a thing really made me **reel**.
I happened to **stumble** across a very pretty chair in a funny old junkshop where I had gone to look for books.

	stagger(ed) (ing)	reel(ed) (ing)	totter(ed) (ing)	stumble(d) (ing)	
When the boy's name was called he	+				to his feet, but could not walk.
Although his leg was injured he managed to	+				as far as the nearest farm, where he found someone to help him.
The sailor had been at sea for so long that he		+			from side to side when he tried to walk on land!
We met a party of drunken students		+			back from a tour of the town's bars.
The wounded man			+		momentarily at the cliff's edge and then fell.
I felt very weak, but managed to			+		up the stairs to bed.
The pony				+	on the rocky path and almost fell.
The survivors of the expedition	+			+	into the desert trading post just before they completely collapsed.

7 Slipping and sliding

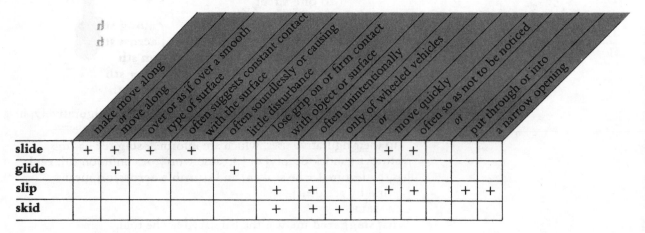

All these verbs are intransitive, and **slide** and **slip** are also transitive. **Slide** and **slip** are often used figuratively in informal circumstances to mean [+ pass gradually] [+ into or out of a state, condition or opinion] [+ often for the worse].

EXAMPLES

He **slid** into bad habits.

In today's permissive society it's all too easy to let one's standards **slide/slip**.

I sort of **slipped** into the habit of visiting him every day for half an hour.

Note the colloquial expression **to let things slide** [+do nothing] [+about things which are wrong].

EXAMPLE

I'm sorry the place is so untidy, I rather **let things slide** when I am here by myself.

	slide (slid)	slip(ped)	glide(d)	skid(ded)	
Children love to	+				down sandhills.
The wardrobe is too heavy to lift, but I think we can	+				it across the floor.
There was too much on my desk and half the papers	+	+			onto the floor and got out of order.
He		+			quietly into the room and took his place at the back.
She		+			on a banana skin and sprained her ankle.
I		+			over in the snow and broke my arm.
The boat			+		smoothly through the calm clear water.
The nurse			+		soundlessly past each patient's bed, checking that they were all peacefully asleep.
The car raced round the corner and				+	to a halt just in front of the house.
He fell off his bicycle when it				+	on the wet road.

8 Moving with force

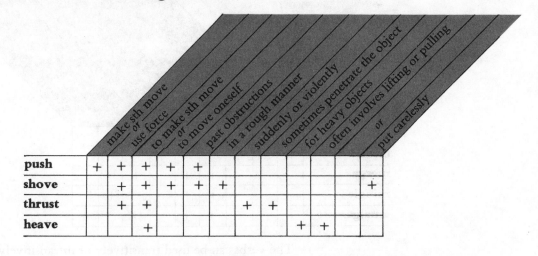

	make sth move or use force	to make sth move or to move oneself	past obstructions	in a rough manner	suddenly or violently sometimes penetrate the object	for heavy objects often involves lifting or pulling	or put carelessly
push	+	+	+	+	+					
shove		+	+	+	+	+				+
thrust		+	+				+	+		
heave			+					+	+	

All the verbs, except **thrust**, can be used transitively or intransitively. **Thrust** is only transitive. **Shove** is colloquial. **Thrust** is not much used in colloquial speech.

	push(ed)(ing)	shove(d)(ing)	thrust (thrust)	heave(d)	
Could you	+				the button to stop the machine?
I	+				my way through the crowds and managed at last to find my friends.
After two hours walking,	+				our way through dense undergrowth, we found the river-crossing.
He	+				back his chair from the table and stood up.
Everyone was	+	+			to try to make sure they got places on the boat.
I just		+			my things in the back of the car and drove off as fast as I could.
He	+		+		his hand down through the soft earth, trying to locate the lost ring.
She suddenly			+		£5 into my hand and ran off, telling me to enjoy myself with it.
We all				+	on the rope together to pull the boat in.
Now we have an oil-fired boiler, no-one has to				+	coal any more.
It took two of us to				+	the heavy trunk into the back of the car.

9 Combining

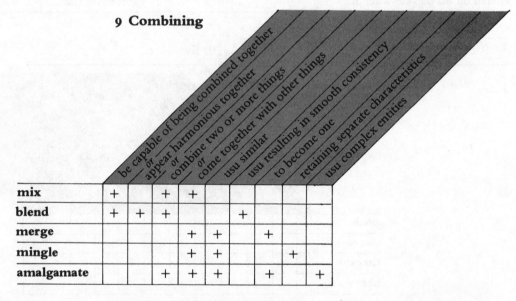

	be capable of being combined together or appear harmonious together	or combine two or more things	or come together with other things	usu similar	usu resulting in smooth consistency	to become one	retaining separate characteristics	usu complex entities
mix	+		+	+				
blend	+	+	+		+			
merge			+	+	+			
mingle			+	+		+		
amalgamate		+	+	+	+		+	

The verbs can be used transitively or intransitively but **mingle** is not often used transitively. All can occur in the construction to **. . . . . sth with sth**, and all can be followed by the preposition **with**.

Note the phrasal verb **to mix up** which means [+ confuse].

EXAMPLES

He **mixed up** all my careful arrangements and managed to arrive at the wrong station two hours late.

The two flocks of sheep got **mixed up** and we couldn't recognize which of them belonged to which farmer.

	mix(ed)(ing)	blend(s)(ed)(ing)	merge(d)(ing)	mingle(d)(ing)	amalgamate(d)	
Water and oil won't	+					
The two groups of students don't	+					with each other at all.
When making a cake you must	+	+				all the ingredients together very well.
She doesn't	+			(+)		with the other children in her class.
The tea we buy is usually the result of	(+)	+				several varieties.
I really don't think those two colours	(+)	+				well together.
It's amazing that such a modern painting		+				in so well with your antique furniture.
The Teacher Training College has			+			with the University.
The two companies			+		+	to form one much larger unit.
Two engineering unions have recently			+		+	to gain greater bargaining power.
The rain				+		with the tears on her cheeks.
It was exciting to				+		with the huge crowds of people out in the streets to celebrate the national holiday.
Two schools have					+	to save on staff and facilities.
Wouldn't it be possible to					+	both theories to achieve wider coverage of the data?

B Synonymous Pairs

1 **hole**
breach | [+esp one in a defence wall] ⇒ [+violation]

Breach usually occurs in set expressions the most common of which are: **a breach of contract/promise/faith/confidence/the peace** (=public disturbance).

2 **to encourage**
to foster | [+certain feelings or ideas in the mind] or [+help to develop]

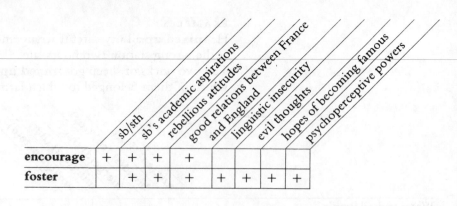

	sb/sth	sb's academic aspirations	rebellious attitudes	good relations between France and England	linguistic insecurity	evil thoughts	hopes of becoming famous	psychoperceptive powers
encourage	+	+	+	+				
foster		+	+	+	+	+	+	+

3   **to speak/write**
　　to ramble　　│　[+at great length] [+usu without ever coming to the point]

Ramble is colloquial.

EXAMPLES

Her letter **rambled** on for pages about how unhappy she was but I couldn't really gather why.

If you think I'm going to listen to that old fool **rambling** on for two hours about his work on dialect differences in West Yorkshire, you are quite wrong!

4   **to browse** ⎫ [+read] ⎧ [+at random] [+for pleasure]
　　to peruse ⎭　　　　⎩ [+carefully]

Peruse is formal and a bit old fashioned.

EXAMPLES

I really enjoy having a long breakfast on Sunday morning and quietly **browsing** through the newspapers.

I spent the afternoon **browsing** through old history books in the second–hand bookshops.

The immigration official **perused** my papers at length but eventually he smiled and told me I could continue.

I occupied myself in **perusing** the titles of the books in his library.

5   **insistent** ⎫ [+determined in ⎧ [+compelling attention]
　　persistent ⎭ pursuing a goal] ⎩ [+over a long period] or [+recurring] or [+continuing for a long time]

EXAMPLES

An **insistent** knocking at my door aroused me at 3 o'clock this morning.

He is so **insistent/persistent** that she may yet give in and agree to marry him.

The Government eventually had to give way to **persistent** pressure from all sides that the laws concerning privacy be changed.

This **persistent** cold weather is really most depressing.

Exercises

1 Find words to fit the following definitions/descriptions.

1 hard covering of bird's eggs, nuts, and of some animals (snails, lobsters)
2 small folds or lines in the skin especially due to age
3 false statement that damages a person's reputation
4 something said or done to cause amusement
5 rough piece of cut tree-trunk; short piece of this for a fire
6 speak or act in a way that hurts or is intended to hurt a person's feelings or dignity
7 showing clever and humorous expression of ideas, being very lively in one's speaking
8 the grounds of a university
9 narrow opening or crack in a rock, wall
10 game of chance in which one buys numbered tickets; only a certain number of tickets are drawn
11 variety of a spoken language peculiar to a region or to a social group

2 Choose the word that best fits a given context and change its form where necessary.

1 She loved to . . . . . in our bookshop when she came over to England. (read, peruse, browse)
2 Despite having a knife in his back, the man managed to . . . . . across to the telephone. (stagger, stumble, reel)
3 The two lost children finally . . . . . up together under a tree and fell asleep. (huddle, cuddle)
4 His way of . . . . . things about other people made him the most unpleasant of companions. (hint, imply, insinuate)
5 He gave a . . . . . of despair when he saw the pile of paper-work still to be done. (sob, groan, moan)
6 There was a long . . . . . of despair from the child as he realised someone had stolen his toy. (scream, shriek, wail)
7 The aroma of freshly-ground coffee . . . . . with the smell of steaming hot rolls sent our appetites soaring! (merge, mingle, blend, amalgamate)
8 The children enjoyed the ice on the roads because they could . . . . . on it. (slide, slip, skid)

3 What kinds of objects/people can be described as:

1 smooth? 2 scared? 3 tangible? 4 soft? 5 potent? 6 sly?
7 appalling? 8 cruel? 9 bold? 10 growing? 11 verbal?
12 horrible? 13 intimate?

4 Which adjectives collocate with which nouns?

a 1 native 2 original 3 wrong 4 valid 5 competent
6 hysterical 7 standing 8 dangerous 9 utopian
10 conceited 11 superficial 12 tangible 13 over-anxious
14 serene 15 wily

b 1 age 2 treatment 3 approach 4 result 5 ovation
6 speaker 7 language 8 lawyer 9 training 10 custom
11 form 12 answer 13 passport 14 character 15 mother
16 evidence 17 road 18 proposals 19 driver 20 salesman

5 What are the main semantic features of the following?

1 cluster   2 shove   3 browse   4 ramble on   5 hint   6 flaunt
7 entail   8 blush   9 cling to   10 intrude   11 bowl sb over
12 rehearse

6 Fill in the blanks with appropriate words from the given list.

vent   second   point   standing   shell   wear   bear   likely   fill
light

1 Why did you . . . . . the candles?
2 What she said was very much to the . . . . .
3 From then on she withdrew into her . . . . .
4 The pianist was given a . . . . . ovation.
5 John is . . . . . to be late.
6 Have you got somebody to . . . . . the position?
7 Why did she . . . . . that weird uniform?
8 He finished . . . . . last.
9 Please . . . . . in mind what I told you.
10 He gave . . . . . to his feelings.

7 What kinds of things can one:

1 aim at?   2 watch?   3 browse over?   4 foster?   5 point out?
6 light?   7 advocate?   8 stake out?   9 face?   10 rehearse?
11 look up?   12 flaunt?   13 deny?   14 assert?   15 cling to?

8 Fill in the following componential grids:

1

	make sth move *or* use force	to make sth move *or* to move oneself	past obstructions	in a rough manner	suddenly or violently	sometimes penetrate the object	for heavy objects	often involves lifting or pulling	*or* put carelessly
push									
shove									
thrust									
heave									

2

	get up unsteadily	*or* strike the foot against sth and *or* almost fall	walk or move unsteadily	swaying from side to side	with weak steps	almost falling with every step
stagger						
reel						
totter						
stumble						

9 Give at least one word which has the opposite sense to:

1 covert 2 smooth 3 frank 4 rigid 5 conceited 6 physical 7 hostile 8 aloof 9 promising 10 luscious (fruit) 11 nasty 12 emotional 13 complex 14 attractive 15 utopian 16 valuable

10 What differences and similarities are there between the following pairs?

1 babble/blab 2 cuddle/huddle 3 remember/remind 4 blend/merge 5 trespass/encroach 6 wail/groan 7 slip/skid 8 notice/point out 9 encourage/foster 10 lure/seduce 11 sigh/gasp 12 tableware/silverware

Revision Exercises

R1 In what sense are the following words negative?

1 debauch 2 unmindful 3 incessant 4 libel 5 wane 6 smirk 7 covet 8 malign 9 infringe 10 pry 11 divulge 12 aggravate 13 scathing 14 hoax

R2 Who or what can you:

1 defame? 2 sprinkle? 3 divulge? 4 betray? 5 pry into? 6 sue? 7 store? 8 stir? 9 trigger (off)? 10 intercept? 11 explore? 12 prohibit? 13 violate? 14 bug? 15 coach?

R3 What differences and similarities are there between the following pairs?

1 restrain/inhibit 2 prohibit/ban 3 arouse/rouse 4 crowd/flock 5 diffuse/disseminate 6 suffuse/spread 7 consent/permit 8 relish/like 9 filthy/dirty 10 blunt/plain 11 witness/see 12 enhance/heighten 13 plunge/thrust 14 inflict/cause

R4 Fill in the following collocational grids:

1

	foment(ing) (ed)	rouse(d)	incite(d)	arouse(d)	
Political agitators deliberately					the crowd to violent action.
He was					to dislike his mother by the attitude of his step-mother.
At 3 a.m. a tremendous storm					everybody from their beds.
His flagrant disrespect for the rules has					everybody to action.
The shortage of food					deep feelings of discontent among the people.
Seeing injustice tends to					all my aggressive feelings.
Militant students are					some kind of direct action against the authorities.
The revolt was in fact					by a small group of people within the Government.

2

	ban(ned)	forbid (forbidden)	prohibit(ed)	
The farmer has				the children to play in the barn.
I				you to use those swearwords to me.
It is				to spit on the floor.
Smoking in cinemas is				by law in many States of the US.
The Government has				all further sales of the drug pending an enquiry.
The controversial film about race relations has been				in many countries.
Many quite harmless books are being				by prejudiced heads of school.
The University has				him from doing any further teaching.
He has been				from entering Britain because of his political activities.

3

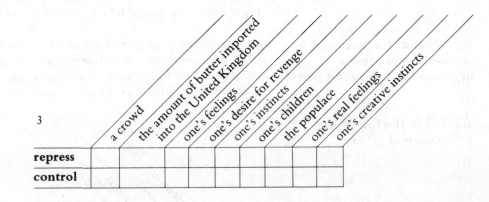

	a crowd	the amount of butter imported into the United Kingdom	one's feelings	one's desire for revenge	one's instincts	one's children	the populace	one's real feelings	one's creative instincts
repress									
control									

R5 Give distinctive semantic features for the following groups of words:

1 strike, slap, clout
2 entrust, confide, consign
3 educate, instruct, coach, tutor, train

R6 Supply appropriate prepositions/adverbs.

1 We are slaves . . . the clock.
2 Egypt is famous . . . its pyramids.
3 People crowded . . . the famous actress to get her autograph.
4 We live . . . a pace that is dissonant with our inner needs.
5 He is oblivious . . . what is going on.
6 Is there anybody looking . . . the children?
7 I will attend . . . this complaint.
8 They were assailed . . . doubts.
9 There must be a way of stopping that dog . . . biting everyone he meets.
10 Nothing could possibly rouse them . . . their beds.
11 What has incited them . . . such extreme behaviour?

12 The shopping centre thronged . . . people taking advantage of the winter sales.

13 They work . . . day.

R7 Guess the right word.

1 There was a b . . . . . of light showing underneath the darkened door.

2 A law was e . . . . . by Parliament to reduce racial discrimination.

3 The judge's long tirade against strikers was a clear a . . . . . of his position.

4 The only pr . . . . . we took before climbing the mountain were to inform the police, and to make sure we had enough provisions.

5 She always wore a p . . . . . smile, as though nothing could ruffle her.

6 He sn . . . . . unkindly behind his hand and immediately straightened his face as if nothing had happened.

7 The literature was considered to be s . . . . . as it clearly aimed at helping to overthrow the government.

8 All the natives of the island spoke in the v . . . . . but none of them could read or write.

9 The lady was re . . . . . about where she had been that day, but the police soon extracted the facts from her.

10 He had a s . . . . . grin on his face which made us distrust and dislike him.

R8 What differences and/or similarities are there between the following pairs?

1 disclose/divulge   2 confirm/establish   3 mould/shape   4 oblivious/unmindful   5 somatic/mental   6 weeds/plants   7 disparity/incongruity   8 admonition/warning   9 subsidy/money   10 surge/movement

R9 Provide a few collocations with which both the given words/expressions can occur.

EXAMPLE: to get rid of ⎱ *unripe strawberries from a basket*
to discard ⎰ *half the texts in the book*

1 to benefit/to profit   2 to postpone/to delay   3 to hinder/to obstruct   4 to initiate/to launch   5 to heighten/to intensify   6 to break/to violate   7 to tend/to look after   8 versatile/many-sided

R10 Fill in the following componential grids:

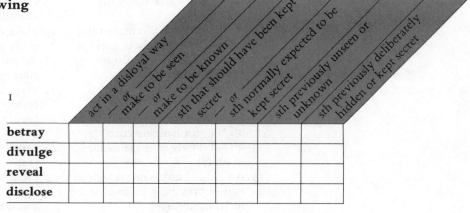

1	act in a disloyal way	make to be seen	make to be known	sth that should have been kept secret	sth normally expected to be kept secret	sth previously unseen or unknown	sth previously deliberately hidden or kept secret
betray							
divulge							
reveal							
disclose							

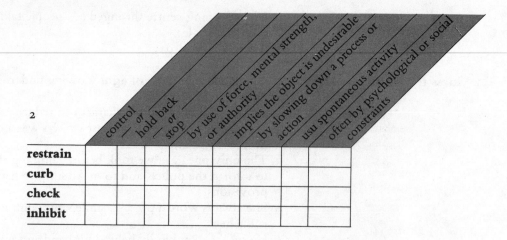

2	control or	hold back or	stop	by use of force, mental strength, or authority	implies the object is undesirable	by slowing down a process or action	usu spontaneous activity	often by psychological or social constraints
restrain								
curb								
check								
inhibit								

R11 Choose from the words in brackets the one which is most appropriate. Modify its form where necessary. necessary.

1 The demonstrators . . . . . together, some thousand strong, to listen to their speakers. (flock, throng, crowd)
2 'Birds of a feather . . . . . together.' (flock, throng, crowd)
3 By driving too fast we were . . . . . the law. (encroach, invade, infringe)
4 The cat . . . . . to the tree-trunk with its sharp claws. (hold, cling, seize)
5 After the match the crowd . . . . . quietly. (scatter, strew, disperse)
6 We were mildly . . . . . to see her back so soon. (amazed, surprised, astounded)
7 The little boy . . . . . the dog with great tenderness. (tend, attend to, care for)
8 Once she had . . . . . her thoughts to paper, she knew there was no turning back. (entrust, commit, confide)
9 Information on the progress of war was . . . . . to the troops. (propagate, diffuse, disseminate)
10 How do you feel about the President's attempts to . . . . . plutonium reprocessing? (curb, restrain, check, inhibit)

R12 Solve the crossword puzzle.

Across
1 We tried to b . . . . . the way by putting a tree across the road. (3)
3 A film or book is censored if it is found to be likely to corrupt and d . . . . . the population. (7)
7 breathe in (6)
10 act or cause others to act immorally (7)
12 Near the door were some p . . . . . for hanging coats. (4)
13 spread slowly over the surface of sth (7)
15 A s . . . . . book is one which is against prevailing political and social norms. (10)
16 animal like a mouse, but larger (3)
18 cut to pieces, roughly and clumsily (4)
19 make coins lower in value by putting less silver in them (6)
23 very religious, praying all the time (5)
24 very important, often in resolving a problem (7)
25 high, windswept, barren area of land (4)
26 person who walks in his sleep (12)
29 I told him it would rain, but he didn't h . . . . . my warning, and went out without a coat. (4)

30 guns (anagram) for 'warm and cosy' (4)

32 passage or hall (5)

34 It's within the r . . . . . of possibility that the weather in England will be good, but it isn't very likely! (5)

35 hit, usu on the head (*coll*) (5)

36 small road in the country (4)

37 part of the body (3)

38 the fact of not being permanent or lasting (10)

Down

2 move on a horse (4)

4 lug pen (anagram) for 'thrust forcibly' (6)

5 Persons aged over 65 are e . . . . . for a pension. (8)

6 quiet, not saying what one thinks (8)

8 I, a lass? (anagram) for 'attack violently' (6)

9 official who checks books, films, etc to make sure they have nothing in them which could corrupt (6)

11 place where you live (5)

12 be widespread (of an idea or belief) (7)

14 pans (anagram) for 'length of life' (4)

17 You must a . . . . . by the rules. (5)

20 money paid by a government to meet the cost of public services (9)

21 call, send for sth (6)

22 a trick, designed to deceive people, pretending that an event has taken place (4)

25 concerned with the speed at which bodily processes (eg digestion) takes place (9)

27 able to move (6)

28 tool which you use for moving, eg coal or snow (6)

31 obvious, clearly noticed (of demands, injustice, etc) (5)

32 allow (3)

33 unwanted plant growing in a cultivated plot (4)

Unit 6   How to keep the doctor away

Exercise for ever!

In our pursuit of good health and shapeliness, most of us think immediately of **dieting**[1]. If only we could eat less, we think, we'd soon be **slim**[2], happy and life would be problem-free. It's true that dieting is one answer, though it can be the most **agonising**[3] and psychologically destructive. So why not think about it another way. Maybe it's not that we eat too much, but that we exercise too little. Most of us lead terribly **sedentary**[4] lives; when we're not sitting at our office desks, we're sitting on a bus or a train or in a car or in front of the **telly**[5], and we very rarely go for a good **brisk**[6] walk, **let alone**[7] **exert ourselves**[8] more **vigorously**[9]. Taking regular exercise can mean that you can eat **decent**[10], satisfying amounts, while not endangering your figure at all. Exercise, or better still sport – since sport is **challenging**[11], exciting and socially enjoyable too – can change your whole attitude to life. It can change a depressive, **lethargic**[12] person into a happy, active one. It can change a **flabby**[13], **clumsy**[14] person into a firm, perfectly controlled, graceful one. Exercise, so the doctors tell us, is a necessary **antidote**[15] to stress, and it will help to keep your heart and lungs working well too.

Tina Bowles, *Honey*

The Morbid Society

A favorite **device**[1] of novelists who think the world is sick is to picture modern society as one vast hospital **ward**[2]. To social critic Ivan Illich, this image is literally true. Illich thinks that from **prenatal**[3] **probes**[4] to **postmortem**[5] examinations, modern medicine has turned the citizens of advanced and industrial nations into lifelong patients who are **presumed**[6] sick until **proven**[7] healthy. The paradoxical result, Illich argues in his brilliant new book 'Medical **Nemesis**[8]' is an epidemic of multiple 'iatrogenesis' – the ancient Greek term for physician-induced illness.

Illich's primary concern is not with the pain, sickness and death caused directly by doctors, hospitals and the indiscriminate use of drugs. These forms of malpractice are, in his radical diagnosis, merely the overt clinical manifestations of the more serious, **pervasive**[9] 'medicalization of life', which makes whole populations **morbidly**[10] dependent upon a dubious – and expensive – system of medical care. Like other critics, Illich insists that better housing and other environmental factors have done more than institutionalized medicine to improve health. He also reminds us that major diseases such as tuberculosis declined *before* physicians intervened with antibiotics.

According to Illich, the expansion of medicine into a multibillion-dollar industry becomes **counterproductive**[11]. Medical bureaucracy, he says, creates bad health by generating painful new needs (**drug dependence**[12] and unnecessary surgery), by lowering the levels of tolerance for discomfort or pain, and 'by abolishing even the right to self-care'. In sum, Illich finds, modern medicine has produced 'a morbid society that demands universal medicalization and a medical establishment that certifies universal morbidity'.

Although he would retain many fruitful methods of modern medicine, including certain forms of **inoculation**[13] and limited **reliance**[14] on experts, he believes that the most important health services can be performed by the people themselves. Medicalized civilization, he argues, is organized 'to kill pain, to eliminate sickness and to abolish the need for an art of suffering and of dying'. By contrast, traditional cultures confront pain, suffering and death as tests of the arts of living – **goads**[15] for producing compassion, patience and the dignified acceptance of death. The ultimate nemesis produced by modern medicine, Illich warns, is the gradual loss of these traditional human virtues.

Kenneth L Woodward,

Newsweek

Art Yarrington's Marathon

When it happened, Capt Art Yarrington was 30 and anyone's image of a **dashing**[1] young fighter pilot. He had youth, he was **ruggedly**[2] handsome, and wore his flight cap **at a rakish angle**[3] over a **crew cut**[4] and a perpetual half smile on his face. Art was a jet pilot, flying the supersonic F-104 *Starfighter*, one of the swiftest and most **glamorous**[5] planes in the sky, and he was good at his job.

Then it happened.

'I was home that night,' Art told me later, 'and I felt this sensation in my **chest**[6]. My chest felt full, and I felt **like**[7] I should get up and exercise or something.'

As fate had it[8], lucky or not, Art **was due for**[9] his annual flight **physical**[10] just two days later, and there it was on his **electrocardiogram**[11]. 'Inverted T waves in **leads**[12] II, III and a Vf, with curving of the ST segment. Diagnosis: **Coronary**[13] **insufficiency**[14] with inferior wall **myocardial**[15] **ischemia**[16].'

In Air Force language, it was a '**serial change**[17] in an electrocardiogram' and in nearly every case an automatic cause for permanent **grounding**[18].

To Art Yarrington, it was the end of the world. After 2300 hours in the air, doing something he had dreamed of doing since childhood, flying the fastest and most-beautiful birds ever created, he was **put out**[19] on the **sidewalk**[20], given a firm handshake, and told he would never climb into a **cockpit**[21] of his own again.

'Isn't there anything I can do, **Doc**[22]? Anything?'

As I read his records, he sat with his hands **clasped**[23] and his eyes **staring**[24] at the floor.

'I think you have one chance in a million, but possibly it can be done.'

Except for the history of an abnormal **ECG**[25], I saw nothing else wrong. We **ran our own tests on**[26] him (his ECG had returned to normal by then), and I asked him to give up smoking. Then we started him walking, first on the **treadmill**[27], then outdoors, slowly progressing up to one mile a day. At the end of the two weeks, he was walking up to two miles a day and some of his confidence had returned.

All this was in May. Then, by letter and by telephone, I began hearing from him.

By July he was running three miles nonstop every day, averaging nearly eight minutes a mile.

By August he was up to four miles.

By September, it was five miles in 40 minutes.

In October, his average daily run was six miles in about 46 minutes.

He came back about that time for another checkup, **all chest and elbows**[28]. 'When do we start?' he asked, as he **rounded the corner**[29] into my office, **rubbing his hands**[30].

We gave him a standard ECG, just to make sure (it was quite normal), then put him on the treadmill. Art Yarrington was in better condition than anyone I had ever examined.

After this demonstration, I thought it was time we tried for a **waiver**[31] through Air Force channels to get Capt Yarrington back on **flying status**[32]. The reply was **perfunctory**[33]: 'Recommend disapproval of waiver.'

Art wasn't discouraged, and suggested something more drastic.

'Why don't I try for the Boston Marathon?'

My **eyebrows**[34] shot up. Drastic, indeed! I had run in it twice while studying at Harvard, and it is a **grueling**[35] race for a healthy man, **let alone**[36] one coming back from a cardiac condition.

'I'm against it,' I told him frankly.

But Art was **adamant**[37]. The race gets newspaper **coverage**[38], and a story about an Air Force cardiac running 26 miles nonstop might raise a few eyebrows besides mine.

'Well, make sure you get yourself into condition for it,' I ended **lamely**[39].

Art did. He increased his program to as much as 70 miles of running a week, and as long as three hours a day. By December, he was running 15 miles averaging nearly seven minutes a mile.

Then a minor tragedy struck. Art developed a foot infection that stopped his running altogether for three weeks. When it healed, it was too late for the race.

But Art was only momentarily discouraged. He **snarled**[40], 'I'll show them'.

Just to prove he could do it, to himself, if no one else, Art worked himself back into **shape**[41] about a month later, **marked off**[42] a **track**[43], and, with four fellow officers standing by as **witnesses**[44], he ran his own marathon, all 25 miles of it, in the respectable time of three hours and 58 minutes.

He was doing all this, remember, without any realistic hope that any of it was ever going to **pay off**[45] other than by improving his health.

I used his marathon run as a basis for a second request for a waiver. It, too, was denied.

Meanwhile, I thought I'd try one more **avenue**[46]. I had heard that civilian insurance companies had changed from more conservative tradition and were now issuing policies at **standard premiums**[47] to men with a history of chest pain if a coronary **angiogram**[48] proved to be normal. This is a test which examines the coronary **arteries**[49] from inside the vessels.

I requested approval from the Air Force's physical-standards section, citing this development, and their response was encouraging. So an angiogram was scheduled for Captain Yarrington at the Baylor Medical School in Houston, Texas.

The cardiologist there stuck a **catheter**[50] (tube) in the large artery of Art's left arm and worked it up until it was very close to the heart. There he injected some special **dye**[51] into the coronary artery and took moving X-ray pictures of the dye as it passed through the arteries supplying the heart. What he saw impressed him.

Among other things he reported, '. . . his coronary arteries appear to

---

31 a document stating that the Air Force gave up its right to ground the pilot
32 the status or position of flying pilot
33 done merely as a duty and without much consideration
34 the hair growing on the bony ridges above the eyes
35 severe, exhausting
36 not to mention, to say nothing of
37 insistent, not changing one's mind under any pressure
38 the fact of being covered or reported
39 without much conviction, lame *lit* unable to walk properly
40 spoke in a harsh, angry voice
41 good condition
42 measured out and designated
43 course on which races are run
44 a person who has first-hand knowledge of an event and is able to testify that something is true
45 give a reward or recompense
46 way of approach
47 premium or fixed sum of money paid for insurance by a normal, healthy person
48 graph of the vascular system, the system of veins or ducts which carry blood
49 the pipes or tubes that carry blood from the heart to all parts of the body
50 tube
51 a substance used for giving colour, usually to material but also to liquids, as here

be larger than we would expect for the size of his heart and this may reflect his excellent physical status.'

That's conservative medical talk for, 'Amazing!' The cardiologist asked Art how his arteries got that way. Art **cocked**[52] his head, '**I run some**[53]'.

There's an amusing **climax**[54] to this meeting. When I **called on**[55] him at Baylor to get the results, the nurse told me that, following the examination, the doctor was so impressed that he waited until dark, then went out in his gym clothes and tried to run a mile himself to find out what kind of condition *he* was in!

Now that I was armed with this favorable medical report, I tried one more time to **request**[56] a waiver for Art's original abnormal electrocardiogram.

This time the request was granted.

So almost two years after he was grounded, Captain Arthur Yarrington of Ridgefield Park, New Jersey, serial number AO-3029402, was returned to flying status after, in official language, a 'history of abnormal electrocardiogram, possibly **schemic**[57] in nature but more likely the result of an inflammatory **carditis**[58]'.

Due to his accomplishment, Art Yarrington became something of a folk hero among his **peers**[59].

Dr Kenneth H Cooper,   *Aerobics*

52 turned upwards showing pride
53 *Br* would say 'I do a bit of running'
54 final point or finishing touch
55 visited
56 ask, demand
57 due to ischemia, cf 16 above
58 inflammation of the muscular substance of the heart
59 equals

Spurious[1] Sedatives

Americans spend as much as $58 million a year on **sedatives**[2], tension relievers and **stimulants**[3] that are available without a prescription at almost any **drugstore**[4] or **newsstand**[5]. But for three years, a **panel**[6] of drug experts working for the US Food and Drug Administration has been analyzing the **ingredients**[7] of these **patent**[8] medicines to see if they really **live up to**[9] their advertising. In a report issued recently, the panel concluded that of the 23 major active ingredients of the pills and capsules, only the stimulant caffeine could be considered both fully safe and effective.

Newsweek

STRESS . . . THE SPICE OF LIFE

By RONALD BEDFORD
Science Editor

Don't complain about stress. According to the world's top expert today it's vital to life.

If we were not under some stress or other, we would all die.

Professor Hans Selye says in a report to the World Health Organisation that stress provides the body's survival mechanism.

But some stresses can be **harmful**[1].

The Montreal University Director advises: 'The best way to avoid harmful stress is to select an environment – a wife, a boss, your friends – **in line with**[2] your preferences.'

Daily Mirror

SPURIOUS SEDATIVES

1 false, not genuine, unnecessary and useless
2 drugs that produce a calming effect
3 drugs that excite or make one feel more energetic
4 *Am* a place where drugs (medicines) are sold, together with goods of many different kinds and where food and soft drinks are served
5 small stall where newspapers and magazines are sold
6 group, team
7 components, elements making up the drugs
8 sold under a legally protected trade name
9 *coll* put into practice, reach the standard that is claimed

STRESS

1 causing harm, damage, injury
2 in agreement with

FIDGETING IS GOOD FOR YOU

1 moving about restlessly, making quick and useless movements
2 turning idly round and round, twisting in an aimless manner
3 causing a thing (eg fingers) to make a sharp (cracking) noise
4 striking one's foot on the floor repeatedly
5 twist and turn the body
6 rub lightly or scrape, especially with the fingernails
7 wind (one thing) about (another) or turn something
8 to draw pictures, symbols, etc abstractedly, on whatever material comes to hand, while the mind is otherwise occupied
9 move (food, etc) about between the teeth or in the mouth
10 give off, set free
11 cause
12 thinner, more slender
13 people who treat pencils like straws. They keep them in their mouths and draw on them as if drinking
14 people who grind their teeth, rub their teeth together with a circular motion
15 people who clench their fists, press their hands firmly together
16 a nervous disease characterized by involuntary muscular twitching, St Vitus's dance
17 push, pull, twist, or move suddenly
18 wriggle, twist the body
19 touch, stroke or caress lovingly
20 keep away, guard against
21 collections of things kept in reserve

MENTAL ILLNESS

1 hide, camouflage
2 agreeable to the mind, *lit* pleasing to the taste
3 claiming, saying

Mental Illness

Mental illness is a myth whose function is to **disguise**[1] and thus render more **palatable**[2] the bitter pill of moral conflicts in human relations. In **asserting**[3] that there is no such thing as mental illness I do not deny that people have problems coping with life and each other.

Thomas Szasz, *The Second Sin*

Carry on fidgeting – it's good for you

Teachers should not tell schoolchildren to stop **fidgeting**[1] in class – for doctors now believe that fidgeting is probably good for us.

Hair-**twiddling**[2], finger-**cracking**[3] and **foot-tapping**[4] may irritate other people but they can calm the worrying type.

Doctors at Graylingwell Hospital in Chichester, Sussex, wired volunteers to 'fidget-meters' which recorded every movement.

Some subjects hardly stirred during the experience, others made as many as 114 movements a minute.

We all tend to **wriggle**[5], **scratch**[6], **twist**[7] or **doodle**[8] when we're worried or kept waiting.

Twiddling

The Queen sometimes **chews**[9] her glasses and when she was visiting the polo at Windsor recently she was photographed standing in a doorway, twiddling her car keys.

Fidgeting helps us **discharge**[10] nervous energy that might otherwise **bring on**[11] a headache or muscle pain.

Fidgeters tend to be **slimmer**[12] than other people. All those little movements burn up calories as effectively as a 10-mile run.

But fidgeting can become a ritual.

When Sir Harold Wilson gets ready to go on TV he goes through an elaborate routine with his pipe.

Doctors believe fidgeting is a sign of anxiety.

Pencil-**suckers**[13] may long for a return to babyhood.

Teeth-**grinders**[14] and fist-**clenchers**[15] are probably fighting to hold back aggression.

Some people may have an underlying wish to do themselves injury, perhaps because of inner conflicts or a feeling of guilt.

But excessive fidgeting can be a sign of illness.

Children suffering from **chorea**[16] – St Vitus' Dance – may **jerk**[17] and **squirm**[18] uncontrollably. They cannot speak properly or even hold a pencil.

Beneficial

Sometimes it is wise to provide the fidget something to fidget with.

The Greeks — and many Arabs — have a string of worry-beads they **fondle**[19] to **ward off**[20] tension.

A doctor said: 'Anything that will stop the speed of modern life for even half a minute is beneficial. I would rather my patients had this than **hoards**[21] of expensive tranquillisers.'

Weekend

Easing a baby's way into the world

For most babies born in hospitals, birth is a **harsh**[1] experience. They are **yanked**[2] out of their warm, dark world into a bright, sometimes air-conditioned room, **slapped**[3] on the **rear end**[4], and the **umbilical cord**[5] cut as soon as possible. It's a cold, cruel world and no mistake.

Many people feel this **bing-bang**[6] approach to childbirth is a bad idea, a convenience to doctors and nurses at the expense of mother and child. One leader in the movement to take the violence out of childbirth is French physician Frederick Leboyer, who practices in a middle-class hospital in Paris.

There, delivery rooms are warm and softly lit. Soft music plays during **labor**[7], the newborn infant is massaged and placed in bath water the temperature of the **amniotic fluid**[8] he just left, and the umbilical cord is usually left uncut until it stops **throbbing**.[9] The baby eases into the world gradually.

The French Science Research Council had one of its psychologists, Danielle Rapoport, do a **follow-up study**[10] on 120 one-, two- and three-year-olds delivered by the Leboyer method and a similar number delivered in conventional ways. She tested the children for **motor skills**[11], language ability, and general development.

The two groups began to speak at the same age, on the average, but the Leboyer children walked earlier (13 months vs. 15 months) and did considerably better on the Brunet and Lezine test for psychomotor functioning.

Even more impressive was Rapoport's report on the Leboyer children's social and emotional development. Only eight of them had even minor problems with **toilet training**[12] or learning to feed themselves. Many of the children, for unknown reasons, were **ambidextrous**[13].

According to Michael Odent, a doctor in the Plitiviers Hospital, which uses Leboyer's method: 'Children born in a serene and peaceful way seem to be secure, in their first months, from such **psychosomatic**[14] symptoms as **colic**[15], as well as the **paroxysmic**[16] crying associated with a new-born baby.

Jack Horn, *Psychology Today*

EASING A BABY'S WAY
INTO THE WORLD

1 rough, hard to bear, cruel
2 *coll* given a sudden, sharp pull
3 struck with the open hand
4 bottom, behind
5 the ropelike tissue connecting the navel of the foetus with the placenta
6 *coll* rough, matter-of-fact
7 the pains of childbirth
8 the liquid substance in the amnion, the membranous sac enclosing the embryo in mammals
9 (of the heart, pulse, etc) beating, quivering rhythmically
10 study which looks at the results of an event, what happens after it
11 abilities of motor muscles and motor nerves (nerves that excite muscles into action)
12 training to keep themselves clean by using the lavatory (WC)
13 able to use both hands equally well
14 physical symptoms caused initially by the mind (ie not originally physical)
15 severe pain in the stomach and bowels
16 periodic, convulsive

DRUG HOARDING[1]

Kent chemists are urging the Department of Health to organize an annual national **spring-clean**[2] of medicine **chests**[3].

The chemists, who organized a fortnight's **clear-out**[4] of family medicine cupboards, ended with more than a ton of drugs, including 1,364,000 tablets and capsules and 84 gallons of liquids, worth altogether £17,565. The collection included **thalidomide tablets**[5], concentrated **acids**[6] in unlabelled beer bottles and enough **strychnine**[7] to kill everyone in east Kent.

According to Rowland Blythe, a Tunbridge Wells pharmacist who helped to organize the collection, people are not taking full courses of treatment and are hoarding unused medicines. Unused pills should be destroyed by **flushing them down the lavatory**[8] and all dangerous liquids should be returned to your local chemist.

John Kemp, *The Daily Telegraph*

DRUG HOARDING

1 collecting, storing up and saving
2 thoroughly cleaning the house during the spring season
3 box for storing things in
4 removing everything unnecessary
5 tablets of a drug that maimed and killed unborn babies in Europe some years ago
6 strong, sour liquids often damaging to material, skin, eyes, etc
7 a stimulant which if taken in large doses is a killer
8 putting them in the WC and flushing the pan by pulling the chain or pressing the button

SKINFUL OF MUD

1 illnesses, sicknesses
2 Bath in mud (=soft, wet earth)
3 town which has natural sources of mineral water
4 small openings in the skin through which sweat comes
5 reduced by a natural chemical process
6 of peat, partly decomposed vegetable material in a solid mass found in marshy places
7 drain-hole in a bath or washbasin

Skinful of Mud
By TERRY GEORGE

*There is no finer cure for backache, liver, stomach or intestinal **ailments**[1] than a **mudbath**[2], according to Professor Otto Stoeber, of Bad Neydharting, Austria. He says there is no need to go to a health **spa**[3]. You simply buy the right mud and fill the bath at home.*

*A warm mud bath relaxes the muscles and opens the **pores**[4] to herbs millions of years old and **rotted down to**[5] a concentrated form.*

*Prof. Stoeber says that 'the **peaty**[6] mud from Bad Neydharting has more than 300 different healing plants in a highly concentrated form and their goodness is absorbed through the skin.'*

*The only problem is getting the mud down the **plug-hole**[7] afterwards. Fortunately, mud packs from the spa come with full instructions.*

Weekend

Discussion

1 When you are ill, do you prefer to go to the doctor, or to try to cure yourself? Give reasons.

2 There are people who claim that all illness is psychosomatically caused. To what extent would you agree? Is it true of you?

3 Szasz asserts that so-called mental illness is used to disguise extreme self-centredness. Do you agree that 'mental illness is a myth'? If so, how would you account for conditions like schizophrenia and paranoia which cause their sufferers so much anguish?

4 Modern medicine has made it possible to avoid much suffering and many deaths which previous centuries took for granted. What are the results of this on our attitude to illness and death? Are all the effects beneficial?

5 What kind of attitude should doctors have to their patients? Is the brisk, 'no-nonsense' approach a good one, or should they be more gentle? Should doctors always be completely truthful with their patients?

6 Do you take enough exercise? If not, why not? Are you just lazy? (Be honest!)

Word Study

A   Semantic Fields

1 Ways of putting things right

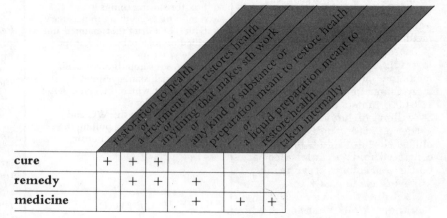

	restoration to health	a treatment that restores health	anything that makes sth work	any kind of substance or preparation meant to restore health	a liquid preparation meant to restore health	taken internally
cure	+	+	+			
remedy		+	+	+		
medicine				+	+	+

EXAMPLES

cure   After six months in the mountains his **cure** was completed and he returned to normal life.

In spite of the large number of research schemes in operation, there is still no real possibility of finding a **cure** for cancer.

The best **cure** for depression is to keep busy and try not to think about the thing which is upsetting you.

remedy   The **remedy** for a fire which won't burn is to adjust the amount of draught it is getting.

My personal **remedy/cure** for a cold is to take two aspirins in some hot lemonade and honey, and go to bed early.

If a field analysis doesn't seem to be working, a good **remedy** is often to try to analyse the difference between the examples.

medicine   I can give you some good **medicine** for your cough.

Children do not like taking nasty-tasting **medicines**.

Chemists' shelves are packed with patent **medicines** whose efficacy is often very doubtful.

Note that the sense of **medicine** may be extended.

EXAMPLE

Laughter is always said to be the best **medicine** when one is ill.

2 Making or getting better

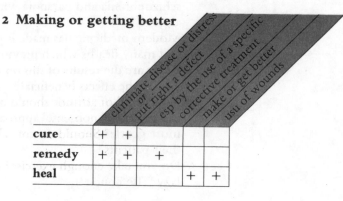

	eliminate disease or distress	put right a defect	esp by the use of a specific corrective treatment	make or get better	usu of wounds
cure	+	+			
remedy	+	+	+		
heal				+	+

Cure and heal can be either transitive or intransitive; remedy is always transitive. They occur in the following constructions:
to cure sb/sth, sb of sth; to remedy sth, sth with sth; to heal sth, up, over

EXAMPLES

cure It's very difficult to **cure** oneself of a bad habit like smoking.
The special treatment she underwent **cured** her completely in six months.

remedy We can **remedy** the patient's lack of appetite with a special diet and lots of exercise.
Once a car develops this fault it is almost impossible **to remedy**.

heal The cut has **healed** much faster than I would have expected.
It's sometimes very difficult **to heal** this type of wound.
Time **heals** all ills.

3 Experiencing something unpleasant

	resign oneself to something painful, unpleasant or offensive	without complaining	over a prolonged period of time	restraining one's feelings of opposition to it	be resistant to —or—	have unpleasant things happening to one
bear	+					
endure	+	+	+			
tolerate	+			+		
put up with	+			+		
stand	+				+	
suffer	+					+

Notice that **bear** and **stand** frequently occur with **can't** and in this construction they may have the features [+strongly dislike] [+usu people]. This use is very colloquial.

EXAMPLE

I can't **bear/stand** Peregrine, he's always boasting about his good marks.

Stand is most commonly used in conjunction with the auxiliary **can** or in interrogative or negative constructions.

EXAMPLES

I **can stand** a lot of discomfort but sleeping on the floor is one thing I really refuse to do.

She is in such a weak condition that it's doubtful whether she **could stand** another operation.

How do you **stand** spending so long working on language tapes every day?

Notice that **stand** is informal and **put up with** is colloquial. **Suffer** can be used intransitively and usually collocates with the preposition **from**.

	a loss	pain	discomfort	great hardship	long hours of work	suffering	a situation	an unlikeable person	a lot of noise
bear	+	+	+	+	+	+	+		
endure		+	+	+	+		+		
tolerate		+	+			+	+	+	
put up with		+	+	+	+	+	+	+	+
stand		+	+	+	+				+
suffer	+	+	+						

4 Fidgeting

	move the body or part of it	or manipulate an object	restlessly	by twisting and turning it	make meaningless marks or drawings	idly or aimlessly	touch or stroke	often to express affection	pull and/or twist	so as to make a sudden sharp noise	close or strain together	firmly	rub together harshly	with a circular motion	so as to produce a dull noise
fidget	+	+	+												
twiddle		+		+		+									
fiddle		+				+									
doodle					+	+									
fondle							+	+							
crack									+	+					
clench											+	+			
grind													+	+	+

Doodle is intransitive, **fidget** can be either transitive or intransitive, and all the other verbs are transitive. In the sense in which they occur here, **crack**, **clench** and **grind** are found only in a limited number of expressions:

	one's toes	one's fingers	one's fists	one's teeth
crack	+	+		
clench		+	+	+
grind				+

Fidget, twiddle, fiddle and **fondle** have a wider distribution, but occur typically in the following collocations. **Fiddle** is probably the most common term.

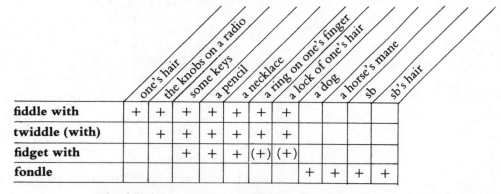

	one's hair	the knobs on a radio	some keys	a pencil	a necklace	a ring on one's finger	a lock of one's hair	a dog	a horse's mane	sb	sb's hair
fiddle with	+	+	+	+	+	+	+				
twiddle (with)		+	+	+	+	+	+				
fidget with			+	+	+	(+)	(+)				
fondle								+	+	+	+

The following illustrate the intransitive use:

EXAMPLES

Children usually have difficulty sitting still for any length of time and tend to **fidget** in their chairs.

Most people **doodle** when they are talking on the telephone.

Who has **doodled** all over the cover of the telephone directory?

Notice the colloquial expression **twiddle one's thumbs** which has the features [+having nothing to do] and [+be bored].

5 Being quick and/or lively

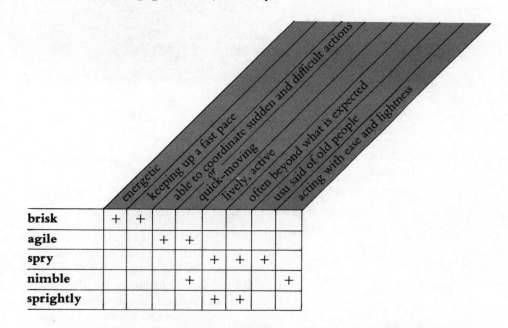

	energetic	keeping up a fast pace	able to coordinate sudden and difficult actions	quick-moving	lively, active	often beyond what is expected	usu said of old people	acting with ease and lightness
brisk	+	+						
agile			+	+				
spry					+	+	+	
nimble				+				+
sprightly					+	+		

The meaning of **brisk** and **agile** is often extended to mental states and attitudes, in which case **brisk** has the features [+abrupt or direct] [+unemotional]. When it has these features, **brisk** modifies, eg the nouns **manner, person, answer**, or is used predicatively.

	walk	pace	manner	exercise	trade	answer	person	climber	monkey	mind	dancer	old lady	fingers
brisk	+	+	+	+	+	+	+						
agile							+	+	+	+	+		
spry											+		
nimble							+	+			+	+	+
sprightly			+								+		

Sprightly is more commonly used as a predicate than as an attribute.

EXAMPLES

George is really very **sprightly**, considering he was still in hospital last week.

When you think she's over eighty, it's incredible how **sprightly** she is.

6 Being unhealthy or nasty

	in bad health	disgusting usu because violent or perverted	having a disease	weak, prone to illness or disease	having strong associations with death	showing an excessive preoccupation with death or very gloomy subjects	likely to be bad for physical, mental or moral well-being or corrupt
ill	+						
sick	+	+					
diseased			+				
sickly				+			
morbid					+	+	
unwholesome						+	+

All these adjectives may be used attributively or predicatively. Note that in British English **to be sick** means 'to vomit', whereas in American English it means 'to be in bad health, have a disease'. British English would use **to be ill**. However, under the influence of American English, British speakers would probably accept 'sick person' to mean 'person who is in bad health'. **To be sick** (to vomit) may not be used in the simple present; **is being sick** is the correct way to express the action in the present.

	food	character	scene	curiosity	house	imagination	film	mind	part	plant	child	person	colour	joke
ill										+	+			
sick					+	+	+							+
diseased							+	+	+					
sickly										+	+	+		
morbid		+	+	+	+	+	+	+		+	+			
unwholesome	+	+	+											

Colloquially **sick** may be used to express 'angry, fed up, upset', and with this sense it is often followed by **of**.

EXAMPLES

If I fail the syntax exam again I shall be really **sick**.

She bought a car because she was **sick** of travelling on crowded rush-hour trains.

7 Being mentally disordered

	disordered in mind	completely	temporarily	often as a result of some specific event or stress	stresses eccentricity of ideas	stresses eccentricity of action	usu only slightly	or apparently the product of a mentally disordered mind
insane	+	+						+
deranged	+		+	+				
mad	+	+						+
crazy	+			+				+
nuts	+			+				
nutty	+			+				+
potty	+				+			+
touched	+					+		
daft	+							+
loony	+				+			+
crackers	+							
bonkers	+							
cranky	+		+		+			+

Nuts, **touched**, **crackers** and **bonkers** are only used predicatively. The following scale shows how formal or informal these words are:

formal	informal	colloquial	slang
insane	mad	crazy daft nuts	nutty
deranged		touched crackers	potty
			loony
			bonkers
			cranky

← ── →

A native speaker of English would certainly recognize all these terms but would only use his own selection from among them.

	insane	deranged	mad	crazy	nuts	nutty	potty	touched	daft	bonkers	loony	crackers	cranky	
He is mentally		+												.
This devilish scheme must be the product of a		+												mind.
Recently he has begun to do really	+		+	+		+	+	+		+		+		things.
She is going	+		+	+	+				+		+			.
The			+											dog had to be shot.
He is probably a bit			+				+	+	+					.
Your			+	+		+		+				+		ideas are not helping us to solve the problem.
He is always coming up with			+	+		+		+				+		projects for saving the world from destruction.
I think he is completely				+	+	+	+	+			+	+		.

The meaning of most of these words is often extended to situations having little or nothing to do with real mental ill health.

Here are a few typical uses of some of these words:

We all went to a **mad** party which took place on the beach.

Your childrens' behaviour is enough to drive anyone **insane**.

I think I must be **bonkers**. I've just locked myself out of my house for the fourth time this week.

Besides the construction **to go insane/mad/crazy/nuts/nutty/potty/bonkers/crackers**, there are a large number of colloquial expressions meaning 'to become or be mentally disordered'. Their use can be extended to situations where real mental illness is not involved:

to go bananas	to have something missing
to have a screw loose	to be not all there
to be soft in the head	to be off one's rocker
	to go round the bend

[+temporarily] to go spare
         to flip one's lid
         to go up the wall

8 Not being broad, thick or dense

	not fat or fleshy	or not full, dense or wide	well proportioned	often graceful, delicate	to the point where the bones under the skin are clearly visible	or with little foliage	may suggest toughness	not of young things	suggests length, tallness	sometimes suggests awkwardness
thin	+	+								
slim	+	+	+							
slender	+	+	+	+						
lean	+									
skinny	+				+					
scrawny	+	+			+	+	+	+		
lanky	+								+	+

The words may be arranged along a scale to show the relative attitudes of the user:

favourable   unfavourable

←   **slim**   **slender**   **lean**   **thin**   **skinny**   **scrawny** →
                                                     lanky

	thin	slim	slender	lean	skinny	scrawny	lanky	
Cucumber should be cut into	+							slices.
Your essay seems rather	+							
Since leaving home he has grown very	+							
The boy had long	+					+	+	legs which he did not seem quite able to control.
They obviously don't feed their dog properly – he is so	+				+	(+)		
Men with	+				+			legs look terrible in shorts.
I wish I was	+	+						enough to wear fashionable clothes!
You need		+						legs to be able to wear shorts!
He presented her with a	.	+						volume of poetry, bound in leather.
The			+					drooping branches of the willow make it a very pretty tree.
The girl had a beautifully		+	+					figure.
The			+					young shoots, just out of the ground, are easily damaged.
I only like				+				meat, please don't give me any fat.
A				+				suntanned arm waved at me from a passing car.
I can't understand why my children look so					+			beside everyone else's, I feed them really well.
Those sort of tall						+		women with greying hair often wear rather austere tweed suits.
A few						+		bushes clung to the cliff edge, torn by the wind and sea.

B   Synonymous Pairs

1   stimulus

goad $\begin{bmatrix} + \text{pointed stick} \\ + \text{for urging cattle on} \end{bmatrix} \Rightarrow \left\{ \begin{array}{l} + \text{sth that rouses} \\ \text{to action} \end{array} \right\}$

As a noun, **goad** is old fashioned. It is now usually used as a verb when it has the features [+rouse to action] or [+annoy or irritate] [+deliberately].

EXAMPLES

The boy would **goad** his sister until she hit him and then he would run and tell his mother.

The men were **goading** a bear with sticks to make it snarl and rear up on its hind legs.

2 **to cause**
to induce | [+a course of action or a state] [+by offering rewards] or [+by using special techniques]

Induce, like **cause**, usually occurs in the constructions
to . . . . .sb to do sth or **to . . . . .sth.**
EXAMPLES
It is possible to **induce** sleep by the use of a machine.
What **induced** her to abandon her research at this stage I simply can't imagine.

3 **to decay**
to rot | [+only of organic matter]

teeth
apples
leaves
buildings } **decay**
societies
cultures

flesh
wood
leaves
apples } **rot(s)**
potatoes
rope

4 **to twitch**

[+move or cause to move]
[+a little]

{ [+with a light movement]

to jerk

[+with a strong or rough movement]

Both verbs can be either transitive or intransitive.
EXAMPLES
He **twitched** the string so that the kitten would chase the shiny piece of paper on the end of it.
The injured dog's body **twitched** as it lay on the ground close to the car which had hit it.
The plank **jerked** just as I was stepping onto it and I missed my footing and fell down.
Jerk the rope twice to signal me to descend.

5 **to wriggle**

[+twist or turn the body]

or [+move with quick, short twistings] ⇒ [+escape from undesirable situation] ⇒ [+feel socially uncomfortable]

to squirm

Notice that **squirm** is an intransitive verb, whereas **wriggle** can also be transitive. Colloquially the meaning of both verbs can be extended to situations where no movement of the body is involved.
EXAMPLES
The monkey did not like being held and **wriggled** about in my hands.
The children **wriggled** into the cherry orchard through a small gap in the fence.
Did you hear how Martin was stopped by customs when he had three cases of whisky in his car? Only he would have been able to **wriggle** out of a situation like that!

It takes a firm hand to dress small babies because they **squirm** and **wriggle** constantly.

The scene which Peregrine caused in the restaurant made me **squirm** with embarrassment.

6   **to pull**
    to yank | [+sharply] [+suddenly]

Yank is informal.

EXAMPLES
Don't **yank** at the bell-pull like that, you will break it.
He **yanked** open the car door and pushed the girl in.

7   **firm**
    adamant | [+unaffected by temptations or requests]

EXAMPLES
Everyone tried to persuade him not to undertake such a dangerous journey but he remained **adamant**.
I'm afraid she's quite **adamant** and refuses to see any member of her family.

Exercises

1 Find words to fit the following definitions/ descriptions:

1 pleasing to the taste
2 preventive injection of germs in small quantities to cause the body to build up resistance to a disease
3 unable to walk, usu because of an injury
4 the pains of childbirth
5 not firm, soft (eg muscles)
6 done merely as a duty and without much consideration
7 partly decomposed vegetable material in a solid mass found in marshy places
8 rub lightly, or scrape, esp with the fingernails

2 What differences and/or similarities are there between the following pairs?

1 illness/disease   2 jet/propeller plane   3 leader/foreman
4 infection/illness   5 discomfort/pain   6 warn/tell   7 brisk/fast
8 arteries/blood vessels   9 dye/colour   10 pull/yank
11 squirm/wriggle   12 cause/induce

3 What kinds of things can you:

1 rub?   2 tap?   3 stir?   4 suck?   5 schedule?   6 deny?
7 climb?   8 give up?   9 twiddle?   10 scratch?   11 grind?
12 hoard?   13 clench?

4 Fill in the following collocational grids:

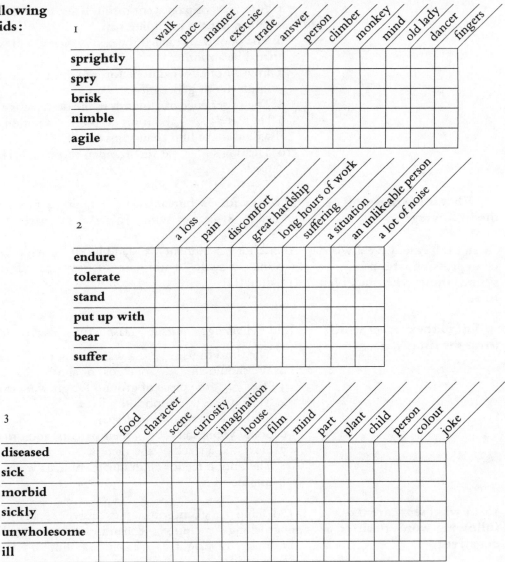

1

	walk	pace	manner	exercise	trade	answer	person	climber	monkey	mind	old lady	dancer	fingers
sprightly													
spry													
brisk													
nimble													
agile													

2

	a loss	pain	discomfort	great hardship	long hours of work	suffering	a situation	an unlikeable person	a lot of noise
endure									
tolerate									
stand									
put up with									
bear									
suffer									

3

	food	character	scene	curiosity	imagination	house	film	mind	part	plant	child	person	colour	joke
diseased														
sick														
morbid														
sickly														
unwholesome														
ill														

5 Explain the meaning of the following:

1 mud   2 spa   3 long for   4 volunteer   5 worry-beads
6 plug-hole   7 tranquilliser   8 routine   9 epidemic
10 survival   11 pore   12 dye   13 cockpit   14 sedative
15 flush   16 massage

6 Guess the right word.

1 The doctor assured the woman that these pr . . . . . depressions would disappear after the birth of the baby.
2 She only showed us her h . . . . . of treasures when we'd promised not to divulge the hiding-place to anyone.
3 She had left out the most vital in . . . . . from her bread.
4 With a sharp y . . . . . we finally managed to get the door open.

5 A t . . . . . of pain went through her entire body as the doctor pulled out the offending nail.

6 The pilot had reached the c . . . . . now, and within minutes he'd be airborne.

7 In view of all we'd done for him, his p . . . . . thanks were an insult to our generosity.

8 The experience of a month in the desert was a gr . . . . . one.

9 He was a . . . . . about his decision and nothing we could say would make him change his mind.

10 The dog s . . . . . at the stranger, showing his huge pointed teeth.

7 What is the meaning of the following?

1 cope with   2 bureaucracy   3 guilt   4 race   5 rot   6 chew   7 strike   8 diet   9 wire   10 jerk   11 snarl   12 twist

8 In each case, give a word or expression which is synonymous with the given one.

1 interior   2 ailment   3 stand by sb   4 endeavour   5 bend   6 yank   7 swift   8 ultimate   9 firm   10 safe   11 rough   12 doubtful

9 Fill in the correct word from the list given.

lead   challenge   pursue   clasp   run   waive   mark off   request

1 The third time I . . . . . a waiver, I got it.

2 We should all . . . . . one goal or another.

3 We . . . . . the piece of ground for growing carrots.

4 Most of us . . . . . unhealthy lives.

5 She . . . . . her hands in despair.

6 Some youngsters . . . . . their parents' authority.

7 He . . . . . a track of 400 meters.

8 The tuition fee for all graduate students was . . . . . at the last minute.

10 In what sense are the following words positive or negative?

1 dashing   2 glamorous   3 excessive   4 adamant   5 frank   6 gruelling   7 clumsy   8 handsome   9 rugged   10 firm   11 brisk   12 bright   13 harsh   14 slim   15 lethargic   16 morbid

11 In each case provide a few nouns or nominal expressions that can collocate with the following:

1 bear   2 endure   3 crack   4 fiddle with   5 wriggle   6 agile   7 sickly   8 diseased   9 scrawny

12 Explain in your own words the meaning of:

1 a ward   2 surgery   3 plug   4 mudbath   5 spices   6 ritual   7 chest   8 marathon   9 newsstand   10 drugstore   11 bureaucracy   12 treadmill

13 What kinds of things/ persons might do the following?

1 shoot up   2 pay off   3 complain   4 dream   5 hoard   6 heal   7 decline   8 rot   9 slap sb   10 grow   11 fidget   12 snarl   13 squirm   14 doodle

14 Choose from the words in brackets the one which is most appropriate in each case. Modify its form where necessary.

1 The only . . . . . for over-tiredness is a good long sleep. (remedy, cure, medicine)
2 She had to wait for the wound to . . . . . before being able to go swimming. (remedy, cure, heal)
3 He could never . . . . . to see her cry. (suffer, endure, bear)
4 I really cannot . . . . . another of these ghastly scenes which end in tears and bad tempers. (tolerate, put up with, stand)
5 Her . . . . . body reminded us of those tall graceful rushes that are to be found by the river, moving in the breeze. (thin, slim, slender)
6 She nervously . . . . . the clasp of her handbag as she waited outside the hospital. (fiddle, twiddle, fondle)
7 'I find him rather . . . . ., with a tendency to dwell on the subject of death.' (morbid, sick, unwholesome)
8 He had an . . . . . mind which would move from one subject to another with an ease and speed that left us speechless. (agile, spry, nimble)
9 Don't leave your tennis racket to . . . . . in the rain. (spoil, decay, rot)
10 Mr Jones was a . . . . . visitor to the seaside resort. (perpetual, eternal, continual, constant)

Revision Exercises

R1 Explain the meaning of the following:

1 widow   2 wrinkles   3 spider   4 alienation   5 peer-group   6 Westerner   7 tangible   8 breach   9 masculinity   10 amnesia   11 skeleton   13 log   14 dichotomize

R2 Supply appropriate prepositions for the following:

1 to huddle . . .   2 to nestle . . .   3 to snuggle . . .   4 to cuddle . . .   5 to encroach . . .   6 to trespass . . . sth   7 to intrude . . . sth   8 to stagger . . . one's feet   9 to stumble . . . sth   10 to reel . . . sth   11 to merge . . . sth

R3 What differences and/or similarities are there between the following?

1 intrude/invade   2 browse/peruse   3 mingle/mix   4 insinuate/intimate   5 scream/shriek   6 totter/stumble   7 slide/glide   8 push/shove

R4 Fill in the following collocational grids:

1

	wane(d)	subside(d)	
The moon has			without the weather improving.
The amount of traffic should			later in the evening.
After a rapid rise to fame the star's career			equally quickly.
The storm finally			after causing considerable damage.
After causing a noisy scene, the girl suddenly			into tears.
The influence of the antigovernment agitation has			in recent months.

2

	invade(d)	encroach(ed)	intrude(d)	trespass(ed) (ing)	
The sea gradually					over the low-lying land.
The green fields are being					on faster and faster by new housing development.
While I don't want to					on your territory, I do feel my experience in this matter may be of some value.
Although this section of coastline is private, people					on it all the time.
We have put up high fences but it is impossible to stop people					in our woods and picking all the spring flowers.
I hope I have not					too much on your time.
England was					by the Normans in 1066.
At holiday times London is					by foreign tourists.
Some people seem quite unaware that they are					on one's privacy.
Please excuse me – I see I have					on a private conversation.

3

	ease(d)	lessen(ed)
The rain		
The number of applicants		
The storm		
The pain		
The situation		

4

	heave(d)	push(ed) (ing)	shove(d) (ing)	thrust (thrust)	
Could you					the button to stop the machine?
He					back his chair from the table and stood up.
Everyone was					to try to make sure they got places on the boat.
I just					my things in the back of the car and drove off as fast as I could.
He					his hand down through the soft earth, trying to locate the lost ring.
She suddenly					£5 into my hand and ran off, telling me to enjoy myself with it.
We all					on the rope together to pull the boat in.
Now we have an oil-fired boiler, no-one has to					coal for it any more.
It took two of us to					the heavy trunk into the back of the car.

R5 Guess the right word.

1 The s . . . . . surface of the golf course was a delight after the rocky terrain we'd been walking on.
2 She gave her dress a couple of tw . . . . ., trying to straighten out the pleats.
3 It was a n . . . . . affair for every piece of evidence revealed something ugly deep down.
4 In a small c . . . . . in the wall, I found the hidden note.
5 The w . . . . . s round her eyes told us that this woman had laughed a lot during her lifetime.
6 Paying his workers such minimal wages was a clear b . . . . . of industrial law.
7 The effect of the alcohol became apparent as he r . . . . . on pathetically about his lost childhood.
8 They g . . . . . time by taking a short-cut.
9 He had been b . . . . . from addressing the gathering.
10 It was restless students who fo . . . . . uprisings and rebellions.
11 He is sitting at home ag . . . . . about tomorrow's exam.
12 A rather awkward situation arose when the farmer whose cherries we had been stealing came into his orchard but we managed to p . . . . . him by offering to pick the rest of the crop for him, for nothing.

R6 Say which verbs can go with each of the given prepositions.

for, in, of, by, at, from

1 educate sb   2 confide   3 take advantage   4 coach sb
5 benefit   6 profit   7 tutor sb   8 restrain sb   9 rouse
10 crowd   11 arouse   12 be famous   13 hint   14 train

R7 What differences and/or similarities are there between these pairs?

1 covet/begrudge   2 fling/throw   3 postpone/delay
4 hold/cling   5 stick to/abide by   6 disparity/incongruity
7 subsidy/money   8 admonition/warning   9 precautions/
measures   10 brief/transient   11 cosy/snug   12 placid/serene

R8 Fill in the following componential grids:

1

	lower in value, quality, or character	make morally bad	(cause to) lose soundness, sense of what is right, or purity	by bad influence	act or cause others to act immorally and/or drink or cause others to drink excessively	turn away from what is right, normal, or true
debase						
deprave						
corrupt						
debauch						
pervert						

2

	reproduce itself by natural process	of cover	cause to be present in	cause itself to be present in	many places or over a wide area	by sending out in many directions	esp of seeds	of ideas, knowledge information	often by separate pieces going to different places	of ideas rather than specific bits of information
spread										
diffuse										
disseminate										
propagate										

R9 Produce a logical and coherent story by filling in the blanks with appropriate words from the list below and modifying their form where necessary. One of the words is used twice.

lethargic, sedentary, perfunctory, flabby, palatable, morbid, appalling, sly, conceited, tangible, nasty, aloof, insistent, pushy, bing-bong, wrinkled, health, breach, postmortem, treadmill, population, exercise, television, to fiddle, to cure, to heal, to remedy, to squirm, to fidget, to yank, to throb, to crowd, to huddle, to encroach, to infringe, to violate, to shove, to stake out, to walk

A 1 . . . . . examination of social habits shows that one of the reasons why most of the 2 . . . . . take such little 3 . . . . . is that they spend an 4 . . . . . amount of time 5 . . . . . in front of their 6 . . . . .. No amount of 7 . . . . . warnings about what this does to their 8 . . . . . will 9 . . . . . them of the habit. Nothing can be allowed to 10 . . . . . the British right to watch football on Saturday afternoons. It is obviously more 11 . . . . . to the ordinary working man, who feels he deserves a change from the 12 . . . . . of his working life, to stay in his own home, than to 13 . . . . . to the football ground, 14 . . . . . his way through the fans 15 . . . . . in, all equally 16 . . . . . on being at the front, and 17 . . . . . a place for himself, which he knows will immediately be 18 . . . . . on by other spectators, more 19 . . . . . than himself.

The last time I went to a football match one player suffered a head injury which would take weeks to 20 . . . . .. A brawl broke out between supporters in the crowd, some arguing that the player who had caused the accident had not 21 . . . . . the rules, others that his 22 . . . . ., 23 . . . . . attack constituted 24 . . . . . proof or a flagrant 25 . . . . . of the rules. A 26 . . . . . looking man, the kind who always thinks he knows best, tried to 27 . . . . . the situation by 28 . . . . . the brawlers apart, and telling them that these 29 . . . . . bored him thoroughly. I tried to remain 30 . . . . . from all this, but it was difficult to concentrate on the match with people 31 . . . . . and 32 . . . . . and 33 . . . . . all around me. I left the match 34 . . . . . with indignation. Never mind if I get old, with a 35 . . . . . waistline and 36 . . . . . cheeks before my time, I'll exchange a 37 . . . . . existence for that kind of 38 . . . . . exercise any time!

Unit 7 To be a woman

THE NEW HOUSEWIFE
BLUES

1 *Br* stop, leave
2 quantity
3 probably

THE NEW HOUSEWIFE BLUES

Young professional women who **quit**[1] work for child care are sometimes surprised by its pleasures, and by the unexpected **amount**[2] of freedom to read or work at hobbies and local causes. But a second surprise is **likely to be**[3] loneliness and the depressing reaction of

A British view of the problems of a working mother.

other women to their new experience of **housewifery**[4]. Valerie Kraus, 34, quit her job as an Illinois teacher last **fall**[5] when she saw her two children 'were losing me and the attention and love that only a mother can give. Soon afterward,' she **recalls**[6], 'at a **pot-luck**[7] dinner at church, we each had to tell about the nicest thing that had happened to us recently. Other women talked about their jobs. When my turn came, I said, "This is the first time I've stayed home and I **thoroughly**[8] enjoy it!" People just said, "Oh." '

Today, when housewives are asked what they do, they tend to answer diffidently 'Nothing really' because they have been made to feel inferior and because the joys and **challenges**[9] of domestic life are unorganized and unmeasured. For centuries, men have told their wives that such problems were not very important, but the novelty is to be patronized by other women for 'not doing anything really'. Kathy Mertz, who enjoyed serving as a **Cub Scout den mother**[10] in North Barrington, Ill., particularly **resented**[11] a newly emancipated part-time secretary who periodically **called on**[12] her to act as chauffeur for her child. Says Mertz: 'She kept telling me that I ought to be "doing something worthwhile"! What I was doing was giving her child care.'

In a success-oriented society the **cumulative**[13] effects of such **treatment**[14] can be demoralizing. One of the few women **so far**[15] trying to do anything organized for the millions of housewives is Jinx Melia, 40, who describes how she became 'a victim of the process that makes a homemaker feel she is worth nothing and her role as creator of the next generation is not important.'

She is one of the **founders**[16] of a national organization to give homemakers more **status**[17]. Named for Martha, who did the household **chores**[18] while her sister Mary listened to Christ **expounding**[19] his wisdom (*Luke 10: 38–42*), the Martha Movement's projects include: short-term child-care and **resource centers**[20] near supermarkets and **hot lines**[21] for counseling housewives with critical problems.

During the past twelve years Arlene Rossen Cardozo, author of 'Woman at Home', has been interviewing and advising women with children, first in Cambridge, Mass., then in Minneapolis, where she now lives with her husband, a professor at the University of Minnesota, and their three daughters. Like the housewives she often speaks to and for, she is no anti-feminist, but she objects **sharply**[22] to the rhetoric of the women's movement – at least in its more extreme forms. It has done considerable **harm**[23], she feels, by **lumping** housework and child care **together**[24] and dismissing them as something that women must escape in order to achieve '**selfhood**[25]'. It has also **deluded**[26] women about both the pleasures and the problems of commercial work and about the ease of being a responsible parent and pursuing a career at the same time. Most potentially dangerous for the family, Cardozo argues, is the fact that the women's movement has **urged**[27] wives to follow men in their

4 housekeeping
5 *Br* autumn
6 remembers
7 ordinary food, not specially prepared because there are guests
8 absolutely, completely
9 calls or invitations to show what one is able to do, to respond to situations
10 female adult leader of an adventure club for boys aged 8–12
11 showed indignation or annoyance at, felt injured about
12 turn to, rely on, ask
13 when several are successively added together
14 the manner of dealing with a person or thing
15 up to now
16 persons who found or establish an institution
17 position or rank of a person, respected position in society
18 the ordinary daily tasks in the home
19 explaining, making clear
20 centres to provide help or information
21 telephone lines for urgent messages
22 quickly, briskly, vigorously
23 damage, injury
24 treat things in the same way, put together as if they were the same things
25 identity, self-realisation
26 deceived, misled
27 encouraged, earnestly persuaded

rush[28] to be **gobbled**[29] alive by the success ethic, **emulating**[30] the American man at a time when he has never been 'less in need of emulation, and more in need of **searching his own soul**[31].'

Instead of helping these women remove the causes of their 'boredom and loneliness at home', as Cardozo believes could (and can still) be done, feminists told them to leave home and become absentee mothers, just like their absentee husbands. Says she: 'Their only **quarrel with**[32] the success ethic was that it excluded women.' The delusion that the mass of men chained to jobs are free or fulfilled (that kind of fulfillment is only sporadically true even for a handful of trained professionals and craftsmen) was never examined. 'Men no longer have jobs; jobs have men,' says Cardozo. 'Now, jobs have women too.'

The problem, as Cardozo sees it, is how to keep people's careers from damaging family life, and how to work out flexible and practical ways of individual child care in an impatient society more and more inclined to turn all problems over to the state. Cardozo, like a number of **public figures**[33], sees no **panacea**[34] in care centers, now being urged by many feminists, because they would become increasingly **compulsory**[35] and would deprive many children of an **affectionate**[36] **upbringing**[37]. An alternative: that women, and men, who take care of their own children be granted Social Security benefits for such work, and that tax benefits be offered to businesses that **devise**[38] **split work shifts**[39] and flexible **schedules**[40] so that young husbands and wives will find it easier to **take turns**[41] in caring for their families – and each other.

'We have **desacralized**[42] marriage,' according to Robert Weiss, chairman of the sociology department at the University of Massachusetts–Boston and author of *Marital Separation*. It is no longer seen as a '**calling**[43]' or a 'social responsibility' but merely as an **adjunct**[44] to the good life. This change, which Benjamin DeMott sums up as scrapping '"in sickness and in health" in favor of "I do my thing and you do your thing",' is not so much the result of sexual permissiveness and easier divorce laws as, like them, an offshoot of what Weiss describes as the 'intensity of our impatience with barriers to self-realization'. Weiss adds: 'To a greater extent than seems true elsewhere in the world, we Americans seem to **cherish**[45] our right to the **unimpeded**[46] **pursuit**[47] of happiness no matter how much **sorrow**[48] that pursuit may **engender**[49].'

Roman Catholic Philosopher-Writer Michael Novak is less cool in his **assessments**[50]. 'Our highest moral principle is flexibility,' he writes; our view, that 'life is **solitary**[51] and brief, and that its **aim**[52] is self-fulfillment. In such a vision of the self, marriage is merely an alliance . . . They say of marriage that it is **deadening**[53], when what they mean is that it drives us beyond adolescent fantasies and romantic dreams . . . Choosing to have a family used to be uninteresting. It is, today, an act of intelligence and courage.'

Time

28 sudden, swift advance
29 eaten fast and greedily, swallowed
30 copying the actions or ideas of
31 examining carefully his beliefs and conduct
32 disagreement with
33 people who play a part in public life
34 remedy for everything
35 obligatory, something one has to do
36 loving
37 training in childhood and youth
38 think out, plan, invent
39 periods of work where day is divided into several sections covered by different workers
40 time-tables, lists of the times at which certain things will be done
41 work alternatively, work in turn, ie one and then the other
42 deprived it of its sacred, holy character
43 vocation, life's work
44 help, auxiliary, addition
45 take care of, care about, want to maintain
46 unobstructed, unhindered
47 the act of pursuing, following, chasing
48 grief, sadness, trouble
49 produce, be the cause of
50 the fixing of the value of something, evaluation
51 lonely
52 purpose, end
53 depriving of feeling, force or brightness

Sandra Day O'Connor, first woman justice of the U.S. Supreme Court.

AND HAVE A DRIVE FOR SUCCESS

1 in or for which there is competition, contest
2 course of action, *lit* method of gripping partner in a wrestling match
3 forbidden, not allowed
4 intimidating by physical force
5 *coll* do not be domineering or conceited
6 the science of morals, the principles of morality
7 pretext, excuse, false claim or reason
8 observed, maintained
9 energy, capacity to get things done
10 leave behind
11 unkind word or utterance showing contempt
12 arithmetic
13 poor and helpless person who usually gets the worst of an encounter, a struggle, etc
14 money allowance legally arranged and paid by a man to his wife if he is separated or divorced from her
15 area of activity
16 (of a woman) like a man
17 dress or appearance of somebody or something else
18 good excuses, *lit* concrete evidence of not being responsible for a crime
19 deaden or muffle the sound of
20 job of one who works in an office, non-manual job
21 full of glamour, mysterious charm
22 abilities, expertise

. . . *and have a drive for success*

The little girl who hears the call of success more sharply than the call of her future wifehood and maternity hears a call to **competitive**[1] action in which no **holds**[2] are **barred**[3]. Her brother has been better schooled than she has been for this expected behaviour in a competitive world. Fair play, no **bullying**[4], **do not throw your weight around**[5], are part of the **ethics**[6] both she and he learned on the playing-fields, but here **the pretence**[7] that all boys are stronger than all girls was **kept up**[8]. Some of her very **drive**[9] for success may come from this comparison, this statement that boys should always **outdistance**[10] girls; some of her drive may come from doors barred to her because 'women always leave and get married', some from a **sneer**[11] from a brother or a father that 'girls have no heads for **figures**[12]'. However this may be, she has been defined as weaker, and there are no rules in American life for the good behaviour of **underdogs**[13]. To the extent that American women – most American women – follow the rules of fair play and give-and-take and no **alimony**[14], they do so because they think of themselves as strong human beings, human like the men of whom they refuse to take an advantage. But to the woman who makes a success in a man's **field**[15], good behaviour is almost impossible, because her whole society has defined it so. A woman who succeeds better than a man – and in a man's field there is no other practical alternative to beating a certain number of men – has done something hostile and destructive. To the extent that as a woman she has beauty or attractiveness of any sort, her behaviour is that much more destructive. The **mannish**[16] woman, the ugly woman, may be treated as a man in **disguise**[17] and so forgiven her successes. But for the success of a feminine woman there are no **alibis**[18], the more feminine she is, the less can she be forgiven. This does not mean that every woman who enters business or fields where she is in an extreme minority is hostile and destructive. But it does mean that any woman who in the course of her childhood had an extra amount of destructiveness developed and repressed is in psychological danger when she is placed in a role that is so destructively defined. To the woman whose maternal attitudes are highly developed, the position may be wholly intolerable.

So brother and sister, boy and girl, educated together, learn what each wishes from what each can give to the other. The girl learns to discipline and **mute**[19] an ambition that her society continually stimulates, as all girls working in **white-collar jobs**[20] are said to have 'careers', and careers are **glamorous**[21], while most men with similar **skills**[22] merely have jobs. And we have the situation that looks so strange on the surface, that as more and more women work, women seem on the whole less interested in the battle that permits them to succeed professionally.

Margaret Mead, *Male and Female.*
A Study of the Sexes in a Changing World

Believe this and you'll believe anything ! !

BELIEVE THIS AND...

1 of long duration
2 argue with, disagree with
3 *coll* members of the women's liberation movement
4 unfriendly, rude, short-tempered
5 *coll* group of persons
6 *coll* wife
7 *coll* test something thoroughly on somebody
8 low, deep, rough sounds
9 generously, extravagantly
10 always, without change or exception
11 skill, cleverness, especially in using the hands
12 a machine for cutting grass on lawns
13 removes, deducts
14 not being honest, deceiving
15 *coll* fancy, like
16 *of* inn or hotel
17 fried too much
18 spoke in a low, indistinct voice
19 words of affection, love
20 not humorous, expressing disappointment or disgust
21 example
22 me

As a Scotsman **of long years standing**[1] (especially at bus stops), **I take issue with**[2] these Continental **women's libbers**[3] who accused Scots of being a **surly**[4] **lot**[5], slow to praise, quick to criticise.

I mean to say, I'm always telling the **missus**[6] she makes a lovely job of cleaning the windows. In fact, she could win a prize for it, and I've said so often. When she **tries out** one of her new recipes **on**[7] me, I'm the first to admit, 'I've never tasted anything like it.' When she brings me breakfast in bed on Sunday, do I just accept it with sleepy-headed **grunts**[8]? On the contrary, I thank her **profusely**[9]. In fact, her toast is so good I **invariably**[10] shout downstairs for more.

Who cleans the car the cleanest? Why, she does, of course – and I frequently tell her I couldn't do it as well as she does.

Another thing. You won't catch me trying to insult her **dexterity**[11] with the **lawnmower**[12] by taking over.

She makes a far better job of it than I do, and again I tell her so.

The minute she puts on a new dress and asks, 'How do I look?' what else can I say but, 'It **takes** ten years **off**[13] you, dear.' Perhaps I'm **cheating**[14] here, since I don't mention the number that the ten is actually deducted from. Besides, if I said she looked like Raquel Welch, she might start thinking I **have a thing about**[15] Raquel Welch – which I do.

Only the other night, I was unavoidably delayed on my way home. That infernal clock in the local **hostelry**[16] was slow. My bacon and eggs were **frizzled**[17] dry. The little woman **muttered**[18] some sweet **endearment**[19] which I didn't quite catch and said she'd make more. I said I

didn't know how she had the patience. She said she didn't know, either. You see, patience just comes naturally to her – and I'm the first to compliment her on that quality.

And she's so understanding. On Sunday I was later home than usual. My missus said I'd just missed her mother. I said that was a pity. She gave me a **wry**[20] smile.

That's a **sample**[21] of her understanding. She really does understand how I feel about her mother. There have been occasions when her mother said she could never see what her daughter saw in **yours truly**[22].

Well, I know. But I'm not saying. I'm no Scottish male chauvinist pig.
– **J R**

The Sunday Post

Women Farmers

Like many working women, Lucille Crawford rises before **dawn**[1], eats a **hearty**[2] breakfast, **teases her hair**[3] and **clips on**[4] a pair of gold earrings. Then the 54-year-old widow **dons**[5] a green-and-yellow **cap**[6], climbs into a bronze **pickup truck**[7] and **sets out**[8] for a sixteen-hour day **tending**[9] her 200-**acre**[10] grain farm in Ashland, Ill.

Lucille Crawford is one of an increasing number of American women who are **running**[11] their own farms. With increased mechanization and a shortage of skilled labor, a woman's role down on the farm is no longer confined to **canning**[12] tomatoes, keeping the books and **mending**[13] the overalls. Today, approximately 74,000 women own or manage farms in the US. Seventeen per cent of all farm workers are now women, and female **enrollment**[14] in agricultural colleges has risen about 90 per cent. 'Agriculture was traditionally a man's program and "**home ec**[15]" traditionally a female one,' says Dr Louis Thompson, associate **dean**[16] of agriculture at Iowa State University. 'Now, women are beginning to recognize that they can do just about any job a man can do.'

The rise of women down on the farm has been **prompted**[17] by a **quest**[18] for better-paying jobs and by **sheer**[19] economic necessity. Many widows of farmers, like Lucille Crawford, are now staying on their **homesteads**[20] instead of selling them off; those married to farmers are becoming full business partners. 'These **gals**[21] are running the **combines**[22] and **hauling**[23] grain in trucks, they attend all the farm meetings and they're usually the **accountants**[24] in the family,' says Jerry Peterson of The Kansas Farm Bureau. 'They're the real liberated woman. They aren't **pampered**[25] too much except on their birthdays. The shortage of **skilled labor**[26] and the mountains of government paperwork involved in **hiring**[27] **hands**[28] have also made women more valuable on the farm, just as they were in centuries past.

Mary Alice Kellogg with Elaine Sciolino in Chicago,
Newsweek

WOMEN FARMERS

1. the beginning of the day, when it gets light
2. large and strengthening
3. combs out her hair
4. puts on, fastens
5. puts on
6. a kind of hat
7. motor vehicle having usually two seats in front and an open or partially covered platform for carrying goods
8. leaves, sets off
9. looking after, taking care of
10. 4000 square metres
11. organising, managing, conducting the operation of
12. putting into a can, esp fruit and other kinds of food into air-tight tin boxes
13. repairing
14. the number of students (who have enrolled)
15. home economics, the management of household affairs
16. head of a faculty at a university in US
17. inspired
18. search
19. unmixed, complete, absolute
20. *Br* farms
21. *Am coll* girls or women
22. combine harvesters, machines which cut corn in the field and separate the grain from the straw
23. transport of large things or large quantities (usually by road)
24. persons who keep accounts in a business
25. treated too kindly
26. trained and experienced workmen
27. *Am* employing for wages, *Br* taking on, employing
28. *Br* workmen

Men at work

Why is it that so many women still want to be treated as women, even though the Sex Equality Act has been passed? It seems to us men that women want to claim all the many benefits and advantages, but none of the worries and disadvantages which we men have daily to **contend with**[1]. At work? We mustn't allow the poor dears to lift anything too heavy! Socially? Hold the doors open, and give up one's seat on public transport! Is it any wonder that men are grey-haired and bent-backed, when we have carried women on our backs for centuries?

She

MEN AT WORK

1. struggle against, solve

For wives only!!

Here's a simple test (**devised**[1] by a male chauvinist) for wives to determine whether they still love their husbands.

1 – At a party, you discover your loved one dancing **cheek-to-cheek**[2] with a **shapely**[3] blonde. Do you . . .

(a) Congratulate yourself on having **landed**[4] a man who **appeals to**[5] other women as a cross between Steve McQueen and Charles Aznavour?

(b) First chance you get, tell him you're glad to see he's enjoying himself, but **point out**[6] tactfully that the blonde's husband is over 6 ft tall – and very jealous?

(c) **Kick**[7] him **viciously**[8] on the **ankle**[9] as he dances past?

2 – Husband goes into **paroxysm**[10] of **rage**[11] when you **crash**[12] the **gears**[13] during first driving lesson. Do you . . .

(a) Apologise, tell him you don't think you'll ever make a driver, and ask him to take you home?

(b) Say you're sorry, but everyone has to learn – and anyway, aren't those gears a bit stiff?

(c) **Swear**[14] back at him and **head for**[15] driving school?

3 – Asked to drive you to supermarket on Saturday morning, husband declines on grounds he's going fishing. Do you . . .

(a) Hope he has a pleasant day and **enlist**[16] the kids to help you with the shopping?

(b) Suggest a compromise – if he drives you there, you'll make your own way back, **laden**[17] like a **pack mule**[18]?

(c) **Scrub**[19] visit to supermarket and serve him a boiled egg for Sunday lunch?

4 – Three months after you first **dropped hints**[20] that living-room needs redecorating, nothing has been done. Do you . . .

(a) Reflect the poor dear is invariably **worn out**[21] after a hard day at work and **tackle**[22] the job yourself?

(b) Tell him you appreciate he hates painting and papering, but if you call in a professional firm it'll cost about £40?

(c) Call in a professional firm and hand him a bill for £40?

If you answer (c) to each of these questions, your love is definitely **on the wane**[23].

If it's (b), you still love the **lad**[24], but you realise he's far from perfect.

If your answers are all (a)s, you're either madly in love with your husband – or you're just mad – **H A**.

The Sunday Post

FOR WIVES ONLY

1 planned, set up, invented
2 very close together so that the cheeks touch
3 well-formed, having a pleasing shape
4 *coll* caught as a husband, *lit* got something as the result of effort
5 interests, attracts
6 call attention to the fact
7 strike with the foot
8 spitefully, delighting in inflicting injury, with evil intent
9 the part that joins the foot and the leg
10 a sudden fit or attack of anger, etc
11 furious anger, a fit of fury
12 *lit* strike violently against something causing damage; *here* cause to make a loud noise
13 the driver of a car has to change gears as he goes faster or slower (except if the car has an automatic gear-box)
14 curse, use bad language
15 go to
16 engage, obtain the help or support of
17 loaded, burdened
18 a mule used for carrying heavy burdens
19 *coll* cancel, *lit* clean by hard rubbing
20 hinted, suggested indirectly
21 exhausted
22 begin to do
23 decreasing, diminishing, losing strength
24 *coll* (young) man

1 having a good temper, not easily made angry
2 a woman who shouts and scolds and is constantly in a bad temper
3 lodging and meals
4 prepares himself to expect the worst
5 furious attack
6 most precious possession, most cherished treasure, *coll* wife
7 shouts, uses extravagant language
8 *coll* spend too much money on something
9 get, receive, *lit, of* harvest a crop
10 angry, fierce stare
11 a woman's dress or gown
12 to obtain a promise of nonintervention by bribing (paying money)
13 speak in a harsh, angry voice
14 is a lecher, one who pursues women for sexual pleasure only
15 front part of the body containing the heart and lungs
16 pacify, soothe
17 *coll* ten pound notes
18 *coll* man
19 easily made angry
20 *lit* money earned by a business and divided among the shareholders; *here* good results

Will a new frock calm her?

What makes a woman **good-tempered**[1]? Many men would like to know the short answer to this question.

Faced with the angry **virago**[2] who shares his **bed and board**[3], your average male either disappears smartly in the direction of the nearest pub or **braces himself**[4] for the **onslaught**[5] and thinks about something else while **the light of his life**[6] **rants**[7] on and on.

But the man who encourages his woman to **splash out**[8] on something new to wear will **reap**[9] several benefits from his generosity: a more amiable creature around the house. A woman readier for love. A woman who feels appreciated.

I do not of course, suggest that all a man has to do to replace that angry **glare**[10] with a sunny smile is buy his loved-one a new **frock**[11]. A lot depends upon why she's ill-humoured. With some women, a new frock would make matters worse. 'You think you can **buy me off**[12], do you?' she might **snarl**[13].

The man who treats his woman like a dog, who **leches**[14] after other women, who keeps his pay-packet so close to his **chest**[15] she never knows what's in it, is not going to **placate**[16] her with a couple of **tenners**[17].

But take the average decent **bloke**[18] and his average **irritable**[19] wife. If he's got the sense to invest in her happiness, he's the one who'll enjoy the **dividends**[20].

The Daily Mirror

Discussion

1 How true in their assessment of the situation of women are the first two articles? Can they be applied to the situation in your country?
2 To what extent is there a difference in the education and upbringing of boys and girls?
3 If a man and a woman, possessing the same qualifications and experience, both apply for the same job, what are the disadvantages of employing the woman? What are the advantages?
4 What effects have the different feminist movements had on:
   (a) men's attitudes towards women?
   (b) women's attitudes towards men?
   (c) the position of women in society?
5 What do you think marriage should be? Describe the ingredients you think essential for a successful marriage.
6 'To a greater extent than seems true elsewhere in the world, we Americans seem to cherish our right to the unimpeded pursuit of happiness no matter how much sorrow that pursuit may engender.' From what you know of the USA, how true is this?
7 Imagine a conversation between a wife who wants to go out and get a job, and her husband who doesn't want her to. What reasons will she give? What objections will he raise?

Word Study

A   Semantic Fields

1 Calming down

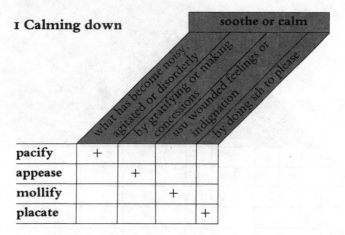

	what has become noisy, agitated or disorderly	by gratifying or making concessions	usu wounded feelings or indignation	soothe or calm by doing sth to please
pacify	+			
appease		+		
mollify			+	
placate				+

All the verbs are transitive. A common construction in which they all occur is **to . . . . . sb/sth** $\begin{cases} \textbf{with} \\ \textbf{by} \end{cases}$ **sth**

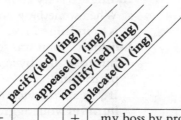

	pacify(ied) (ing)	appease(d) (ing)	mollify(ied) (ing)	placate(d) (ing)	
I	+			+	my boss by promising to work an extra hour each evening this week.
Although the professor spoke reasonably to his discontented students he was unable to	+			+	them.
The customer demands his money back and nothing else will	+			+	him.
The government hoped to	+	+		+	the rebellious population by announcing tax reforms, but this did nothing to ease the situation.
The scanty meal did nothing to		+			their hunger.
It might		+			his anger if we offered him a free dinner.
Margot is very upset and all my excuses did not seem to			+		her.
Although he was angry I think my explanation			+		him a little.

2 Pleasing others and oneself

	gratify one's own or another's wishes or desires	comply with the moods or whims of another, often out of weakness	in order to placate	do special and often unnecessary things for	do things for sb which they could easily do themselves	excessively	to the point of being ridiculous	usu suggests providing physical comfort	have injurious effects on the character
indulge	+	+							
humour		+	+						
pamper				+	+			+	
spoil				+	+	+			+
mollycoddle				+	+	+	+	+	

All the verbs are transitive. **Indulge** is also intransitive and collocates with the preposition **in**.

EXAMPLES

indulge Tony adores his wife and **indulges** her every whim.
When something goes wrong in life, the worst thing one can do is to **indulge** in self-pity.

humour John was so angry when he came home that I had to **humour** him by agreeing with everything he said in order to pacify him.
If you are the victim of a kidnapping, it's usually safer to **humour** your aggressors than to try and fight back.

pamper The old lady **pampered** her little dog in every way – even buying it chocolates for it to eat while it watched television.

spoil Since you worked so hard to get this job finished, I think you deserve to be **spoiled/pampered** just for once.
People who feel inadequate as parents often **spoil** their children to try to compensate.

mollycoddle Don't **mollycoddle** the child! How will he ever manage by himself when he grows up?

3 Softening or lessening

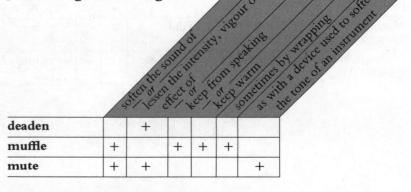

	soften the sound of	lessen the intensity, vigour or effect of	keep from speaking	keep warm	sometimes by wrapping	as with a device used to soften the tone of an instrument
deaden		+				
muffle	+		+	+	+	
mute	+	+				+

Mute is not often used in active constructions.

	deaden(ed)	muffle(d)	muted	
The tooth is so damaged that it will be necessary to	+			the nerve.
I feel that my ability to react in emotional situations has been	+			by all that I have suffered.
The doctor gave her an injection to	+			the pain.
The thick walls tend to	+	+		any sound.
We	+	+		the sound of the horse's hooves by tying rags around them.
She was		+		up in scarves, a big coat and a hat against the cold.
First reaction to the play was a bit			+	, perhaps because the audience didn't understand it all.
They sat in a corner, talking in low			+	tones.

4 Utter indistinctly and quietly

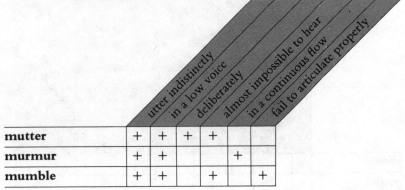

	utter indistinctly	in a low voice	deliberately	almost impossible to hear	in a continuous flow	fail to articulate properly
mutter	+	+	+	+		
murmur	+	+			+	
mumble	+	+		+		+

All the verbs can be used either transitively or intransitively and all collocate with the preposition **at**. **Murmur** may be used for sounds which are not speech, in which case it means [+ low pitched, gentle continuous sound].

EXAMPLE

From our room overlooking the bay we could hear the sea constantly **murmuring** on the beach below.

	mutter(ed)	murmur(ed)	mumble(d)	
When I asked him where he had been he	+		+	something indistinct and looked embarrassed.
Don't	+		+	! Tell us clearly who you are and what you want.
He leant towards me,		+		that he had to leave, and quietly left the room.
'I'm sure I can make you happy', she		+		tenderly.
He		+		to his companion, who nodded, and they both smiled.
The boy			+	a few embarrassed words and fled from the room.
The old man			+	so much that it was impossible to understand him.

5 Sounding like animals or birds*

	utter by producing sounds which are											often expressing							resembling the sounds produced by							
	loud	high-pitched	low	deep and hollow	short	short and successive	prolonged	feeble	sharp	harsh	like 's' or a forceful whisper	anger or	pain or	dissatisfaction or	impatience or	sadness or	disapproval or	nervousness	lions	dogs	bulls or cows	wolves	pigs	lambs, goats	birds	snakes
roar	+											+	+						+							
growl	+		+									+		+						+						
snarl									+	+		+								+						
bellow	+						+					+									+					
bark	+				+				+	+		+			+					+						
howl	+						+					+	+	+		+				+		+				
grunt			+		+									+			+						+			
bleat		+					+							+			+							+		
twitter		+				+												+							+	
hiss							+				+						+									+

* Based partly on G. Miller and P. Johnson-Laird (1976) p 625.

These verbs can all follow a direct quotation and may precede it if they occur in conjunction with another verb. All, except **twitter** and **howl**, take direct objects which name the type of message. The direct object of **snarl**, **grunt**, **twitter** and **howl** is not usually a **that**-clause. When used intransitively with a [+human] subject all these verbs, except **growl**, **snarl**, **bark**, **bleat** and **twitter**, can also denote sounds not accompanied by words.

EXAMPLES

roar He **roared** at us to get off his land as we were trespassing.
When we asked him what he was doing he **roared** some obscenity and marched away angrily.

growl He **growled** a curt order to the man next to him.
'Why have you come to disturb me again?' he **growled**.

snarl The guard turned and **snarled** at us to keep quiet.
'You couldn't even find the way to your own front gate,' he **snarled**.

bellow The gardener **bellowed** at us because we walked across his seed beds.
He ran after us **bellowing**, 'Get out of here and never come back!'

bark The captain **barked** an order to his men.
'Pay attention when I'm talking to you,' she **barked**.

howl Both the children are **howling** because I took away their trumpets.
'He'll never come back, never,' she **howled**.

grunt 'Their work had better have improved since last time,' **grunted** the teacher.
When I tried to wake him he just **grunted** and went on sleeping.

bleat What are you **bleating** about now?
'It's raining and I got wet and I haven't had any supper,' **bleated** the small child.

twitter 'I'm not quite sure how to answer you,' she **twittered**.
For heaven's sake, stop **twittering** and tell me what you want to do.

hiss She leant towards me and **hissed**: 'What a dreadful hat Mrs Tomkins is wearing!'
The audience booed and **hissed** at the unpopular singer.

Note the colloquial expressions **to roar with laughter** (to laugh heartily) and **to howl one's head off** (to cry loudly).

EXAMPLES

Everyone **roared with laughter** when I told them how I broke my arm playing snowballs.

She has locked herself in her room and is **howling her head off** because she can't go to England with the others.

6 Feeling or expressing contempt

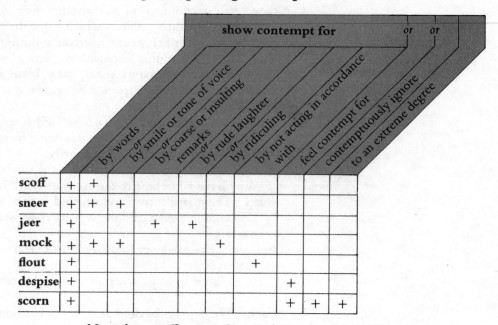

	by words	by smile or tone of voice	by coarse or insulting remarks	by rude laughter	by ridiculing	by not acting in accordance with	feel contempt for	contemptuously ignore	to an extreme degree
scoff	+	+							
sneer	+	+	+						
jeer	+			+	+				
mock	+	+	+		+				
flout	+					+			
despise	+						+		
scorn	+						+	+	+

Note that **scoff**, **sneer**, **jeer** and **mock** can be either transitive or intransitive and all collocate with the preposition **at**. **Flout**, **despise** and **scorn** are transitive.

	sb's accent	sb	what sb says	the ragged old man	sb's efforts	warnings to be careful	social conventions	sb's advice	the rules	the law	a political regime
scoff at	+	+	+	+	+	+	+	+	+		
sneer at	+	+	+		+	+					
jeer at	+	+	+	+	+		+	+			
mock	+	+		+							
flout						+	+	+	+		
despise		+	+	+	+	+	+	+			+
scorn					+	+	+	+	+		

7 Cleaning

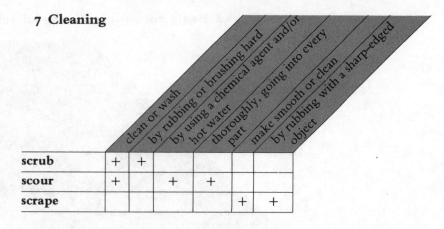

	clean or wash	by rubbing or brushing hard	by using a chemical agent and/or hot water	thoroughly, going into every part	make smooth or clean	by rubbing with a sharp-edged object
scrub	+	+				
scour	+		+	+		
scrape					+	+

The verbs occur in the following constructions:
to scrub sth; out sth; sth out; down (sth)
to scour sth; out sth; sth out
to scrape sth (off sth); sth off; sth out of sth; sth up; up sth

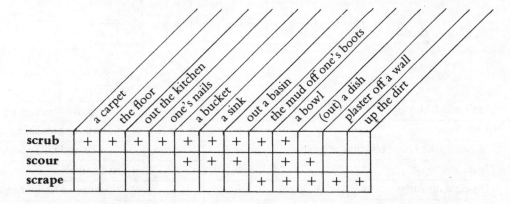

	a carpet	the floor	out the kitchen	one's nails	a bucket	a sink	out a basin	the mud off one's boots	a bowl	(out) a dish	plaster off a wall	up the dirt
scrub	+	+	+	+	+	+	+	+	+			
scour				+	+	+		+	+			
scrape								+	+	+	+	+

Colloquially **scrub** extends to mean [+cross out] or [+drop] and **scour** to mean [+search throughout].

EXAMPLES
Someone has **scrubbed** his name off the list of participants.
Well, we may as well **scrub** that idea since no-one seems to approve of it.
I have **scoured** the town looking for yellow roses but there are none to be had.
Note also the colloquial expression **to scrape the bottom of the barrel** which has the features [+use the last of one's resources] and [+usu the least good ones].

8 Being uncomfortable in social situations

	feeling or showing self-consciousness in the presence of others	avoiding close contact with others	being anxious not to impose oneself on others	because lacking in self-confidence	hesitant	often associated with youth	pretending to be modest or self-conscious in an affected way	easily frightened or lacking courage in social contacts
shy	+							
diffident		+	+	+				
bashful	+				+	+		
coy						+	+	
timid							+	+

	shy	diffident	bashful	coy	timid	
He's much too	+					to go into a shop by himself
I felt very	+					about approaching such an eminent man.
When I asked her about it she gave a	+		+			smile and said nothing.
Mice are very	+				+	creatures.
It's difficult for a	+				+	person to make friends.
She's a very		+			+	young girl who finds it difficult to ask people for help.
He's very		+				about his own talents and hardly mentions them.
The	+		+		+	child hid behind his mother's skirts.
No-one could persuade the			+			youth to dance.
Don't be so				+		– tell us about your new girlfriend.
A					+	little knock was heard at the door.

B   Synonymous Pairs

1   **to explain**
to expound   [+ in a systematic and thorough way] [+ often done by an expert] [+ usu lengthy]

EXAMPLES
We had to listen to the lecturer **expounding** her theories on language teaching for two hours.

Apart from giving a general introduction to linguistics, the Professor also **expounded** on the subject of the relationship of language and social change.

2 **to growl**   ⎰ [+make a low, threatening ⎱
     to snarl   ⎱ sound] ⎰ ⎱ [+show the teeth]

(For the extended senses, see grid 5.)

EXAMPLES

The dog **growled** at anyone who tried to enter the house.
Something **growled** at the back of the cave and we saw it was a large brown bear.
The dogs **snarled** and barked around us.
As the tiger **snarled** we could see his large fierce teeth.

3 **to mend**
   to repair

The difference between **mend** and **repair** is almost entirely collocational. **Mend** may be preferred for situations where there is a visible hole or break in something but the collocations show that **repair** is not necessarily excluded from these cases. **Repair** is preferred for larger things like cars, ships, etc.

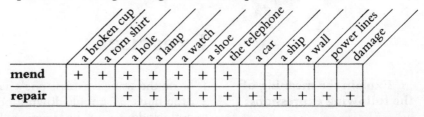

	a broken cup	a torn shirt	a hole	a lamp	a watch	a shoe	the telephone	a car	a ship	a wall	power lines	damage
mend	+	+	+	+	+	+	+					
repair			+	+	+	+	+	+	+	+	+	+

4 **to reject**   │ [+exclude]   [+to accept]
                                                          ⇒ ⎰ [+refuse] ⎰ [+definitely and finally]
   to dismiss │ [+send away]   [+to consider]

EXAMPLES

He was **dismissed** from his job for cheating.
He **dismissed** all my ideas for improving efficiency as either ridiculous or too expensive.
The committee **rejected** my proposal.
The company maintains a very high standard for its products by **rejecting** any imperfect items before they come off the production line.

5 **to deceive** │
   to delude   │ [+cause false illusions]

EXAMPLES

Do not **delude/deceive** yourself about his real motives for marrying her – it's quite obvious he is doing it for her money.
He deliberately **deluded** her into believing money would be available for her research.

6   **to imitate** ⎱ [+copy] ⎰ [+exactly]
to emulate ⎰   ⎱ [+the example of sb else] [+usu because one thinks it is good]

EXAMPLES
Malcolm made us all laugh by **imitating** the professor giving a lecture.
Teenagers often **emulate** film stars or singers in their style of dress.
It is a pity he's chosen to **emulate** the bad behaviour of his elder brother.

7   **lonely** ⎱ [+without companionship or association] ⎰ [+often sad or gloomy]
solitary ⎰   ⎱ or [+preferring solitude]

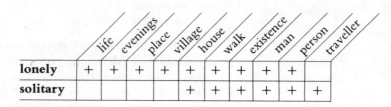

	life	evenings	place	village	house	walk	existence	man	person	traveller
lonely	+	+	+	+	+	+	+	+	+	
solitary				+	+	+	+	+	+	+

Exercises

1 Explain the meaning of the following expressions:

1 be on the wane   2 tease one's hair   3 take issue with
4 drop hints   5 gobble down food   6 success-oriented society
7 potluck dinner   8 hot lines   9 household chores   10 success ethic   11 flexible schedules   12 split work shifts

2 Fill in the correct word from the list given.

run, try out, resent, howl, roar, pass, call, lift, mend, reap, scrape, sack, pamper, keep, challenge

1 to . . . . . with laughter   2 to . . . . . sb for help   3 to . . . . . one's dog   4 to . . . . . a law   5 to . . . . . a sack of potatoes
6 to . . . . . a new recipe   7 to . . . . . the bottom of the barrel
8 to . . . . . garments   9 to . . . . . the books   10 to . . . . . sb's success   11 to . . . . . benefits   12 to . . . . . an opponent
13 to . . . . . a worker   14 to . . . . . one's head off   15 to . . . . . a shop

3 What differences and/or similarities are there between the following pairs?

1 look/glare   2 dawn/dusk   3 mollify/placate   4 indulge/humour   5 deaden/mute   6 grunt/bleat   7 explain/expound
8 growl/snarl   9 shy/bashful   10 lonely/solitary

4 When and why would one:

1 apologise?   2 congratulate sb?   3 feel insulted?   4 hire a car?
5 bully sb (into doing sth)?   6 eat a hearty breakfast?   7 enroll in evening classes?   8 use a combine?   9 buy a pick-up truck?
10 use a lawnmower?

5 Fill in the following collocational grids:

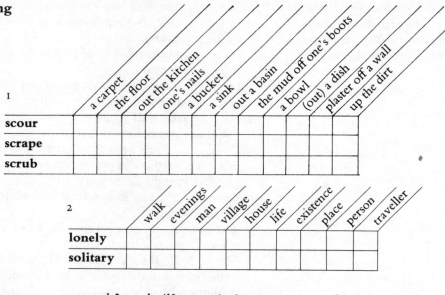

1	a carpet	the floor	out the kitchen	one's nails	a bucket	a sink	out a basin	the mud off one's boots	a bowl	(out) a dish	plaster off a wall	up the dirt
scour												
scrape												
scrub												

2	walk	evenings	man	village	house	life	existence	place	person	traveller
lonely										
solitary										

6 What kinds of things can you:

1 scrub? 2 boil? 3 paint? 4 paper? 5 frizzle? 6 run?
7 damage? 8 scrape off? 9 drive? 10 don? 11 clip?
12 pursue? 13 sum up? 14 achieve? 15 haul? 16 crash?

7 Guess the right word.

1 They have d . . . . . a completely new method of teaching vocabulary.
2 The only income she received was the a . . . . . paid by her divorced husband.
3 The criminal's a . . . . . that he was at the cinema at the time the crime was committed was not accepted.
4 At the end of the day, the greengrocer l . . . . . together all grades of apples and sold them at the same price.
5 Although her up . . . . . had been very strict, she was in no way inhibited.
6 After the night's storm we waited impatiently for the d . . . . . to see what damage had been done.
7 Wanting to go and play football, the boy g . . . . . his food like a hungry dog, and with much the same noisy relish!
8 The q . . . . . of the expedition was to locate the treasure.
9 He h . . . . . her up from out of the hole in which she'd fallen by using a strong rope.
10 Because of the terrible weather, there was no corn to h . . . . . that summer.
11 His anger mounted to r . . . . . when he found that his plan had been turned against him.
12 The b . . . . . I work next to at the factory is getting married next week.

8 In each case provide a few nouns or nominal expressions that can collocate with the following:

1 a wry . . . 2 a jealous . . . 3 a tactful . . . 4 a sunny . . .
5 a decent . . . 6 a surly . . . 7 a trained . . . 8 a cool . . .
9 a mannish . . . 10 a cumulative . . . 11 a responsible . . .
12 a hearty . . .

9 Choose the word which is most appropriate in each case and modify its form where necessary.

1 We . . . . . the little boy's resentment at not being allowed to go to the circus by buying him a huge ice-cream. (pacify, appease, mollify, placate)

2 He . . . . . a retort which of course she overheard. (mumble, mutter, murmur)

3 He . . . . . something about going out but we couldn't really catch what he said. (mumble, mutter, murmur)

4 He . . . . . the wall vigorously with the brush, but the words could not be eradicated. (scour, scrape, scrub)

5 The . . . . . of the natives was remarkable, for shown a new task just once, they could perform it perfectly thereafter. (dexterity, skill, cleverness)

6 She . . . . . the tear in her dress with almost invisible stitches. (repair, mend)

7 The one . . . . . house on the cliff was occupied by a family of seven. (lonely, solitary, alone).

8 He . . . . . his theory at length but what he was saying was completely unintelligible to his audience. (expound, explain)

9 Although he didn't say anything, George clearly . . . . . his sister for her dishonesty. (scoff, scorn, sneer, despise, flout)

10 The parents had . . . . . the boy so much that he was incapable of doing anything for himself. (indulge, humour, pamper)

10 Fill in the following componential grids:

1

	by words _or_	by smile or tone of voice _or_	by coarse or insulting remarks _or_	by rude laughter _or_	by ridiculing	show contempt for — by not acting in accordance with	feel contempt for — contemptuously ignore _or_	to an extreme degree _or_
scoff								
sneer								
jeer								
mock								
flout								
despise								
scorn								

2

	clean or wash — by rubbing or brushing hard	by using a chemical agent and/or hot water	thoroughly, going into every part	make smooth or clean — by rubbing with a sharp-edged object
scrub				
scour				
scrape				

3

	utter indistinctly	in a low voice	deliberately	almost impossible to hear	in a continuous flow	fail to articulate properly
mutter						
murmur						
mumble						

R1 Explain the following words and expressions in your own words:

1 patent   2 panel   3 cupboard   4 chemist   5 label   6 tension reliever   7 bing-bang approach   8 umbilical cord   9 labour 10 follow-up study   11 sedentary life   12 antidote   13 flabby muscles   14 telly   15 checkup

R2 What differences and/or similarities are there between the following pairs?

1 trespass/encroach   2 nestle/snuggle   3 speak/ramble (on) 4 chatter/prattle   5 whine/moan   6 thrust/heave   7 remedy/heal 8 bear/stand   9 rub/grind   10 fidget/twiddle   11 brisk/nimble

R3 What is the occupation or function of the following?

1 a psychiatrist   2 a burglar   3 a judge   4 a pharmacist 5 a carpenter   6 a foreman   7 a postman   8 a technician 9 an astronomer   10 a surgeon   11 a shopkeeper   12 a pilot 13 a superintendent   14 an electrical engineer

R4 Fill in the following componential grids.

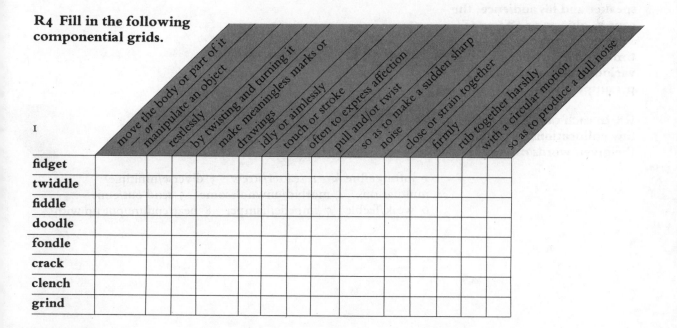

1

	move the body or part of it — or manipulate an object	restlessly	by twisting and turning it	make meaningless marks or drawings	idly or aimlessly	touch or stroke	often to express affection	pull and/or twist	so as to make a sudden sharp noise	close or strain together	firmly	rub together harshly	with a circular motion	so as to produce a dull noise
fidget														
twiddle														
fiddle														
doodle														
fondle														
crack														
clench														
grind														

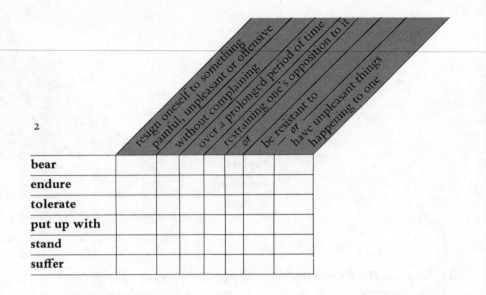

2

	resign oneself to something painful, unpleasant or offensive	without complaining	over a prolonged period of time	restraining one's opposition to it	be resistant to — or have unpleasant things happening to one
bear					
endure					
tolerate					
put up with					
stand					
suffer					

R5 Give the figurative senses of:

1 reel   2 ease   3 slip   4 stagger   5 assail   6 propagate
7 stumble   8 crowd   9 slide   10 breach

R6 When would one . . . ?

1 doodle   2 squirm   3 snarl at sb   4 stumble   5 scratch
6 clench one's fist   7 shriek   8 begrudge sth   9 sob   10 grind
one's teeth   11 gasp   12 reel

R7 For each word give as many contextual details as you can (eg information about the status, age or emotional state of the speaker and his audience, the causes, objects or effects of actions, the spacing or timing of events, or the various implications and presuppositions).

1 to go bananas   2 scrawny   3 sprightly   4 morbid   5 hoax
6 to goad   7 doodle   8 to go up the wall   9 to squirm
10 to sponsor   11 placid   12 to sue   13 take legal action
14 realm   15 inhibit

R8 In each case, provide a few collocations in which all the given words can occur.

EXAMPLE: fiddle with
twiddle with } *some keys/a pencil/a necklace*
fidget with

1 infringe/break   2 scatter/strew   3 diverse/multiple/
multifarious   4 morbid/unwholesome   5 send out/emit
6 weak/feeble   7 impede/hamper   8 bear/endure/put up with

R9 Fill in the following componential grids.

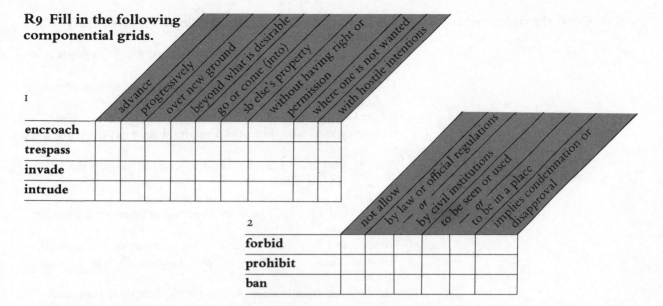

1	advance	progressively	over new ground	beyond what is desirable	go or come (into)	sb else's property	without having right or permission	where one is not wanted	with hostile intentions
encroach									
trespass									
invade									
intrude									

2	not allow	by law or official regulations — or	by civil institutions	to be seen or used — or	to be in a place	implies condemnation or disapproval
forbid						
prohibit						
ban						

R10 Choose the word which is most appropriate in each case, modifying its form where necessary.

1 Part of the . . . . . involved spending eight weeks in the pure Swiss mountain air. (medicine, cure, remedy)

2 The lacemaker's . . . . . little fingers mended the tear in the girl's new dress in next to no time. (springly, spry, nimble)

3 She was . . . . . about not wanting to see him, and, when we had heard her reasons, we completely agreed with her. (insistent, unyielding, adamant)

4 The tight-fitting dress showed her . . . . . figure to advantage. (lanky, lean, slim, scrawny)

5 There was no one among his . . . . . who was as young as John. (peers, equals)

6 Their presence . . . . . the free flow of conversation. (hinder, hamper, obstruct)

7 We . . . . . her ear-ache by the application of olive oil; but this would not . . . . . her of future attacks. (cure, remedy, heal)

8 He grew rather peevish in his . . . . . ing years. (deteriorate, worsen, decline)

9 He was very . . . . . as a child so now he expects his poor wife to run around after him and do everything he wants. (spoil, mollycoddle, humour)

10 The new doctrine has been widely . . . . . by its followers. (diffuse, disseminate, propagate)

R11 Which of the given words have the feature [+hard] included in some of their senses; which have the feature [+excessively] and which [+violent]? Notice that not all of the words mentioned are relevant.

1 malign   2 batter   3 ill   4 strike   5 morbid   6 debauch
7 hit   8 clout   9 humour   10 pamper   11 defame   12 punch
13 mollycoddle   14 assail   15 destroy   16 tear down
17 squirm

R12 Guess the right word.

1 She took a m . . . . . delight in sending her own obituary notices to the local paper.
2 His diet has to be very a . . . . ., so he must eat citrus fruits every day.
3 The c . . . . . on her belt would not fasten because part of it was broken.
4 When I was younger I did a lot of swimming and my arms were very muscular, but now I'm afraid they have become very f . . . . . .
5 Powder, and indeed most make-up, tends to clog up the p . . . . . in your skin.
6 The birds s . . . . . at the sound of the shotgun.
7 He received a n . . . . . bang on the head as he entered through the low door.
8 He tried to r . . . . . his own shoes but was not very successful.
9 What you g . . . . . on the one hand, you usually lose on the other.
10 Children are usually very d . . . . . with their books and toys until they have been taught to be careful and gentle.
11 I had known John's integrity in the past, so his ruthlessness now made him fall in my e . . . . . .
12 He had a d . . . . . brain, which no amount of coaching would change.
13 Why is he always so pr . . . . . in the praise of others?

R13 Solve the crossword puzzle.

Across

1 fall down when walking (7)
4 plant products used to flavour food (5)
8 make fun of, laugh quietly at sb (7)
9 the ability to be amusing (3)
10 Famine and war . . . . . unnecessary suffering on thousands of innocent people. (7)
12 I'd house (anagram) for 'very ugly'. (7)
15 Western countries must . . . . . their use of energy resources. (4)
16 rough, unrefined, unpleasant (5)
17 cause a train to come off its tracks (6)
18 He's not . . . . . bad as you think! (2)
20 nailer (anagram) for 'being in a line' (6)
21 persuade to engage in sexual intercourse (6)
23 bones which make up the human body (8)
24 I like this shirt but it doesn't . . . . . me, it's too small. (3)
25 want sth which belongs to sb else (5)
26 piece of wood (3)
27 gaps (anagram) for 'breathe with difficulty' (4)
28 silly, stupid, mad (*coll*) (4)
31 speak in a harsh, rough voice (5)
32 assess by placing on a numerical scale (4)
33 tape (anagram) for 'earthy substance you can burn' (4)

Down

2 shy and nervous (5)
3 Conservatives often try to . . . . . subversive books. (3)
5 deliberately stimulate sb or a group of people to bad action (6)
6 being which exists (6)

7 walk unsteadily swaying from side to side when you have drunk too much (4)

10 An offence against the law for which one can be charged is an i . . . . . offence. (10)

11 the state of having lost one's memory (7)

12 restrain freedom of movement or action (6)

13 organise and carry out (eg a series of tests) (7)

14 One who has turned away from true, right or just actions or opinions is p . . . . .. (9)

19 bring legal charges against sb (3)

21 almost fall, when walking (7)

22 The baby koala likes to . . . . . into his mother's pouch. (7)

23 express a bad opinion of sth (*coll*) (5)

24 forest (anagram) for 'encourage' (6)

26 thin and bony but healthy (4)

29 animal closely related to man (3)

30 striking one's foot rhythmically against sth to make a noise (3)

Unit 8

Make the punishment fit the crime

CRIME AND PUNISHMENT

1 spoilt, ruined, suffering
2 change one's place of residence (suggests one is strongly motivated to leave)
3 tendency
4 sudden desire or inclination to act, without reflection or thought about the consequences
5 crimes, breaking the rules
6 record, systematically observe
7 *lit* position from which one can see clearly, or a long way
8 kill by suspending from the neck with a rope
9 stick to, go on believing in
10 develop, invent
11 spread out in the most effective way
12 legal system
13 prisons which are like schools, for young criminals
14 who don't break the law
15 restore to a useful and socially acceptable state
16 suspension of a prison sentence on condition that the guilty person is supervised by social workers
17 release of a prisoner from jail before the end of his sentence on condition of future good behaviour
18 designed for a specific trade or skill
19 lead, direct towards sth
20 dissimilar, radically different
21 unfavourably, not likely to be helpful
22 almost entirely
23 peculiar to an individual
24 freedom to choose and make decisions
25 made to feel different from and separated from
26 not useful or helpful

Crime and Punishment

Secretary, bus conductor, solicitor, teacher, shop assistant, welder – no matter who you are or where you live, you probably feel concerned about Britain's rising crime rate. According to some recent statistics, London now has some 7,000 crimes per year per 100,000 of its population. For many people living in dismal urban areas **ravaged**[1] by crime, the only answer is to **move up and out**[2] to more pleasant surroundings. What is happening? Can anything be done to stop this **trend**[3]?

The exercise yard of a British prison.

Basically, there are two opposing general attitudes which a society can take towards crime and criminals. One view says that punishment (usually in the form of long prison sentences) discourages the criminal **impulses**[4] in most of us, and deters criminals who are punished from repeating their **offences**[5]. It is only to be regretted that this simple solution is not borne out by trends observed since we began **keeping track**[6] of the crime rate. Not only does it continue to rise, but also the trend among once-convicted offenders is for them to commit further offences.

From the **vantage**[7] point of two hundred years, we are shocked to learn that it used to be normal to **hang**[8] a man for stealing a loaf of bread. Yet we in Britain **cling to**[9] just such a punishment-based system, instead of **evolving**[10] new methods of dealing with crime. One reason for this might be that the 'punishment deters' view expressed above is a cover-up for a pessimistic acceptance that all societies naturally produce criminals and that the best thing is to have a **well-deployed**[11] police force and efficient **judiciary**[12] which will simply remove them to prisons, **borstals**[13] and psychiatric hospitals where they won't bother us **law-abiding**[14] citizens.

According to the second general attitude to crime, a society accepts responsibility for creating its criminal element, and takes steps to **rehabilitate**[15] and train offenders so that they will no longer feel the impulse to commit crimes. Such a society will use **probation**[16] and **parole**[17] systems, counselling services and **vocational**[18] training schemes to **channel**[19] criminals' energies more positively, regarding them more as people needing help than as people who have done something wrong.

The problem in Britain (and in many other countries) seems to be that we are operating both these **disparate**[20] systems at once. It just does not make sense to place criminals in the **adverse**[21] social conditions of a prison for the length of their sentence and then expect them to adjust to society outside through a brief period at a rehabilitation or retraining centre. Our present system **virtually**[22] leaves the choice of punishment or rehabilitation to the **idiosyncratic**[23] **discretion**[24] of our judges. A criminal mind, either actual or potential, can only be confused and **alienated**[25] by a society which treats one criminal with loving care and help, and another with hate and punishment, when both have committed the same crime.

Our society is in danger of being overburdened by the totally **negative**[26] deployment of resources involved in running the punishment system. We not only should, but must move away from the old punishment-based judicial system to one which genuinely cares for all men.

VANDALISM AND VIOLENCE IN SCHOOL AND SOCIETY

WILLIAM W BRICKMAN

With growing frequency, statistics reveal a considerable **prevalence**[1] of vandalism and violence in schools all over the country. The annual reports by the **FBI**[2] attest to the **perennial**[3] rise of **juvenile delinquency**[4] and crime in society at large.

Information released by the New York City Board of Education in December, 1975, should cause considerable anxiety. In 'Fun City', the number of acts of crime in the public schools during September–November, 1975, was 55% higher than for the corresponding period in 1974. The major criminal actions were **assaults**[5] on teachers and robberies of teachers, pupils, and others. In a large suburban high school in Illinois, considered by principals to be one of the 'best' 100 in the US, incidents of **larceny**[6] went up from 26 in 1970–71 to 105

in 1973–74; of vandalism, from 27 to 71; and of other **infractions**[7], various increases. Assaults decreased from 12 to 11 at this school, but bomb threats rose from four to six. Finally, an estimate by the National Association of School Security Directors indicates that, during 1974, there were 12,000 armed robberies, 270,000 burglaries, 204,000 **aggravated assaults**[8], and 9,000 rapes in American schools, and that the price of vandalism reached $600,000,000.

The blame for this situation has frequently been laid at the door of the current status and mood of society. Among the contributory factors cited are the **deplorable**[9]

economy, racial tensions and **clashes**[10], the availability of weapons, the widespread accessibility of drugs and liquor, the daily depiction of violence in television programs, the inconsistent and light punishment **meted out**[11] by the courts, and parental and pedagogical permissiveness. Efforts at **coping with**[12] the waves of school vandalism and crime have been **hampered**[13] by **judicial**[14] and social restrictions upon **suspension**[15], **exclusion**[16] and corporal punishment, accompanied by an insistence upon a broad definition of pupil rights.

Intellect

VANDALISM & VIOLENCE

1 common occurrence or practice
2 Federal Bureau of Investigation (of US)
3 continuing year by year
4 anti-social conduct by young people, often breaking the law
5 violent attacks
6 stealing, theft
7 instances of breaking or offending against the law
8 assaults with intention to permanently injure
9 that is to be deplored, regretted
10 conflicts
11 given
12 struggling successfully with
13 obstructed, hindered, made difficult
14 connected with a judge or court of law
15 temporary removing from a position
16 shutting or keeping out

LIFE'S LIKE THAT

While some young volunteers were cleaning and painting an old lady's kitchen, a social worker came to see how work was progressing. 'Doesn't it look nice!' she enthused. 'Aren't you glad you agreed to have it done?'

'Well,' sighed the old lady. 'I don't really mind. I'd do anything to help solve the delinquency problem.'
– Mrs M P, London

Reader's Digest

When the guns **blaze**[1]

by FENTON BRESLER

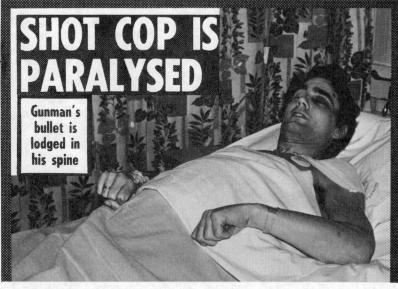

SHOT COP IS PARALYSED

Gunman's bullet is lodged in his spine

How much longer can we expect the ordinary unarmed young policeman **on the beat**[2] to face armed **thugs**[3]?

That is the question posed by the death of 21-year-old Police Constable Stephen T, who was not even on duty when he chased after the **runaway**[4] suspect who suddenly turned on him and shot him dead.

* * *

Last week, Mr Ronald G, Chief Constable of the 5,000-strong West Yorkshire Metropolitan Force, in whose area crime rose by 20 per cent last year, said: 'We shall use **lethal**[5] means if necessary to stop the sort of characters that are **preying on**[6] society today.'

Five hundred of his men are already trained to shoot. 'I am contemplating whether or not they should carry firearms in certain cars. If the situation gets any worse, we would contemplate making firearms more easily available to officers who go into these dangerous situations.'

DILEMMA

It is a vicious dilemma. Violence breeds violence. At the moment, merely the threat of his gun is often enough to ensure the criminal's safe escape.

But if the policeman also has a gun, which he is at liberty under the law to use, will not almost inevitably one of them be tempted to try to beat the other to the **draw**[7]?

On the other hand, if the one fired is that held in a policeman's hand, should we **grieve**[8] all that much?

After all, if one of those three plain-clothes officers questioning young Stephen T's killer before he suddenly broke off and ran had been carrying a gun, Constable T might not have died.

Can we any longer afford not to arm our police?

Daily Express

A thief gives back the booty[1] . . .

Blind Stanley H, 50, was heart-broken when his home was **ransacked**[2] . . .

The burglar took £150 worth of property including his special radio for use by the blind.

But now the thief has made Stanley happy again — by sending the booty back! The stolen items were found by Stanley's wife Elfriede when she opened the back door of their cottage in Southfield Road.

A carrier bag had been left, containing missing cuff links, an electric razor — and the radio. A **scrawled**[3] letter read: 'Sorry for stealing your property. I didn't know your husband was blind.

'Sorry I can't return everything. But an associate had the other half of your property and I can't recover them.'

Detective Chief Inspector Dawson Horn said yesterday: 'This gesture gladdens my heart.

'At least one thief has a conscience and realises the heartbreak and suffering that can be caused. He is, of course, still being sought.'

Daily Mirror

WHEN THE GUNS BLAZE

1 fire (ammunition) very quickly
2 on patrol in their regular area
3 violent criminals
4 escaped
5 causing death, fatal
6 robbing, *lit* killing for food
7 the pulling out of a gun, ready to fire
8 feel grief, feel deep sorrow or suffering

A THIEF GIVES BACK THE BOOTY

1 goods/money obtained illegally
2 searched roughly for anything worth stealing
3 written quickly and badly

The champion shoplifter

One morning last week, an attractive, dark-haired woman in her thirties walked into a large department store in Glasgow. She wore a **bulky**[1] coat with **hood**[2] attached. She carried a large, square parcel in one hand, a shopping bag in the other.

In the **outfitting department**[3], the woman admired a row of suits. **In a twinkling**[4], she **tucked away**[5] a £60 tweed suit into a big secret pocket in her **coat lining**[6].

In the jewellery department she tried on a pearl necklace. **Deftly**[7] she slipped it in the hood of her coat.

Next stop, the rainwear counter. She picked up an umbrella, glanced about, coolly tore off the price tag, and walked away with it. After a visit to the electrical goods department, the closed umbrella contained a transistor radio, a tape recorder, and four torches.

She then laid her shopping bag on top of a **sweater**[8] on a nearby counter. When she lifted the bag, the sweater went with her – pulled in through the bag's false bottom. On to the toy department, where she slipped a variety of toys into the 'parcel' she was carrying. The parcel was actually a gift-wrapped empty cardboard box. It had a **flap**[9] in the side with a **spring-device**[10] behind it.

Ten more minutes in the store, and the woman also lifted two pairs of slacks, a wig, three cigarette lighters, five wristwatches, and several bottles of perfume. Total **haul**[11] – more than £200 worth.

The lady with the light fingers is acknowledged as Scotland's champion shoplifter. She steals around £10,000 of goods every year. But everything she steals is returned!

She's a supervisor with Group 4, a security firm that trains and supplies store detectives. Her job is to give new recruits first-hand knowledge of the job. Several times a month she becomes a shoplifter – to let trainees see the **dodges**[12] shop thieves get up to.

Nobody is more qualified to act the thief than this lady.

She's **nabbed**[13] more shoplifters in her time than she cares to remember. She knows every trick in the book.

The Sunday Post

THE CHAMPION SHOPLIFTER

1 large, very thick
2 a soft and flexible covering for the head fastened to a coat
3 department or section where men's clothes are sold
4 *coll* in an instant, in a moment, very quickly
5 put away, hid
6 inside fabric layer of a coat
7 by skilful movement of the hands
8 pullover
9 a piece of something that hangs down or over or at the side of something
10 contrivance of metal which tends to return to the original position or shape after being pulled out of position
11 *coll* amount stolen or gained
12 tricks
13 *coll* caught

THE TOUGH GUYS FLED

1 quickly and skilfully
2 *sl* young rough who starts trouble or disturbance; *lit coll abbr* of name Edward
3 fell suddenly, dropped heavily
4 moved suddenly to one side in order to escape something
5 violent criminal
6 fled, ran away
7 struggled successfully with, controlled
8 unable to work because of illness or injury

The Tough Guys Fled!

A Glasgow taxi driver picked up two youths in Buchanan Street last Friday night. Once inside the cab it was obvious they'd been drinking. They swore and argued with each other.

The street they'd asked for was dark and quiet. They stepped out and told the driver if he wanted paid, he'd have to come out and get the money.

As the driver calmly got out of the cab one youth bent to pick up a stone and the other moved in and swung his boot.

The driver **smartly**[1] stepped back, then his foot darted out catching the **ned**[2] in the stomach. As he **slumped**[3] to the ground his mate threw the stone. The driver **dodged**[4] it and drove his fist into the **thug's**[5] stomach. After that the neds weren't so brave. One gave the driver two pound notes and **took to his heels**[6]. The other raced after him.

How come the driver **coped**[7] so easily with the thugs?

A year ago he was beaten up when three drunks refused to pay their fare and he was **off work**[8] three weeks. As soon as he was fit, he joined the Kobe Osaka Karate Club in Classford Street. He was determined he'd be able to defend himself if he was attacked again.

Taxi drivers, bus drivers, conductors, policemen and even postmen attend the club. They're taking up karate as a means of defending themselves. So now the neds aren't getting things all their way.

The Sunday Post

Crime in a cashless society

In a cashless society of the future, **disruption**[1] of the electronic **flow**[2] of **funds**[3], images, and data may be the dominant mode of criminal conduct. Street robberies may **virtually**[4] disappear.

Electronic criminals have already appeared and are robbing businesses and the public through a wide variety of **ingenious**[5] schemes.

In 1964, a computer programmer stole $5 million worth of programs from his employer and attempted to sell them. He was caught, convicted of **grand theft**[6], and served five years in prison. In 1973, a cashier at the Union Dime Savings Bank in New York City used a computer to **embezzle**[7] $1.5 million. In Washington, D.C., a man opened a bank account and made a quick $100,000 in three days through a simple scheme: When he obtained his individualized, computer-coded **deposit slips**[8] from the bank, he promptly substituted them for the blank uncoded deposit slips in the bank's *lobby*. **Unwary**[9] customers filled out the slips, and their money was credited to the thief's account. A few days later, the thief **withdrew**[10] the money and vanished.

Computers are 'Kidnapped'
As they become increasingly recognized as sources of money and power in society, computers are beginning to be treated as if they were real people. They are **assaulted**[11], stolen, and kidnapped and held for **ransom**[12]. In the state of Washington, in 1968, someone fired two pistol shots into a computer at a state employment office. In 1969, a group of Massachusetts college students took over the campus computer center in an attempt to force the administration to meet their demands. The 1970 bombing of an Army **data center**[13] in Wisconsin by political **dissidents**[14] destroyed 20 years of important data and caused $1.5 million in damage. That same year, students in New York held an Atomic Energy Commission computer for $100,000 ransom.

The Futurist

CRIME IN A CASHLESS SOCIETY

1 breaking up
2 stream
3 sums of money
4 almost, more or less
5 clever and skilful
6 *Am* theft of goods or money over a certain fixed value
7 steal money that has been entrusted to one's care
8 small printed form which must accompany any payment into one's bank account
9 incautious, unsuspecting, not realising the real situation
10 took out
11 attacked
12 the sum paid for the liberation of a kidnapped person
13 centre where certain facts are collected and filed for future reference
14 people not in agreement

Discussion

1 What do you think of the view that 'all societies naturally produce criminals'? If this is true, try to find reasons for it.
2 Evaluate the reasons for increases in crime given in the final paragraph of Brickman's article. How applicable are they to the different crimes reported here? Can you suggest any other reasons for crime?
3 'Stealing from large organisations is not really a crime.' Does this view seem to you prevalent, and how do you feel about it?
4 When discussing treatment of criminals, shouldn't some distinction be drawn between those who are mentally ill and might be cured through therapy, and those who are not? Or would you see all criminals as being mentally ill?
5 What effect does the fact that the British police are not armed have on criminals and the public? Compare this situation with that in your country.
6 What justifications can you find for the idea that the large amount of publicity that crime receives in the media contributes to its increase?
7 Comment on the following excerpt from *The Second Sin* by Thomas Szasz.
'Punishment is no longer fashionable. Why? Because – with its corollary, reward – it makes some people guilty and others innocent, some good and others evil; in short, it creates moral distinctions among men, and, to the "democratic" mentality, this is odious. Our age seems to prefer a meaningless collective guilt to a meaningful individual responsibility.'

Word Study

A Semantic Fields 1 Being guilty

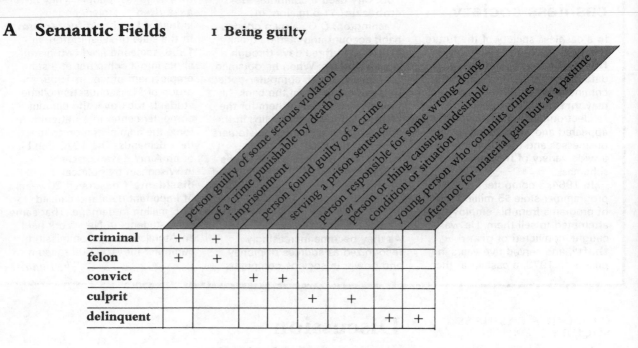

	person guilty of some serious violation of a crime punishable by death or imprisonment	person found guilty of a crime	serving a prison sentence	person responsible for some wrong-doing or	person or thing causing undesirable condition or situation	young person who commits crimes often not for material gain but as a pastime
criminal	+	+					
felon	+	+					
convict			+	+			
culprit					+	+	
delinquent							+	+

Note that **felon** is the legal term for one popularly called **criminal**.

EXAMPLES

criminal   It is usually very difficult for convicted **criminals** to find jobs when they come out of prison.

felon   The **felons** apparently entered the house by climbing a drain-pipe, and after locking the owner in a cupboard they removed all the silver and valuables.

convict   Two **convicts** have escaped from a nearby prison and the police are scouring the countryside for them.

culprit   We knew someone was systematically stealing paper from the office and today we caught the **culprit** in the act.

The car kept breaking down and it turned out that a leaky fuel-line was the **culprit**.

delinquent   Two young **delinquents** appeared in court today charged with causing severe and irreparable damage to the equipment in the local children's playground.

	cause not to be alive	as a result of previous decision	object must be human	object has political power or significance	by using force or a weapon	stresses the ugly nature of the action	object usu animal	for food	brutally	object is usu a group of defenceless people	object is sb condemned to death by a legal or pseudo-legal procedure	object is usu large number of pests	deliberately
kill	+												
murder	+	+	+										
assassinate	+		+	+									
slay	+		+		+	+							
slaughter	+						+	+					
butcher	+						+	+	+				
massacre	+								+	+			
execute	+										+		
exterminate	+											+	+

Slay is more literary than the other words. In extended senses, **kill** is informal and can take a [+ animate] or a [+ non-material] object. **Slaughter**, **butcher** and **exterminate** can all apply to [+ human] objects but **slaughter** and **butcher** stress the feature [+ violent], whereas **exterminate** implies [+ a whole (usu ethnic) group of people].

EXAMPLES

kill We must **kill** these rumours of revolution before they become widespread.

The lights failed in the last scene of the play and completely **killed** the dramatic effect.

slaughter The Prince ordered his soldiers to **slaughter** any of the enemy regardless of age or sex.

butcher All the women and children were cruelly **butchered** in a surprise attack on two border villages.

exterminate The Spanish conquerors drove most of the South American Indians into the distant mountains, and systematically **exterminated** those who remained.

In colloquial speech, **kill** and **slay** are used to exaggerate the effect of what is being said. No literal meaning is intended.

EXAMPLES

If I have to type this page again, I'll **kill** myself!

The next person who comes in with dirty feet on my clean floor will be **slain** alive!

★ Based partly on A. Lehrer (1974) p 113–115.

Everyone **killed** themselves laughing when they heard about my adventures on the cross–Channel ferry.

	oneself	trees	birds	flowers	a prime minister	a man	a king	a brother	calves	lambs	a whole village	innocent victims	a traitor	rats	locusts
kill	+	+	+	+	+	+	+	+	+	+	+	+	+	+	+
murder					+	+	+	+				+			
assassinate					+	+	+								
slay						+	+	+					+		
slaughter									+	+					
butcher									+	+					
massacre											+	+			
execute					+	+	+					+	+		
exterminate														+	+

3 Taking another's property

	search through another's property										take another's property	*or*	
	in order to steal	in a rough manner	causing widespread damage	thoroughly	involves many participants	at times when social order is disturbed	by using violence or threats	by any other unjust means	on a large scale	esp food or valuables	from a building	search through	roughly
ransack	+	+	+										
rifle	+	+		+								+	+
rob							+	+					
plunder	+	+	+		+	+	+		+	+			
loot	+	+	+		+	+			+				
burgle													

The direct object of all the verbs, except **rob**, is the place where the action happens. The direct object of **rob** is usually [+human] or [+institution]. **Plunder** and **loot** may also be intransitive. **Rifle** may be followed by the preposition **through**.

Plunder is usually used to describe events in past centuries.

	ransack(ed)	rifle(d)	rob(bed)	plunder(ed)(ing)	loot(ed)	burgle(d)	
The thieves	+						the house looking for valuables.
Soldiers ran wild in the town and	+			+	+		any building which contained valuables.
Enemy troops	+			+	+		each house as they came to it, and then set fire to it.
She		+					desperately through drawers and cupboards, searching for the missing documents.
Please don't		+					through my papers, you will put them out of order.
I'm convinced my desk has been		+					while I have been out.
He was set on by a gang of delinquents who			+				him of his money, watch and cheque book.
She was			+				of all her jewellery while she slept.
Highwaymen used to			+				travellers on lonely roads.
The troops are				+			and looting wherever they go.
Gangs and individuals took advantage of the power-cut to					+		the big department stores in the centre of town.
Our house was						+	while we were on holiday.
Police are searching for a gang which is thought to have						+	several houses in the area in recent weeks.

4 Freeing from blame

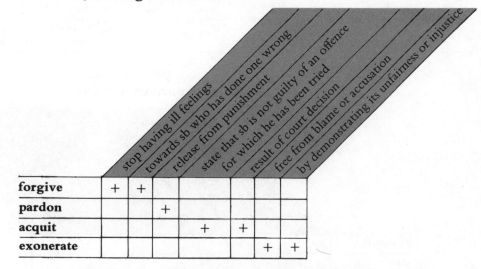

	stop having ill feelings towards sb who has done one wrong	release from punishment	state that sb is not guilty of an offence for which he has been tried	result of court decision	free from blame or accusation by demonstrating its unfairness or injustice	
forgive	+	+				
pardon			+			
acquit				+	+	
exonerate						+	+

These verbs are all transitive. **Forgive** can also be intransitive.
Pardon is very formal, or a little old-fashioned. They occur in the
following constructions:

to forgive sb; sb sth; sb for sth; sb for doing sth
to pardon sb; sb sth; sb for sth
to acquit sb; sb of/on sth (usu charges)
to exonerate sb from/of sth
Pardon is quite widely used, especially in the United States, in the imperative as an expression of politeness.
EXAMPLE
Pardon me for intruding, interrupting.

	forgive (forgave) (forgiven)	pardon(ed)	acquit(ted)	exonerate(d)	
My sister has never	+				me for losing her favourite doll when she was seven.
I can	+	(+)			you your ignorance, but there is never any excuse for bad manners.
'	+				and forget' is an old saying but it is good advice to anyone.
He said he had	+				her for that insulting remark she made.
The king		+			all the rebels and let them go free.
'		+			my ignorance.'
He was charged with murder but was			+		for lack of evidence.
The Court of Appeal			+		him of the charge of libel.
The tribunal				+	the Minister of all blame for the breach of security.
I won't				+	the Government – they are guilty of imposing excessive taxation.

5 Changing purpose or route

	cause to turn away	try to make sb turn away from a purpose or project	by advice or persuasion	by arousing fear, doubt or anxiety	by weakening his enthusiasm, sense of purpose or will power	by directing attention or interest towards a new object or from its original course or route	of sth travelling or water
dissuade	+		+	+			
deter	+		+		+		
discourage		+	+			+	
divert	+					+	+	+

The verbs are transitive and can be used in the following phrases:

to dissuade sb; sb from sth; sb from doing sth
to deter sb; sb from sth; sb from doing sth
to discourage sb; sb from sth; sb from doing sth
to divert sb/sth; sb/sth from sth; sb/sth from doing sth

	dissuade(d)	deter(red)	discourage(d)	divert(ed)	
I did my best to	+				him from this crazy project, but he is determined.
At least we	+				her from inviting all our 45 cousins to the wedding.
We intended to walk along the coast to the next town but were		+			by the stormy weather.
Although he has had so many setbacks, nothing will		+	+		him from completing his research.
I shall do anything in my power to			+		my daughter's relationship with this young man.
Everyone			+		me from going on such a tiring journey, but it was not nearly as difficult as they feared.
Because of fog my plane was				+	from London to Paris.
They				+	the stream to fill the new artificial lake.
All traffic has to be				+	round the town centre on market day.
You must				+	the guard's attention while I slip in through the door.
People call on me and				+	me from doing what I had intended.

6 Bringing about death or disaster

	leading to disaster of	leading to a certain death	lasting until death of	capable of killing	because powerful enough or sufficient to do so
fatal	+	+		+	+
deadly		+		+	
lethal				+	+
mortal			+	+	

	weapon	drug	dose of a poison	wounds	danger	combat	enemies	blow	disease	poison	injuries	accident	mistake	step
fatal			+	+							+	+	+	+
deadly								+	+	+				
mortal				+	+	+	+	+	+	+				
lethal	+	+	+											

Deadly is used in colloquial speech either as an intensifier, or with the sense of [+ not pleasing to the senses].

EXAMPLES

His lectures are so **deadly** boring that most students fall asleep during them.

They have painted their house a really **deadly** shade of pink.

The party was so **deadly** that we left after only half-an-hour.

B Synonymous Pairs

1 **to exclude**
   to suspend [+ by a higher authority] [+ usu temporarily] [+ as a punishment] [+ often from a privilege, right or position]

	a possibility	persons under twenty-five	foreign students	a student from school	sb from teaching	sb's driving licence	a ferry service	lectures	sales of a drug
exclude	+	+	+	+					
suspend				+	+	+	+	+	+

2 **to interrupt**
   to disrupt [+ completely] [+ throw into confusion] [+ lasting some time]

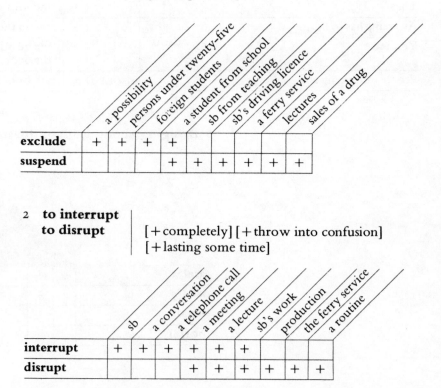

	sb	a conversation	a telephone call	a meeting	a lecture	sb's work	production	the ferry service	a routine
interrupt	+	+	+	+	+	+			
disrupt				+	+	+	+	+	+

3 **to put away**
  to tuck away | [+into a small place] [+often with the intention of concealing]

Tuck away is very colloquial.

EXAMPLES

I'm afraid I have mislaid your letter which I had **tucked away** in a safe place and now cannot find.

She tends to **tuck** her money **away** in obscure places in an attempt not to spend it.

4 **to admit** { [+accept as true or valid] } or [+confess] or [+acknowledge] or [+allow to enter]

  to concede or [+give up] or [+give away to opponent]

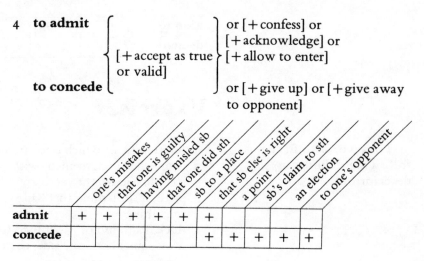

	one's mistakes	that one is guilty	having misled sb	that one did sth	sb to a place	that sb else is right	a point	sb's claim to sth	an election	to one's opponent
admit	+	+	+	+	+	+				
concede						+	+	+	+	+

5 **hateful**
  odious | [+because of particularly offensive or disagreeable quality of behaviour]

Like **hateful**, **odious** occurs in the phrase **to be . . . . . to sb**.

EXAMPLES

He is so **odious** it's difficult to believe anyone could actually like him.

I did not see any necessity for the telephone operator to be so **odious** to me when I complained that he had connected me with a number in Spain instead of one in Holland.

6 **clever**
  ingenious | [+original and skilful] or [+product of original thought]

Clever is more informal than **ingenious**.

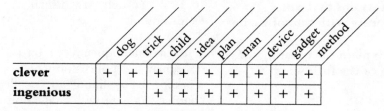

	dog	trick	child	idea	plan	man	device	gadget	method
clever	+	+	+	+	+	+	+	+	+
ingenious			+	+	+	+	+	+	+

7 **gloomy** $\Big\{$ [+dark] $\Rightarrow$ [+depressing] $\Big\}$ or [+unhappy] or [+pessimistic]
   dismal

The extended use of **gloomy** is colloquial.

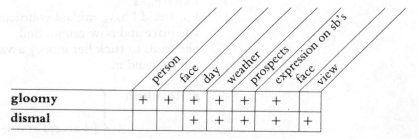

	person	face	day	weather	prospects	expression on sb's face	view
gloomy	+	+	+	+	+	+	
dismal			+	+	+	+	+

Exercises

1 Find words to fit the following definitions/descriptions.

1 position from which one can see clearly, or a long way
2 people not in agreement with certain norms
3 electric hand-light and battery
4 piece of something that hangs down or over or at the side of something
5 thick, stiff kind of paper used for making boxes, binding books
6 move quickly to one side, change position or direction in order to escape or avoid
7 release of a prisoner from jail prior to the expiration of his term on condition of future good behaviour
8 institution for the care of the mentally ill, or the aged, or the poor
9 facts that are certainly known and which can be processed, for example, by computer
10 money (to be) paid in exchange for the release of a captive
11 string of beads, pearls worn as an ornament
12 violent attack

2 What differences and/or similarities are there between the following pairs?

1 kill/slaughter   2 injuries/bruises   3 cash/cheques   4 larceny/crime   5 ransom/hostage   6 dodge/avoid   7 sigh/breathe
8 steal/kidnap   9 acknowledge/thank   10 put away/tuck away
11 discourage/deter   12 interrupt/disrupt

3 In each case provide a few nouns or nominal expressions that can collocate with the following:

1 academic   2 stable   3 lethal   4 brief   5 irrational
6 idiosyncratic   7 ingenious   8 suburban   9 widespread
10 fatal   11 deft   12 dismal   13 bulky   14 mortal
15 profound

4 Explain the meaning of each of the following:

1 juvenile delinquency   2 bird of prey   3 plain-clothes policeman   4 police constable   5 a suspect   6 a thug   7 social worker   8 coat lining   9 jewellery department   10 rainwear counter   11 bag with a false bottom   12 corporal punishment

13 first-hand information   14 £60 tweed suit   15 dart out one's
foot   16 take to one's heels   17 be convicted of grand theft
18 have light fingers   19 nab a shoplifter   20 be off work
21 swing one's boot   22 in a twinkling

**5 Fill in the correct word
from the list given.**

fire   meet   destroy   hold   release   credit   withdraw   pick up
bend   cope with   take up   scrawl

1 to . . . . . information   2 to . . . . . money from one's account
3 to . . . . . sb for ransom   4 to . . . . . a hitch-hiker   5 to . . . . . a
piece of metal   6 to try to . . . . . sb's demands   7 to . . . . . with a
problem   8 to . . . . . an old house   9 to . . . . . a note
10 to . . . . . the money to sb's account   11 to . . . . . a sport
12 to . . . . . a few shots

**6 Which of the following
words have the feature
[+ violent] or [+ brutally]?**

1 ransack   2 ravage   3 attack   4 acquit   5 deter   6 butcher
7 tear down   8 rape   9 burgle   10 flee   11 massacre   12 kill
13 grieve   14 slump   15 smash   16 plunder   17 take over
18 swear   19 attack   20 exonerate   21 cane   22 slander

7 Guess the right word.

1 The government released the prisoner on p . . . . . .
2 The thief complained to the judge that he didn't know what the
latter meant when he referred to la . . . . . .
3 He was the kind of reviewer who delighted in giving ad . . . . .
criticism of an artist rather than the constructive, appreciative
kind.
4 The verdict was 'guilty' and justice was duly m . . . . . out on
the criminal.
5 The kidnappers demanded a £100,000 r . . . . . for the
businessman.
6 The pirates l . . . . . everything of value on the ship and could
barely carry away their b . . . . . .
7 The h . . . . . of the car was badly damaged in the accident.
8 The busy politician sc . . . . . his signature hastily at the bottom
of the letter.
9 We had to admire the i . . . . . way in which he produced a
magnificent meal out of next to nothing.

**8 What differences and/or
similarities are there between
the following pairs?**

1 acquit/exonerate   2 ransack/rifle   3 shoplift/steal   4 slip in/
put in   5 murder/assassinate   6 lethal/mortal   7 convict/culprit
8 jug/bottle   9 infraction/action   10 cab/car   11 sweater/
cardigan   12 slacks/trousers

**9 Choose the word which is
most appropriate in each
case. Modify its form where
necessary.**

1 When he heard what conditions were like in Alaska, he was
. . . . . from going once and for all. (deter, discourage, divert)
2 The whole of the heath was . . . . . by fire. (damage, ruin,
ravage)
3 'What . . . . . weather for summer, not one day of sunshine!'
(regrettable, deplorable, unfortunate)
4 The treasurer was found guilty of . . . . . ing last year's financial
contributions to the Union. (steal, rob, embezzle)

5 What a . . . . . looking penknife you've got there! (lethal, fatal, deadly, mortal)

6 He . . . . . down in the armchair, bearing all the weight of the day's worries with him. (fall, slump, drop)

7 The . . . . . form beneath his raincoat made us suspect he was carrying a revolver. (thick, large, bulky)

8 Her new evening dress . . . . . to her body in a most seductive way. (adhere, cling, stick)

Revision Exercises

R1 Supply appropriate prepositions for the following:

1 to mock . . . sb/sth   2 to sue sb . . . sth   3 to take pity . . . sb   4 to give vent . . . sth   5 to stagger . . . one's feet   6 to resign . . . sth   7 to refer . . . sth/sb   8 to aim . . . sth   9 to fidget . . . sth   10 to live . . . . . . sth   11 to stare . . . sth/sb   12 to cure sb . . . sth   13 to suffer . . . sth   14 to twiddle . . . sth   15 to jeer . . . sb/sth   16 to scour . . . sth   17 to growl . . . sb   18 to remedy sth . . . sth

R2 Fill in the following componential grids:

1

	utter by										usu expressing								
	loud sounds	high-pitched, shrill sounds	short sounds	long, drawn-out sounds	all on the same note	low-pitched sounds	soft sounds	breathing sharply and irregularly (often while crying)	taking a deep breath	short sounds, as if short of breath	anger *or*	excitement *or*	fear *or*	complaint *or*	despair or distress *or*	sadness *or*	relief *or*	resignation *or*	tenderness *or*	surprise
scream																				
shriek																				
whine																				
wail																				
groan																				
moan																				
sob																				
sigh																				
gasp																				

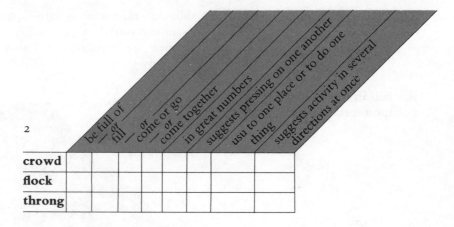

2	be full of __ or __ fill	__ or come or go	__ or come together	in great numbers	suggests pressing on one another	usu to one place or to do one thing	suggests activity in several directions at once
crowd							
flock							
throng							

R3 What words are derivationally related to the following?

1 rely   2 cover   3 shape   4 agony   5 ritual   6 pursue
7 stimulate   8 alone   9 pretend   10 endear   11 recognize
12 generous   13 present   14 dexterous   15 intensive
16 account

R4 Guess the right word.

1 The g . . . . . s that came from the wood told the huntsmen the wild boar were near.
2 He was contemptuous of those beneath him and s . . . . . at their opinions.
3 The prisoner was put into s . . . . . confinement and his only contact was with his gaoler.
4 With d . . . . . loving hands, the woman bandaged up her husband's wounds.
5 In these woods, the unw . . . . . walker risks treading on a snake if he doesn't keep a careful look out.
6 As a head master one has the pe . . . . . problem of deciding how much freedom pupils should be allowed.
7 From the de . . . . . with which she could return his witty remarks we gathered this must be an emancipated woman!
8 I s . . . . . my fingernails with the small brush until all the earth from the garden was gone.
9 Women are b . . . . . from certain all-male clubs in London.
10 The dog gave a low g . . . . . of warning.

R5 In each case provide a few nouns or nominal expressions that can collocate with the following:

1 to tackle   2 to dismiss   3 to muffle   4 to scour   5 to foster
6 to gratify   7 to hire   8 to run   9 to flout   10 to gobble (up)
11 to induce   12 to bar   13 to can   14 to mend   15 to drop

R6 What differences and/or similarities are there between the following pairs?

1 mock/flout   2 scrape/scratch   3 tolerate/suffer   4 doodle/fondle   5 tap/touch   6 despise/scorn   7 rot/decay   8 wriggle/squirm   9 clench/close   10 agile/spry   11 coy/timid
12 morbid/sickly   13 competitive/ambitious   14 lanky/slender

R7 Explain the meaning of each of the following:

1 alibi   2 craftsman   3 ethics   4 bloke   5 vicious   6 buy sb off
7 room and board   8 onslaught   9 lecherous   10 cheeky
11 tenner   12 panacea   13 chauvinist   14 paroxysm
15 alimony

R8 Fill in the following componential grids:

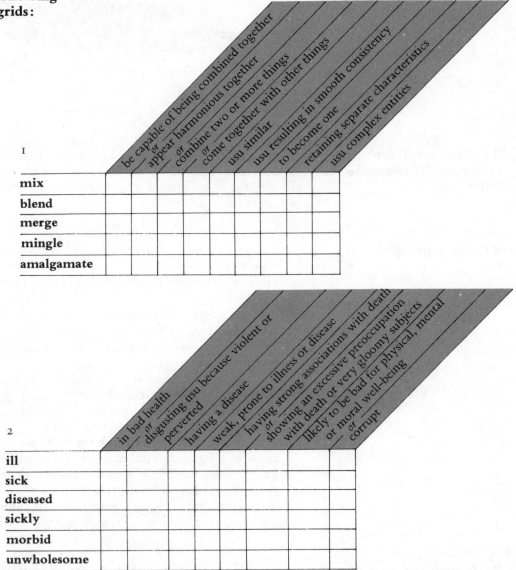

1

	be capable of being combined together	or appear harmonious together	or combine two or more things	or come together with other things	usu similar	usu resulting in smooth consistency	to become one	retaining separate characteristics	usu complex entities
mix									
blend									
merge									
mingle									
amalgamate									

2

	in bad health	or disgusting usu because violent or perverted	having a disease	weak, prone to illness or disease	having strong associations with death	showing an excessive preoccupation with death or very gloomy subjects	likely to be bad for physical, mental or moral well-being	or corrupt
ill								
sick								
diseased								
sickly								
morbid								
unwholesome								

R9 How does the meaning of the words change in the given collocations? Use a dictionary if necessary.

1 **to kill** pain/time/a bill/a proposal/a person
2 **to pick up** information/a parcel/a language/a hitchhiker/speed
3 a **healthy** child/appetite/climate/way
4 a **hearty** meal/appetite/welcome/support/person
5 **life** –span/–jacket/–boat/insurance/expectancy/guard/size/time/
cycle

R10 Produce a logical and coherent story by filling in the blanks with appropriate words from the list given and modifying their form where necessary. Notice that not all of the words mentioned are relevant.

dismal, blind, ingenious, hearty, lethal, wry, surly, constricting, profusely, viciously, laden, loaded, cheek-to-cheek, independent, goal, challenge, clashes, shoplifting, theft, infractions, vandalism, delinquency, culprit, to sneer, to resent, to pamper, to haul, to reap, to glare, to assassinate, to snarl, to smash, to slash, to swear, to convict, to dart out, to exonerate, to slump, to dodge, to slip in, to nab, to lump, to pick on, to deter, to loot, to divert

From being a rather 1 . . . . . mother's boy, Giles had grown up to be quite 2 . . . . ., with a 3 . . . . . laugh that seemed to add a couple of years to his age. He had been rather a 4 . . . . . failure at school and indeed he himself said that his school years had had rather a 5 . . . . . effect on him. He 6 . . . . . the way he had always been so 7 . . . . . 8 . . . . . by the other boys, and 9 . . . . . that if he ever had children he'd make sure they had a better time than he'd had. Strangely enough, all this had not rendered him 10 . . . . ., rather, he was a very sociable person.

Wanting to 11 . . . . . some benefit from his education, Giles decided to join the police force. His friends 12 . . . . . at the idea but for Giles it was a real 13 . . . . ., for it meant a job 14 . . . . . with responsibility. Of course, if one 15 . . . . . together all the more unpleasant aspects, such as the 16 . . . . . that occurred during demonstrations, petty 17 . . . . . such as 18 . . . . ., one could sneer at the job. Giles was not 19 . . . . . . With a large youth unemployment problem, juvenile 20 . . . . . was on the increase where he lived. Cases of 21 . . . . . were reported every day in which telephone boxes were 22 . . . . . up and train seats 23 . . . . . . It was difficult to 24 . . . . . people though, as there were never any witnesses and the 25 . . . . . were only too good at 26 . . . . . ing the police. One day Giles saw an old man 27 . . . . . wearily down on a park bench. He asked if he could help but the man first 28 . . . . . angrily at him, then realising that he was a policeman, gave him a 29 . . . . . smile and told him that there'd been a 30 . . . . . at his house and that he'd seen the culprit 31 . . . . . of the bushes and make away. 'If I'd been able to 32 . . . . . him, he'd have got what for!' 33 . . . . . the old man. 'It was 34 . . . . . folly to have left that kitchen window open . . . he must have 35 . . . . . while I was out getting the milk . . . to think that I must have been almost 36 . . . . . with the villain as I walked up the path past the bush where he was hiding!'

Unit 9 Eat, drink and be merry

The food you eat

JEROME GOLDSTEIN

THE FOOD YOU EAT

1 the amount of money involved in the operations of a firm or industry
2 businesses which sell ready-cooked food to the public, esp those offering standardized food produced in large quantities
3 not produced in a factory, not containing unnatural additives
4 causing to become less and less healthy
5 the process of supplying and receiving nourishment

In spite of the $75 billion a year **turnover**[1] of the **food service industry**[2], some Americans believe that eating natural food, the kind that you prepare in your own kitchen from fresh, **unprocessed**[3] produce and meat, is better than the typical supermarket and food service diet. We have many reasons for this belief, including the fact that in countries where natural foods are eaten almost exclusively, most **degenerative**[4] conditions like heart disease and cancer are relatively rare.

Now, probably for the first time, we have the results of a scientific comparison of the health effects of a natural foods diet and a food service diet. These findings have been revealed by Michele Bremer, Ph.D., in the *Ecology of Food and* **Nutrition**[5], an international journal which studies all aspects of nutrition.

Dr Bremer used 600 white mice for the study, divided into three equal groups. One group was fed the food service diet, the second was fed a diet consisting wholly of natural foods, and the 'control' group received a scientifically prepared mixture designed to keep experimental animals at peak physical condition.

A major manufacturer of restaurant and supermarket foods donated five of its most popular suppers for the food service diet, and traditional American foods such as apple pie, **bologna**[6] and spaghetti were added to approximate the typical diet of people interviewed in ten different states.

The natural foods diet was high in vegetables and grains, with a modest amount of meat.

By the time the mice reached early adolescence, some differences were beginning to show. The natural foods group, along with the control group, looked like normal, slim, healthy mice. But the supermarket mice were beginning to divide themselves into two fairly distinct groups. Some had soft, smooth coats but were becoming noticeably **chubby**[7]. The others appeared **scrawny**[8], and their coats began to look **matted**[9] and yellowish.

The technician responsible for the daily care of the animals noticed a subtle behavioral difference between the supermarket group and the other two groups. The food service group seemed more nervous. When the cages were opened, all the mice **fussed**[10] and ran around, but then most quickly settled down. However, mice in the food service cages remained in disorder for a noticeably longer time than those in the other cages. A less subtle difference was that the supermarket mice *bit* people handling them, a problem which did not arise with the others.

The mouse experiment was continued for over two years, by which time most of the mice had died. The primary finding was a significant difference in size. Many supermarket mice were more than twice as large as the average natural foods and control mice, with much more fat around their abdomens. Analyses also showed that they had proportionately less body protein than the other two groups.

Commenting on the significance of Dr Bremer's research, *Prevention* executive director says:

'Analyses of the nutritional content of the three diets showed that all contained adequate levels of vitamins, though the natural foods diet had higher levels of vitamins A and C than the supermarket diet. Protein content was about the same, and the supermarket diet had just slightly more fat. The biggest difference between these two was in **fiber**[11] content. The natural foods diet had about $3\frac{1}{2}$ times as much fiber as the supermarket diet.

'The importance of this is that the differences in fatness, in skin health, and in disposition observed between the supermarket group and the natural foods group were *not* a result of a severe deficiency of any of the major nutrients, such as vitamins, protein, calories or iron. Yet, these **nutrients**[12] are usually considered to be the only yardsticks of dietary excellence. It seemed clear that there was something else about the natural foods diet, as yet unidentified which made a big difference in the physical and even the emotional health of the animals. . . .'

Organic Gardening and Farming

6 bologna sausage, a highly seasoned sausage of mixed meats
7 round and plump
8 too thin and skinny, so that the bones show through the skin
9 tangled or knotted
10 got excited or nervous
11 thread structure of many animal and vegetable substances (eg cotton, wool, wood, cereals)
12 something that nourishes

Why not dogs?

As a vegetarian I am amazed at the outcry about eating dogs, from people who quite happily eat fish, cows, pigs, sheep and birds. What, may I ask, is the difference between eating dogs and pigs, particularly as the latter are every bit as intelligent?
S.T.A.

Daily Express

HOUNDED OUT

1 *fig* driven out, *lit* chased out by hounds
2 of no special breed, or mixed breed
3 moved silently and secretly
4 snatch, seize suddenly
5 exposed
6 complete, fully-developed, *lit*, of a bird when it gets its adult feathers
7 allowing to fall out
8 twisted around tightly together
9 *fig* and *coll* a sudden inspiration
10 a line of things dropped or left behind at intervals after sth has passed
11 *coll* swallowed down greedily like a wolf
12 *coll* eat fast and greedily
13 china plates, bowls, cups etc

SINGING THE JUNK FOOD BLUES

1 rubbish, things of little or no value
2 cause or precipitate
3 a form of recurrent, very severe headache
4 persons who are accused of a crime or offence
5 *Am* hard biscuits, made in the shape of a knot, salted, and eaten with beer
6 *coll* fanatics; people who like sthg very much

Hounded[1] out!

I usually take my lunch in a small café around the corner from my office. I like it because it's clean and cheap and most of all because it's quiet. At least, usually it is. One day recently things were different.

The cafe was busy with lunch-time customers as two large **mongrel**[2] dogs **sneaked**[3] in un-noticed through the door, attracted, no doubt, by the smell of food and the crumbs they found on the floor. The trouble started when both dogs tried to **grab**[4] the same piece of bread. They **bared**[5] their teeth and circled around preparing to fight. Suddenly they leapt on each other growling, barking and scratching. A **fully-fledged**[6] dog fight was taking place right in the middle of the cafe. Customers (including me!) fled, knocking over tables and chairs and **spilling**[7] food in a mad rush for the door.

The proprietor **wrung**[8] his hands in despair. Suddenly he had a **brainwave**[9]. He seized some hot pies and threw them on the floor, making a **trail**[10] of pies leading towards the door. When the dogs smelled the pies they stopped fighting and began to **wolf down**[11] as many as they could, following the trail to the door. Once outside they **gobbled up**[12] the rest on the pavement.

Not only did those dogs cost a small fortune in **crockery**[13] breakages – they also deprived me of my regular lunch order – pie and chips!

Deanford News

SINGING THE JUNK[1] FOOD BLUES

Most chronic. headache sufferers already know that chocolate, cheese, good whisky and wine, and dishes loaded with mono-sodium glutamate are apt to **trig**-ger[2] **migraines**[3] and are therefore 'off limits'. Now recent research adds some other **culprits**[4] to the list: salted snack foods (**pretzels**[5], potato chips, nuts and the like), especially when eaten on an empty stomach.

When a person is tired, or hasn't eaten, the sudden load of salt can bring on a migraine attack within 6 to 12 hours, reports Dr John B Brainard, who has a private practice in St Paul, Minn. By controlling or virtually eliminating the intake of salty foods, as well as the other known headache-causers, 10 of the 12 patients he checked for six months were able to prevent the onset of recurrent headaches. Sorry, junk food **freaks**![6]

Family Health

Back to basics

Oatmeal, corn meal and other old-fashioned, no-nonsense foods are making a dramatic sales comeback, the Quaker Oats Company reports, as housewives rediscover the economy and **nutrition**[1] of natural foods.

'It seems that now, for the first time in decades, supermarket shoppers are taking a look at the price tags on **convenience**[2] and **super-convenience**[3] food packages and opting for the kind of product mother or grandmother used to buy,' comments *Chicago Sun-Times* writer Edwin Darby.

Organic Gardening and Farming

BACK TO BASICS

1 the property of supplying nourishment
2 easy to prepare
3 very easy to prepare

The Experts have done it again!

Contrary to popular belief, it has been proved conclusively an apple a day rots your teeth away.

Is nothing sacred?

Time was, if anything was worrying me, I'd just have a cigarette and let my anxieties drift away in a **blissful**[1] **haze**[2] of **tar**[3] and nicotine.

But as the screams of the experts grew more persistent – 'It kills you! It kills you!' – I looked about desperately for an alternative **soother**[4].

I found it in food.

Nothing for easing the mind – and the appetite – like a **chip butty**[5] washed down with **gallons**[6] of sugary tea.

No sooner had I downed the last morsel when the experts started screaming again.

'Chip butties? Shriek! Think of the poisonous white bread, full of **bleach**[7] and **starch**[8] and who knows what else!

Think of the butter, **oozing**[9] with cholesterol, just **itching**[10] to gather round your poor old heart in a fatty mass!

'Tea! **Gasp**![11] The caffeine! That nasty white sugar! What are you trying to do to yourself?'

All right, then, I said, I'll eat more healthily. Fresh, wholesome additive-free cheese and milk.

Even that didn't please them.

'Dairy produce! Good grief! You'll have **brick-hard**[12] **arteries**[13] before you know it!'

Clearly, there was more to this staying alive business than met the eye.

Result is I break out in a cold sweat at every mealtime.

What unknown horrors are **lurking**[14] in the macaroni and cheese?

Will I collapse with an overdose of **custard**[15]?

My hand trembles visibly as I pause to drop some saccharin in my de-caffeinated coffee. Is this wise – bearing in mind the Americans' discovery that feeding a rat 4,000 saccharins a day for five years gives it cancer?

I would pack it all in and go on a **fast**[16]. But, then, you never know what they're putting in the water these days, do you?

Trouble is, I seem to be the only one giving myself **ulcers**[17] worrying about it all.

All I can see about me are people happily poisoning themselves, smoking, drinking, and bursting with what can only be described as **rude**[18] health.

I can't help feeling the experts have gone wrong somewhere. – T R S

The Sunday Post

Baffling[1]

The Common Market has paid out over £21 million to buy up and destroy fruit and vegetables this year.

Under the rules, they can step in like this when prices fall too low to give producers a **set**[2] return.

Amongst the money paid out was £7.3 million for surplus Italian pears, and £6.9 million to France for surplus apples.

Peaches, tangerines, oranges, cauliflowers, and tomatoes, were among other produce destroyed.

What a waste.

The Sunday Post

BAFFLING

1 puzzling, too difficult to understand
2 fixed or arranged in advance

Austrians 'too fat'

VIENNA: Julius ('Let me have men about me that are fat') Caesar would have had the time of his life in present-day Austria.

For no less than 11.3 per cent of the 8,500,000 inhabitants of the Austrian Republic suffer from **obesity**[1], shortness of breath and excessive perspiration.

So, with a finger held up in warning, the medical association of this country of rich cream cakes, huge **schnitzels**[2] and juicy hams, has told the **chubby**[3] ones to stop **gobbling**[4] so much food.

AUSTRIANS 'TOO FAT'

1 excessive corpulence
2 *German food*, thick slices of meat, cooked and served for one person
3 round and plump
4 *coll* eating fast and greedily

THE EXPERTS HAVE DONE IT AGAIN!

1 very happy
2 a very thin mist
3 a black sticky liquid
4 something that soothes or tranquilizes
5 *coll* sandwiches with fried sliced potatoes in them
6 *lit* a measure used for liquids; here *fig* large quantities
7 substance to make linen white
8 white tasteless powdery substance which stores carbohydrate, found in bread, potatoes, cakes etc
9 giving off or exuding
10 *coll fig* having a restless longing to
11 a sudden catching of the breath through fear, astonishment, etc
12 hard as bricks, elements used for building houses and walls
13 blood-vessels that carry blood from the heart to all parts of the body
14 lying in wait
15 a mixture of eggs and milk, sweetened and flavoured, and baked or boiled
16 going without food
17 open sores produced in the stomach and intestines as a result of stress
18 strong, sturdy

WON'T YOU TRY THIS SPRING SALAD?

½ cup salad oil
2 teaspoons vinegar
1 small **clove**[1] **garlic**[2]
    minced[3]
½ cup finely **chopped**[4] onion
½ teaspoon sugar
Dash salt
Dash pepper
1 cup **coarsely**[5] **shredded**[6]
    cabbage[7]
3 cups **torn**[8] lettuce
2 tomatoes, peeled, **cubed**[9]
    and **drained**[10]
2 tablespoons sliced green
    olives
2 hard-boiled eggs, chopped
1 cup **diced**[11] cooked pork
⅓ cup **grated**[12] Parmesan
    cheese

Mix first 7 ingredients. Combine cabbage, tomatoes, olives, pork and eggs; **toss**[13] lightly with **dressing**[14]. Refrigerate ½ hour. Add lettuce and toss. **Sprinkle**[15] cheese over salad. Makes 8 **servings**[16].

WON'T YOU TRY THIS
SPRING SALAD

1 one section of a plant bulb
2 strong-tasting and strong-smelling onion-like bulb
3 cut or chopped into small pieces
4 cut into small pieces
5 so that the pieces remain quite large
6 cut or torn into shreds, strips, scraps
7 a vegetable with thick leaves round a hard centre
8 pulled apart
9 cut into solid bodies with six equal square sides
10 made dry by letting the water flow away
11 shaped like a dice, cut up into small pieces like cubes
12 rubbed to small pieces
13 mix by raising a few inches in the air over the bowl and dropping, repeatedly
14 sauce for salad
15 scatter in small drops or tiny bits
16 portions, quantities sufficient for one person

Discussion

1 Cooking and eating habits vary from country to country. To what extent do eating habits reflect the differing personalities of different races and cultures? Compare any that you know.

2 Why do most people in Western countries eat more than they need? Is it just habit, or are there social reasons?

3 Do you eat to live, or live to eat? Are you sure? Supposing that as from tomorrow you were to be fed on nothing but tablets containing all the nourishment you needed, what would you lose?

4 The list of foods and drinks which are 'bad for us' gets longer and longer as more research is done. If we know that things like alcohol, coffee, butter, sugar, white bread or chemical sweeteners are bad for us, why do we go on eating them? Have we *no* self control? Or aren't we afraid of the consequences? Or are we too stupid to believe the warnings?

Word Study

A Semantic Fields 1 Large and small pieces of things

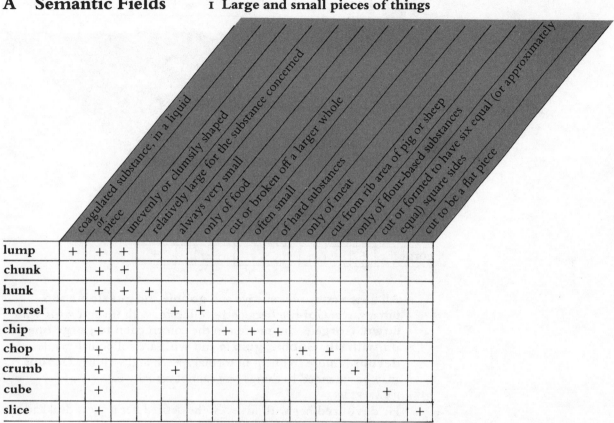

	coagulated substance, in a liquid	or piece	unevenly or clumsily shaped	relatively large for the substance concerned	always very small	only of food	cut or broken off a larger whole	often small	of hard substances	only of meat	cut from rib area of pig or sheep	only of flour-based substances	cut or formed to have six equal (or approximately equal) square sides	cut to be a flat piece
lump	+	+	+											
chunk		+	+											
hunk		+	+	+										
morsel		+			+	+								
chip		+					+	+	+					
chop		+								+	+			
crumb		+			+							+		
cube		+											+	
slice		+												+

Some of the words take the preposition **of** while others are more (or equally) common in compounds. The use of **lump**, **chunk** and **hunk** to apply to food is rather colloquial. **Piece** would be the neutral equivalent.

		dough	mud	fat	meat	cheese	bread	wood	glass	china	cake	melon	carrot
lump		+	+	+	+	+							
chunk					+	+	+	+					
hunk	of				+	+	+	+					
morsel				+	+	+	+				+		
chip							+	+	+				
slice					+	+	+				+	+	+

Compounds: **wood-chip, lamb chop, cake crumb, breadcrumb, sugar cube, meat cube, stock cube.**

2 Eating

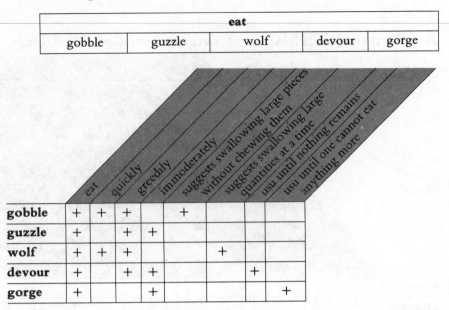

eat				
gobble	guzzle	wolf	devour	gorge

	eat	quickly	greedily	immoderately	suggests swallowing large pieces without chewing them	suggests swallowing large quantities at a time	usu until nothing remains	usu until one cannot eat anything more
gobble	+	+	+		+			
guzzle	+		+	+				
wolf	+	+	+			+		
devour	+		+	+			+	
gorge	+			+				+

All these verbs are transitive and **gobble** and **guzzle** are also intransitive. **Gobble** frequently collocates with **up** and **wolf** with **down**. **Gorge** is commonest in the construction **to gorge oneself on/with sth**. **Gobble**, **guzzle** and **wolf** are colloquial, while **devour** is more frequent in formal speech and writing. **Devour** may be extended to things one cannot actually eat.

EXAMPLES

He **devoured** her with his eyes. (he desired her a great deal and showed that he did)

She is quite **devoured** by jealousy of her successful sister.

Her **devouring** ambition is to go to England. (= she cannot think of anything else)

	gobble(d)	guzzle(d)	wolf(ed)	devour(ed)	gorge(d) (ing)	
The children	+	+				their supper as fast as possible.
The chickens hungrily	+	+		+		everything we threw down for them.
The dog			+	+		its food as though it had not eaten for a week.
It was disgusting to behold the guests					+	themselves on huge quantities of delicious food.
After eight weeks of voyage we					+	ourselves on food and wine for the first three days after our return.

3 Biting

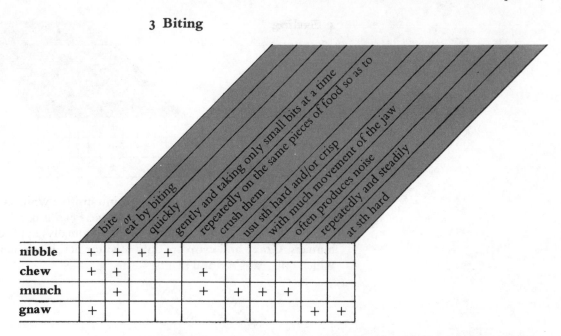

	bite	or eat by biting	quickly	gently and taking only small bits at a time	repeatedly on the same pieces of food so as to crush them	usu sth hard and/or crisp	with much movement of the jaw	often produces noise	repeatedly and steadily	at sth hard
nibble	+	+	+	+						
chew	+	+			+					
munch		+			+	+	+	+		
gnaw	+								+	+

The verbs can be used transitively or intransitively. **Nibble** and **gnaw** often collocate with the preposition **at** and sometimes with **on**. **Munch** is common in the construction **to munch away at sth**. In its figurative sense, **chew** has the feature [+ think over carefully] and is used with **over**. This usage is colloquial. **Gnaw**, figuratively, has the feature [+ torment] and is usually used as a present participle.

EXAMPLES

Don't make up your mind immediately. Go away and **chew** over everything I said and let me know tomorrow.

I have this **gnawing** anxiety all the time that something must have gone wrong, even though I know quite well someone would have let me know if it had.

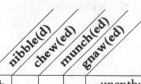

	nibble(d)	chew(ed)	munch(ed)	gnaw(ed)	
She did not eat a proper meal, but	+				unenthusiastically at a lettuce leaf or two.
Mice have	+				at this cheese – I can see their little teeth marks!
The meat was very tasty but I had to		+			it a lot because it was rather tough.
The puppy has		+			up my shoe and completely ruined it!
Puppies will		+			on anything they can find.
Each child			+		his apple contentedly.
The Koala bears			+		on Eucalyptus leaves.
Rats have				+	a hole in the bottom of the door.
Dogs				+	bones to exercise their teeth.

4 Feeding

	provide nourishment	or cause grass to be eaten in	or eat	grass	until it is left very short
feed	+		+		
graze		+	+	+	
crop			+	+	+

Feed and **graze** may be transitive or intransitive while **crop**, in the sense in which it appears here, is transitive. **Feed** is usually used for animals but may be humorously (and colloquially) applied to humans. **Graze** and **crop** are only used for herbivores (animals which only eat grass and plants).

	feed (fed)	graze(d)	crop(ped)	
The farmer	+			his calves each evening.
We	+			our pigs with pigmeal and water.
Giraffes	+			chiefly on green leaves from trees.
There was no grass so we had to	+			hay to the cattle instead.
I must go home and	+			my family.
Sheep and cows		+		peacefully in a meadow in front of the house.
We usually		+		the top fields in the late summer.
The goats have neatly			+	the grass like a lawn.

5 Drinking

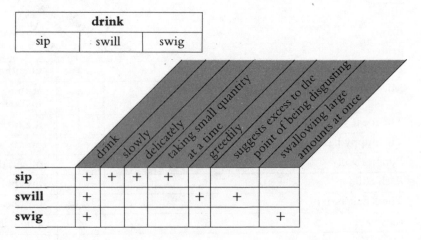

		drink	
	sip	swill	swig

	drink	slowly	delicately	taking small quantity at a time	greedily	suggests excess to the point of being disgusting	swallowing large amounts at once
sip	+	+	+	+			
swill	+				+	+	
swig	+						+

All three verbs are used transitively. They occur with the following prepositions; **to sip up/at, to swill down, to swig at. Swill** and **swig** are colloquial.

EXAMPLES

sip   At my mother's tea parties the guests **sip** their tea delicately out of bone-china tea-cups while discussing the weather.
The cat **sipped** experimentally at the wine, then sneezed because she did not like it.

swill   We found ourselves in a bar near the docks, filled with sailors who were **swilling** beer as though it was the last time they would ever have the chance.
It was the kind of society occasion where everybody **swills** down far too much drink because they are so bored.

swig   We were surprised to see even the female members of the expedition cheerfully **swigging** whisky straight from the bottle.

6 Reducing to small pieces

	cut through with a blow or blows from a sharp-edged instrument	or	cut	or tear	reduce to small pieces	by forcing under pressure through small holes	rub against a surface containing small sharp-edged holes	into small pieces	into small cubes	into cubes	into small irregular strips or long narrow pieces	into flat pieces
chop	+	+	+					+				
dice			+						+			
cube			+							+		
shred			+	+							+	
slice			+									+
mince					+	+						
grate							+				+	

Chop, **dice**, **shred** and **slice** may occur with **up**. **Chop** may also occur with **down**.

EXAMPLES

Could you **chop** the onions **up**?
We had to **chop down** the oak tree because it was rotten.
He carefully **shredded up** the documents so that they could not be reconstructed.

Chop is often used in colloquial speech as a synonym of **cut**.

EXAMPLES

What a pity you have **chopped off** all your beautiful hair.
This article is far too long and will have to be **chopped**.

	wood	nuts	off one's finger	onions	potatoes	apples	carrots	cheese	liver	meat	bread	lettuce	cabbage	paper	chocolate
chop	+	+	+	+		+		+							
dice			+	+		+									
cube							+		+	+					
shred						+					+	+	+		
slice				+	+	+	+	+	+	+	+				
mince									+	+					
grate						+	+								+

7 Throwing

cast	throw		
	toss	hurl	fling

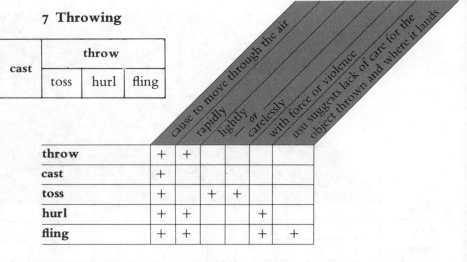

	cause to move through the air	rapidly	lightly or carelessly	with force or violence	usu suggests lack of care for the object thrown and where it lands
throw	+	+			
cast	+				
toss	+		+	+	
hurl	+	+		+	
fling	+	+		+	+

Although **cast** is a synonym of **throw**, its contemporary use is restricted to a few set phrases and expressions, in some of which its sense is extended.

EXAMPLES

The fishermen **cast** their nets in deep water.

The oak tree **cast** a deep shadow across the lawn.

She **cast** a quick glance at her companion.

Martin must be angry about something – he has been **casting** black looks at everyone all day.

He **cast** caution to the winds and plunged into the icy river.

Recent tests have **cast** doubts on the efficacy of this new wonder drug.

Why did you **cast** aspersions on my ability to teach advanced students?

All the verbs collocate with **at** and **on**, and **hurl** and **cast** can also take **upon**. The verbs (except **cast**) occur in the following constructions: **to . . . . .sth at/to/on sth/sb.**

Hurl is used figuratively with the sense 'to say forcibly' and often occurs with **insults**.

EXAMPLE

He **hurled insults** at the driver who had crashed into him.

	coins	sth on the ground	oneself to the ground	a book	a ball to sb	salad
throw	+	+	+	+	+	
toss				+	+	+
hurl			+	+		
fling		+	+		+	

8 Behaving furtively

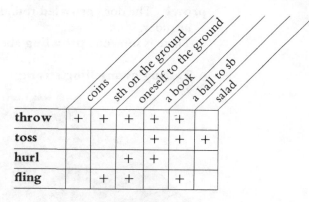

	deliberately wait in hiding to attack — or	stay somewhere unobserved — or	move in a stealthy way to avoid duty or work — or		move in a dejected way as a result of anger — or	as a result of fear or guilt — or	to avoid being noticed	looking, or as if looking, for sth to eat or steal
lurk	+	+	+					+
skulk		+	+	+	+	+	+	
slink			+			+	+	
sneak			+				+	
prowl			+					+

Slink often collocates with **away**, **off** and **out**, and **sneak** with **in** and **out**. **Prowl** is common with **about**, **round** and **around**. Notice that because of their negative implications these verbs, with the possible exception of **sneak**, are not usually used with first-person subjects in present and future tenses.

EXAMPLES

lurk A suspicious character is **lurking** in the trees opposite the house.
 The possibility of failure always **lurked** in the background.
 Suspicion always **lurks** in her mind.

skulk The students who had failed **skulked** about outside the hall where the presentation of diplomas was taking place.
 I'm afraid I have upset John and he is **skulking** around in the garden, probably planning revenge.

slink The dog **slunk** off with its tail between its legs.

sneak Teachers do not usually like students who **sneak/slink** away before the end of a class.

The door was locked but I **sneaked** in through a window round the back.

prowl The dogs **prowled** round the yard, sniffing for signs of an intruder.

There is someone **prowling** about downstairs in the dark.

9 Tasting or smelling strong

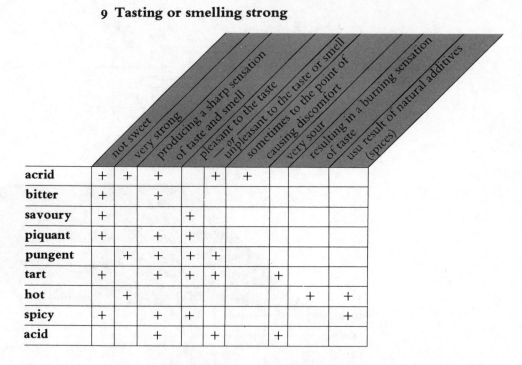

	not sweet	very strong	producing a sharp sensation of taste and smell	pleasant to the taste	unpleasant to the taste or smell	sometimes to the point of causing discomfort	very sour	resulting in a burning sensation of taste	usu result of natural additives (spices)
acrid	+	+	+		+	+			
bitter	+		+						
savoury	+			+					
piquant	+		+	+					
pungent		+	+	+	+				
tart	+		+	+	+		+		
hot		+						+	+
spicy	+		+	+					+
acid			+		+		+		

Although these words may all apply to taste or smell, the collocational grid shows that **acrid** and **pungent** are more usually used only for smells, while the rest are more usually used for tastes.

	smoke	fumes	smell	taste	flavour	sauce	dish	rice	chocolate	aroma	curry	peppers	apple	wine
acrid	+	+	+	(+)										
bitter			+	+					+					
savoury			+		+	+	+							
piquant			+	+	+				(+)					
pungent		+	+						+					
tart			+	+								+		
hot			+	+			+				+	+		
spicy			+	+	+	+				+	+			
acid			+	+									+	+

The following words are used figuratively, with the senses shown:

acrid [+ sharp and direct] [+ of speech]

bitter [+ resentful and unforgiving]

tart [+ rude and direct] [+ of speech]

acid [+ rude, expressing anger] [+ of speech]

EXAMPLES

acrid His **acrid** comments suggest that he feels very strongly about the matter.

bitter Clearly she feels very **bitter** about the way in which she was dismissed from her job.

tart He obviously feels bitter about my good exam marks, because when I asked him if he wanted to borrow any of my notes I got a very **tart** reply indeed.

acid It would help if you could stop making **acid** comments and produce some constructive criticism.

10 Being fat

	carrying excessive fat or flesh	to an extreme degree	detrimental to health	suggests unattractiveness	slightly	naturally as with age	usu. of elderly men	carried with dignity	sufficiently well-covered with flesh	usu. of a pleasing appearance	usu. of children and young people
fat	+										
obese	+	+	+								
corpulent	+			+		+					
stout	+				+	+					
portly	+					+	+				
plump									+	+	·
chubby									+	+	+

Obese is less common than the other words and is usually reserved for medical contexts.

The words can be placed on the following scale:

complimentary   uncomplimentary

<--->

**chubby   plump   portly   stout   corpulent   fat
                                                                    obese**

	man	woman	child	baby	arms	legs	face	gentleman	dog	cheeks	horse	mouse	thighs	fingers
fat	+	+	+	+	+	+	+	(+)	+	+	+	(+)	+	
obese	+	+	+											
corpulent	+	+						+						
stout	+	+						+	+					
portly	+							+						
plump		+	+	+	+	+	+							+
chubby			+	+						+				+

B   Synonymous Pairs

1 **crawl**   [+move or go slowly] or [+move on all fours] ⇒ [+degrade oneself]

   to creep   [+move furtively] ⇒ [+progress slowly]

EXAMPLES

One by one the explorers **crawled** through the narrow opening into the cave.

A sudden shower brought the rush-hour traffic **crawling** to a halt.

She only gets such good marks because she **crawls** to the professor and flatters him excessively.

The number of accidents occurring to children in school has been **creeping** up year by year.

The house was in total darkness as we **crept** in and tiptoed to our rooms, hoping not to awaken anyone.

A feeling of euphoria **crept** over me as I realized that the months of anxious waiting were over.

One or two mistakes **crept** in towards the end because I was getting tired.

2 **to run away**
   to flee   [+hastily or abruptly] [+often out of fear]

EXAMPLES

After the revolution, many people were obliged to **flee** the country because of their political opinions.

I surprised an intruder who dropped the things he was in the act of stealing, leapt through the window and **fled**.

3 **to give**
   to donate   [+usu to some charitable, educational or religious cause]

EXAMPLES

When he retired he **donated** most of his large collection of books to the University library.

Everyone in the town is being asked to **donate** some money towards putting up a statue in memory of the last mayor.

4   **to close**
    to bang   [+noisily]

EXAMPLES

He left the room hastily, **banging** the door angrily behind him.
Patrick seems to be incapable of shutting a door without **banging**
it, but I suppose he just doesn't realize he's doing it.

5   **intermittent**   [+of sth that   [+stresses the pauses
                        repeatedly stops   and their irregularity]
                        and starts again]
    recurrent   [+stresses the fact that
                                         it comes back insistently]

EXAMPLES

Despite **intermittent** rain, we managed to complete the whole 25
mile walk.
An air service of a rather **intermittent** kind operates between the
island and the mainland.
My work programme has suffered a lot this winter from my
recurrent bouts of bronchitis.
An increasingly **recurrent** phenomenon in our society is that of
people who refuse to work not from laziness but because they
question the general principle of the necessity to work.

Exercises

1 Explain the meaning of the following:

1 custard   2 freak   3 junk food   4 apple pie   5 price tag
6 supermarket shopper   7 brick-hard arteries   8 trail of
devastation   9 degenerative conditions   10 yardstick of dietary
excellence   11 a fully-fledged dog-fight   12 look matted
13 ease the mind   14 go on a fast   15 have the time of one's life

2 What differences and/or similarities are there between the following pairs?

1 onset/beginning   2 snack/dinner   3 cream/milk   4 mongrel/
pedigree dog   5 spill/leak   6 close/bang   7 eat/gobble   8 flee/
leave   9 slice/cut   10 mince/chop   11 burst/break
12 intermittent/recurrent

3 When (or why) would you use the following?

1 dressing   2 mustard   3 saccharine   4 additives   5 bleach
6 an oven   7 a shredder   8 crockery   9 a dustbin

4 Explain the figurative senses of the following words:

1 chew   2 gnaw   3 acrid   4 bitter   5 tart   6 acid   7 crawl

5 Make compounds by combining words in list A with words in list B.

A: wood   meat   sugar   bread   cake   lamb   stock
B: cube   chip   crumb   chop

6 What kinds of things can you . . . ?

1 shred   2 pour   3 peel   4 drain   5 sprinkle over soup or salad   6 refrigerate   7 chop   8 bake   9 boil   10 freeze   11 mix   12 munch   13 chew   14 grate   15 cube   16 mince   17 sip   18 dice   19 toss   20 cast

7 Fill in the correct word from the list given.

burst   show   comment on   creep   baffle   gobble up   catch   opt   lurk   collapse   ooze   feed   hound

1 Many houses . . . . . during the earthquake.
2 The film star is . . . . . by pressmen and photographers every time she goes out.
3 I would rather . . . . . for the second solution.
4 He didn't want to . . . . . the affair.
5 Her reaction . . . . . me completely.
6 The differences started to . . . . .
7 Blood was . . . . . from the wound.
8 Do you breast- . . . . . your baby? No, I bottle- . . . . . him.
9 The dogs . . . . . silently into the kitchen.
10 The police . . . . . the thieves red-handed.
11 He was so hungry that he . . . . . the whole cake.
12 She . . . . into tears when she learned the truth.
13 The police . . . . . in the bushes that were growing by the side of the road.

8 What nouns can the following apply to? Under what circumstances?

1 mild   2 coarse   3 stale   4 spicy   5 piquant   6 bitter   7 slim   8 wholesome   9 hot (taste)   10 pungent   11 savoury   12 acid

9 Guess the right word.

1 Everyone in the club d . . . . . a little money towards the cost of an additional tennis court.
2 If childhood is the happiest period of one's life, then a . . . . . must be the most difficult so most of us are glad to reach twenty and pass into adulthood.
3 Though not pretty, her plump, ch . . . . . face made her look quite angelic.
4 She complained of pains in her a . . . . ., and sure enough it was found that she had appendicitis.
5 A d . . . . . of certain vitamins, notably vitamins B and C, will ultimately lead to illness.
6 The chef m . . . . . the meat in a machine.
7 After d . . . . . the water from the tank, they were able to repair the leaking valve.
8 Our society tends to label someone a f . . . . . as soon as he doesn't conform to the norm.
9 To clean itself, the cat l . . . . . itself from head to tail.
10 Because of the wet summer, the harvest was poor and there would be no s . . . . . for export.

10 In each case provide a few nouns or nominal expressions that can collocate with the following:

1 adequate   2 average   3 major   4 emotional   5 portly   6 persistent   7 acrid   8 poisonous   9 nasty   10 sugary   11 chronic   12 private   13 stout   14 recurrent   15 chubby   16 tart

11 What differences and/or similarities are there between the following pairs?

1 crawl/creep 2 give/donate 3 shred/grate 4 sip/swill 5 graze/crop 6 nibble/chew 7 guzzle/gorge 8 hunk/morsel 9 cube/slice 10 chubby/corpulent 11 tart/acrid 12 lurk/skulk

12 Fill in the following collocational grid:

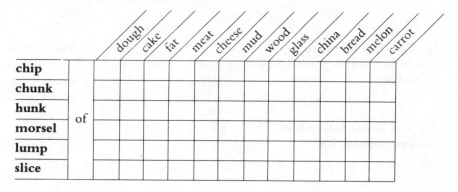

		dough	cake	fat	meat	cheese	mud	wood	glass	china	bread	melon	carrot
chip	of												
chunk													
hunk													
morsel													
lump													
slice													

13 Choose from the words in brackets the one which is most appropriate in each case and modify its form where necessary:

1 She . . . . . her head haughtily, not deigning to reply to the young man's cheeky remark. (throw, cast, toss, hurl)
2 You should always . . . . . a pinch of salt onto boiling potatoes. (sprinkle, strew, scatter)
3 The letter was . . . . . into tiny pieces and only then thrown into the fire. (mince, grate, chop, shred)
4 We . . . . . the cheese and sprinkled it over our spaghetti. (mince, grate, chop, dice)
5 He . . . . . up behind her, put his hands over her eyes, and told her to guess who it was. (slink, sneak, prowl)
6 We . . . . . along the side of the five-foot wall, heads and shoulders bent so that we wouldn't be seen on the other side. (creep, crawl, drag)
7 He . . . . . the door behind him, showing only too clearly his ill-temper. (shut, close, bang)
8 The . . . . . of senility comes when one no longer remembers people's names! (onset, outset, beginning)
9 There was nothing left of the new loaf except a few . . . . . which we gave to the birds. (chunk, hunk, piece, lump, crumb, chip)
10 The unfairness of the High Court's decision on the case provoked a public . . . . . . (outcry, protest, objection)

Revision Exercises

R1 What differences and/or similarities are there between the following pairs?

1 imitate/emulate 2 appease/pacify 3 pamper/mollycoddle 4 muffle/mute 5 twitter/hiss 6 roar/bellow 7 mutter/murmur 8 scoff/sneer 9 scrub/scour 10 shy/diffident

R2 Supply the missing prepositions.

1 to scoff . . . . . sb/sth 2 to placate sb . . . . . sth 3 to discourage sb . . . . . sth 4 to indulge . . . . . sth 5 to murmur . . . . . sb 6 to snarl . . . . . sb 7 to mumble . . . . . sth 8 to

forgive sb . . . . . sth   9 to dissuade sb . . . . . sth   10 to scrub . . . . . sth   11 to hiss . . . . . sb   12 to scrape . . . . . sth   13 to bellow . . . . . sb   14 to sneer   . . . . . sb/sth   15 to rifle . . . . . sth   16 to exonerate sb . . . . . sth   17 to deter sb . . . . . sth   18 to cling . . . . . sth

R3 In what sense are the following words positive or negative?

1 sprightly   2 brave   3 bureaucratic   4 tough   5 prompt   6 lethal   7 deplorable   8 inconsistent   9 serene   10 libel   11 foment   12 deft   13 vicious   14 embezzle   15 slander   16 modest   17 convict   18 slang   19 subversive   20 pious

R4 Fill in the following collocational grids.

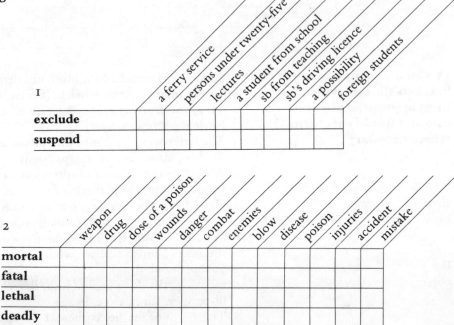

1	a ferry service	persons under twenty-five	lectures	a student from school	sb from teaching	sb's driving licence	a possibility	foreign students
exclude								
suspend								

2	weapon	drug	dose of a poison	wounds	danger	combat	enemies	blow	disease	poison	injuries	accident	mistake
mortal													
fatal													
lethal													
deadly													

R5 Group the following words into fields and place them on appropriate scales:

1 thin   2 touched   3 lean   4 obese   5 mad   6 plump   7 scrawny   8 slim   9 insane   10 skinny   11 portly   12 lanky   13 loony   14 stout   15 slender   16 crazy   17 fat   18 nuts   19 crackers   20 cranky   21 chubby   22 corpulent

R6 Describe the relationship between the words in the following groups, using a dictionary if necessary:

1 sea, puddle, pond, ocean, lake, river, brook, trickle
2 laugh, roar, giggle, smile, snicker, grin
3 browse, read, skim through, peruse
4 speak, shout, stutter, hem and haw, cry, bawl, curse, mutter, mumble, babble
5 territory, land, province, plot, state, zone, area, site
6 shove, push, pull
7 shrink, deplete, dwindle, diminish, decrease
8 salary, money, coins, cheques, deposit slips, banknotes, wages

R7 Choose from the sets of synonyms the word which is most appropriate in each case and modify its form where necessary.

1 The dog . . . . . a gentle warning. (growl, snarl, bark, howl)
2 If only we could . . . . . hold of her, we could pull her up from out of the deep hole! (take, seize, grab)
3 The clever mathematician . . . . . for an arts degree at University. (opt, select, choose)
4 She . . . . . the key quickly and quietly into the keyhole, and turned it. (glide, slide, skid)
5 The gun was certainly . . . . ., it was loaded, a bullet was in the breech and the safety catch was open. (mortal, lethal, fatal)
6 The inventor was congratulated, for it was a(n) . . . . . method of overcoming a problem that had bothered scientists for years. (clever, ingenious, skillful)
7 The blizzard that was blowing did not . . . . . her from joining the search party, as she was used to harsh weather. (divert, deter, dissuade)
8 The elderly man . . . . . down in his seat, trying to get his breath back after running for the bus. (fall, drop, slump)
9 The snake . . . . . and then . . . . . away into the tall grass. (twitter, hiss, bleat; lurk, sneak, slink)
10 The people sitting in front of me on the bus were . . . . . so loudly that I couldn't help overhearing their entire conversation. (mutter, blab, speak, bleat, bellow)

R8 What differences and/or similarities are there between the following pairs?

1 firm/adamant 2 ill/sick 3 gloomy/dismal 4 insane/deranged 5 diseased/unwholesome 6 lean/thin 7 pull/yank 8 twitch/jerk 9 accuse/charge 10 malign/defame 11 disseminate/propagate 12 decline/wane

R9 Fill in the following componential grids:

1

	search through another's property					take another's property			*or*
	in order to steal	in a rough manner	causing widespread damage	thoroughly	involves many participants	at times when social order is disturbed	by using violence or threats	by any other unjust means	on a large scale	esp food or valuables	from a building	search through roughly
ransack												
rifle												
rob												
plunder												
loot												
burgle												

2

	person guilty of some serious violation	of a crime punishable by death or imprisonment	person found guilty of a crime serving a prison sentence	person responsible for some wrong-doing — or	person or thing causing undesirable condition or situation	young person who commits crimes	often not for material gain but as a pastime
criminal							
felon							
convict							
culprit							
delinquent							

R10 Guess the right word.

1 The baby kept up its shr . . . . . for what seemed like hours.
2 He d . . . . . all traces of the love letters.
3 It is recommended to c . . . . . each mouthful some 35 times before swallowing it.
4 She often s . . . . . from severe headaches.
5 Army life demands s . . . . . adherence to rules.
6 We had to r . . . . . them entry, as they were under age.
7 The young girl gave out a suppressed g . . . . . that made her sound more like a frightened mouse.
8 After days of trekking the desert, we reached our g . . . . ., the pyramids of Egypt.
9 Grandmother is still very l . . . . . for her age.
10 She c . . . . . her hand while picking up the broken glass.
11 The old professor r . . . . . on about the history of the University.
12 The c . . . . . fox knew exactly which paths to take to shake off the pursuing hounds.
13 The p . . . . . for treason is death.
14 Even at the age of 92, his health was s . . . . . .
15 Unfortunately he overheard his boss saying that he wasn't very ef . . . . ., and now he's very upset.
16 The doctor emphasised the importance of p . . . . . exercises to each group of pregnant mothers at the clinic.

R11 Solve the crossword puzzle.

Across

1 claps (anagram) for 'hold tightly' (5)
4 very critical, of sth sb says (8)
6 gloomy, dark, depressing (6)
10 clever and quick movement, of the hands (4)
11 soften the sound of sth (4)
12 wait in hiding, unobserved (4)
13 draw (anagram) for 'room in a hospital' (4)
17 produce deep, short sounds, like a pig, to express dissatisfaction (5)
18 taste of sth which has too much salt in it (5)
20 small, deep crack or space in a wall or rock (7)
22 seen cob (anagram) for 'morally offensive' (7)
25 spread resources in the most effective way (6)

27 sudden dramatic increase, eg in crime (5)

28 give off or allow to leak, usu a liquid (4)

29 produce a high-pitched, feeble sound, like a lamb (5)

31 sprites (anagram) for 'continue' (7)

32 pull sharply, on a rope (4)

33 way of speaking, directly and rudely (7)

39 end of the sleeve of a jacket (4)

41 instances of breaking the law (11)

43 touchable, concrete (8)

44 contrary, negative, of comments or criticism (7)

46 thin, well-shaped, attractive (4)

49 complain, repeatedly, about unimportant things (7)

51 large or thick (5)

56 proof that one was elsewhere when a crime was committed (5)

57 trove (anagram) for 'obvious, direct' (5)

58 pretending to be modest or self-conscious (3)

59 part of a plane where the pilot sits (7)

61 Although she is 80, she is still very s . . . . . and active. (4)

62 I must complain to my neighbours about the noise they make, but I don't want to start a r . . . . . . (3)

64 sleepy, lacking in energy, unnaturally tired (9)

65 place a regular order for a magazine or journal (9)

66 crafty, often clever at persuading sb to do sth (4)

Down

2 heavily loaded (5)

3 cooking vessel (3)

4 drug which calms you (8)

5 pull, using a lot of effort (4)

7 mix with other similar things or with people (6)

8 crazy, mad, from 'lunatic' (*sl*) (5)

9 bustle (anagram) for 'hard to notice, not obvious' (6)

14 The concert was cancelled . . . . . to bad weather. (3)

15 Don't f . . . . . about every little detail! (4)

16 twist or turn the body or part of the body (7)

19 small piece of food (6)

21 very bouncy, aggressive, making an impact (10)

23 collection of items which have been stolen (5)

24 mad – connected with 3 down! (5)

26 an equal in age and social status (4)

30 tall and thin, esp with very long legs (5)

34 male (anagram) for 'having difficulty walking' (4)

35 write very badly and illegibly (6)

36 You didn't have to r . . . . . through everything to find what you wanted, you could have asked me where it was. (5)

37 pronounce that sb is not guilty of a crime for which he has been charged (6)

38 thin rope (4)

40 allow to cook in fat until burnt (7)

42 complete or absolute (5)

45 of the body, as distinguished from the mind (7)

47 A fight or argument between rival persons or groups is a . . . . . . (5)

48 move slightly, usu the body or part of the body (6)

50 eat by keeping in the mouth and licking (4)

52 pull sharply (on a rope) (4)

53 squeezed a small piece of skin between forefinger and thumb (7)

54 pear (anagram), for derive profit from (4)

55 stand unsteadily, almost falling over (6)

60 When the roads are slippery, cars may . . . . . . (4)

61 cry, noisily (3)

63 describes a smile which expresses dissatisfaction (3)

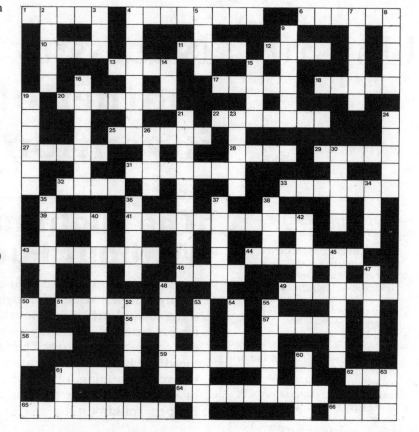

Unit 10 Necessity is the mother of invention

The Nightmare Life Without Fuel

Americans are so used to limitless energy supplies that they can hardly imagine what life might be like when the fuel really starts to **run out**[1]. So *Time* asked Science Writer Isaac Asimov for his vision of an energy-poor society that might exist at the end of the 20th century. The following portrait, Asimov noted, 'need not prove to be accurate. It is a picture of the worst, of **waste**[2] continuing, of oil running out, of nothing in its place, of world population continuing to rise. But then, that could happen, couldn't it?'

So it's 1997, and it's raining, and you'll have to walk to work again. The **subways**[3] are crowded, and any given train breaks down one morning out of five. The buses are gone, and on a day like today the bicycles **slosh**[4] and **slide**[5]. Besides, you have only a mile and a half to go, and you have **boots**[6], raincoat and rain hat. And it's not a very cold rain, so why not?

Lucky you have a job in **demolition**[7] too. It's **steady**[8] work. Slow and dirty, but steady. The **fading**[9] structures of a decaying city are the great mineral mines and **hardware**[10] shops of the nation. Break them down and re-use the parts. Coal is too difficult to dig up and transport to give us energy in the amounts we need, nuclear **fission**[11] is judged to be too dangerous, the technical **breakthrough**[12] toward nuclear **fusion**[13] that we hoped for never took place, and **solar batteries**[14] are too expensive to maintain on the earth's surface in sufficient quantity.

Anyone older than ten can remember **automobiles**[15]. They **dwindled**[16]. At first the price of **gasoline**[17] climbed – way up. Finally only the **well-to-do**[18] drove, and that was too clear an indication that they were **filthy**[19] rich, so any automobile that dared show itself on a city street was overturned and burned. **Rationing**[20] was introduced to 'equalize sacrifice', but every three months the ration was reduced. The cars just vanished and became part of the metal resource.

There are many advantages, if you want to look for them. Our 1997 newspapers continually **point** them **out**[21]. The air is cleaner and there seem to be fewer colds. Against most predictions, the crime rate has dropped. With the police car too expensive (and too easy a **target**[22]), policemen are back on their **beats**[23]. More important, the streets are full. Legs are king in the cities of 1997, and people walk everywhere far into the night. Even the parks are full, and there is mutual protection in crowds.

If the weather isn't too cold, people sit out front. If it is hot, the open air is the only air conditioning they get. And at least the street lights still burn. Indoors, electricity is **scarce**[24], and few people can **afford**[25] to keep lights burning after supper. . . .

Energy continues to decline, and machines must be replaced by human muscle and beasts of burden. People are working longer hours and there is less leisure; but then, with electric lighting restricted, television for only three hours a night, movies three evenings a week, new books few and printed in small editions, what is there to do with leisure? Work, sleep and eating are the great **trinity**[26] of 1997, and only the first two are guaranteed.

Where will it end? It must end in a return to the days before 1800, to the days before the **fossil fuels**[27] **powered**[28] a vast machine industry and technology. . . .

And what can we do to prevent all this now?

Now? Almost nothing.

If we had started 20 years ago, that might have been another matter. If we had only started 50 years ago, it would have been easy.

Time

Make it quick

An Edinburgh **locksmith**[1] has a lot of customers these days for telephone **padlocks**[2]. Usually he sells them to landladies.

But more and more mothers of teen-agers are buying them.

With phone charges up, they're making sure their sons and daughters won't run up **huge**[3] bills, chatting to their **pals**[4]!

The Sunday Post

MAKE IT QUICK

1 one who makes and repairs locks
2 a small movable lock (means by which something may be fastened and which needs a key to work it)
3 very large, enormous, immense
4 *coll* friends

Only one snag . . .

A *Sunday Post* man's been doing his best to obey the Government's **plea**[1] to save energy.

His latest electricity bill showed that, compared to the same quarter last year, he'd used 1000 units less.

Well done, he thought. Only one **snag**[2]. The bill was £4 more.

Can't win, can you?

The Sunday Post

ONLY ONE SNAG

1 appeal
2 *informal* unexpected difficulty or obstacle

Solar Energy[1], the Ult

The heat of the universe is produced by the sun.   **Leonardo da Vinci**

Since the legendary **Prometheus**[2] first stole the fire of heaven, **virtually**[3] all energy consumed by man has been **fathered**[4] by the sun. Coal, oil, and gas are **residues**[5] of plants and animals once fired to life by the warm rays of our nearest star. Solar heat also drives the earth's rain cycle, powering modern **hydroelectric**[6] **generators**[7]. Windmills that pump water or produce electricity turn because of solar-heated currents of air.

Even the wood with which I **stoke**[8] my fireplace is a form of solar energy. Like oil and coal, wood is merely solar power captured in convenient packaging.

But the earth is fast running out of these precious reserves of 'stored sunshine'. At our current pace, we will consume in the next 25 years alone an amount equal to *all* the energy used by man in recorded history. If such consumption continues, obviously **alternative**[9] sources must be found. And the majority of experts with whom I have talked agree that **mankind**[10] must look to the sun to help solve our energy needs.

Sun's Energy Is Boundless

'The solar energy that falls upon the Arabian Peninsula in one year is greater than twice the oil reserves of this entire **globe**[11],' declares Dr George C Szego of InterTechnology Corporation in Warrenton, Virginia. **Put another way**[12], the sunshine falling onto Connecticut **roughly**[13] equals the total energy used in all 50 states of the US.

Already the sun's energy is being put to limited use in homes and buildings around the world. The most common examples are rooftop solar **heaters**[14] that provide cheap hot water for washing and bathing. Estimates vary, but certainly more than a million of these simple heaters are now in use world-wide.

In the United States alone, more than 200 houses and buildings are, or soon will be, partially heated (and some partially cooled) by solar energy. Solar-heated government buildings and schools are being built in half a dozen states; sun-heated **condominiums**[15] are going up in Vermont and Colorado.

During the winter in Florida, I tested one of the several thousand solar-heated swimming pools in this country. Even though a **chill**[16] **norther**[17] was **rattling**[18] the palms, the water was warm. Electric heating for the same pool would be **prohibitive**[19] in cost.

SOLAR ENERGY

1 energy produced by the sun
2 character from Greek mythology
3 practically, almost
4 produced
5 that which remains after a part has been removed, destroyed, etc
6 of electric energy made from water-power or steam
7 a machine for generating or producing energy
8 put fuel on a fire
9 other, different
10 humanity
11 earth
12 in other words
13 approximately
14 something which creates artificial heat
15 an apartment building in which the units are owned separately by individuals and not by a corporation or cooperative; also, a flat in such a building
16 unpleasantly cool
17 *Am* for north wind, *Br* northerly
18 causing a movement which produces short, sharp sounds
19 of a size which prevents a project from being carried out – usu of cost or time
20 noisy
21 things that float on water to show where ships may go with safety
22 the whole apparatus for extracting oil from the earth
23 *Am* place where a road crosses a railway line, *Br* level crossing
24 *Am* way encircling a city, *Br* ring road
25 flown, gone up very fast into the sky
26 material for lining roofs
27 fastened with small nails
28 connected with a device to make an electric connection
29 circling in space around a planet
30 insects with four brightly coloured wings
31 doing something at the same speed as something else
32 a million watts
33 exaggerated, improbable

ate Powerhouse By JOHN L WILHELM

A solar heated house in California.

Today the sun's **roaring**[20] hydrogen-fueled furnace powers educational-television sets in Africa, offshore Coast Guard **buoys**[21], and navigation lights on Gulf of Mexico **oil rigs**[22]. Even the crucial warning bell and lights of a Georgia **railroad crossing**[23] rely on the sun to power them. So do emergency call boxes on the Washington, DC, **beltway**[24]. And nearly every spacecraft that has ever **rocketed**[25] skyward has depended on purple-blue panels of solar cells.

Time to Switch on the Sun

The day may arrive when solar cells are delivered to a house like rolls of **roofing paper**[26], **tacked**[27] on, and **plugged**[28] into the wiring, making the home its own power station.

The imaginative brain of energy expert, Peter Glaser, has conceived what he considers the ultimate solution to the world's energy needs – a solar power station **orbiting**[29] in space.

At his Cambridge, Massachusetts, office, Dr Glaser showed me a design for such futuristic satellites. They look like gigantic **butterflies**[30], with solar-panel wings 6 by $7\frac{1}{2}$ miles in size. A single one of these power stations in **synchronous**[31] orbit 22,300 miles above earth might provide as much as 5,000 **megawatts**[32], half the present capacity of New York City's generating plants.

Farfetched?[33] Perhaps not, if we learn to switch on more of the sunshine that warms us all.

National Geographic

WAR ON WASTE

1 strong, tough
2 waste material, rubbish
3 non-metric weight used in GB (1016.048 kg)

SOBERING THOUGHTS

1 making one become serious
2 reprocessed to be used again
3 an alcoholic drink made in France
4 short in comparison to its width
5 shelf over a fireplace

Underground architecture
What lies ahead may be beneath us by Roy Mason

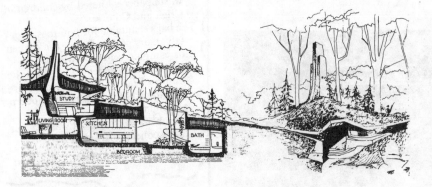

Drawing by Malcolm Wells

Concrete house designed by author Malcolm Wells is covered with earth and plants to simulate nature. The sunken court (between kitchen and bath) allows sunlight to flow in.

Some architects and engineers believe that in the future more buildings will be built under the earth. Underground buildings have many advantages over surface structures, including an unusual ability to conserve energy.

'I don't want to be a **mole**[1]!'

That is a typical response to the idea that houses, offices, and factories be built underground to ease the increasing **congestion**[2] of the earth's surface areas. Nonetheless, an innovative architectural movement is now **focusing**[3] on structures that lie partially or fully beneath the surface of the earth.

Underground structures (sometimes called geotectures or terratectures) are, of course, nothing new. Prehistoric people lived in caves (as many people still do). Ancient Egypt had temples in caves. Early Christians held services in the **catacombs**[4] of Rome. More recently, the US Pavilion at the 1970 World's Fair in Osaka, Japan, was a circular **earth mound**[5] covered by an **inflatable**[6] **membrane**[7].

St Louis University now has underground classroom facilities. The University of Texas at Austin has placed its computer center and administrative offices under **terraced**[8] **malls**[9]. At the University of Illinois campus at Urbana, Illinois, a two-story, 98,000-square-foot library has been constructed underground. The Mormon Church in Salt Lake City has **entrusted**[10] its valuable documents to underground **vaults**[11], and 700 New York corporations have placed their essential records in a vault beneath Iron Mountain, 100 miles north of the city.

The city of Montreal has a delightful system of attractive underground shops, offices, restaurants, cinemas, and pedestrian walkways, all of which are safely away from the Canadian weather. Life functions normally during the worst **blizzards**[12].

ADVANTAGES OF BUILDING UNDERGROUND

There are good reasons why organizations often choose to go underground.

The constant temperature of the underground creates the

UNDERGROUND
ARCHITECTURE

1 a small animal with thick, dark, velvet-like fur that lives underground most of the time
2 overcrowding
3 concentrating

4 underground passages with shelves on the sides used for burying the dead in ancient Rome
5 a bank or heap of earth and stones
6 that can be filled with air or gas so that it swells out
7 a soft, thin, skin-like covering
8 built up in the form of a terrace or

terraces (level spaces above and beside each other, often cut into the side of a hill or slope)
9 *Am* covered streets; *Br* no exact equivalent, but *precinct* or *centre* may be used for specially constructed shopping area
10 given into the care of

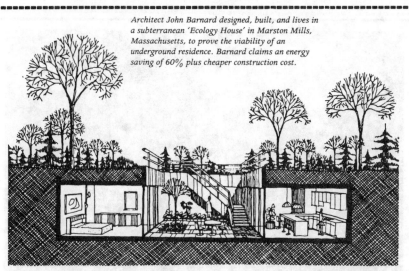

Architect John Barnard designed, built, and lives in a subterranean 'Ecology House' in Marston Mills, Massachusetts, to prove the viability of an underground residence. Barnard claims an energy saving of 60% plus cheaper construction cost.

Drawing by John Barnard

condition for dramatic savings in fuel cost. At Sampum, Pennsylvania, and elsewhere, laboratories have been built underground to benefit from the almost constant temperature of 54 degrees Fahrenheit (12.2 degrees Celsius) underground.

Neither snow nor rain nor sleet[13] nor blazing[14] sun can touch an underground building; thus its exterior is largely maintenance free. Pipes won't freeze nor customers slip, fall, and sue[15]. No roofs need replacing. And since the danger from external fire is minimal, insurance rates drop.

The efficient use of energy for both heating and cooling in underground buildings is, of course, one of the reasons they are attracting more attention today. Day or night, summer or winter, from the frigid[16] north to the tropics, all that an underground building requires is enough energy to raise the temperature from the constant, 54 degrees temperature in the ground, to perhaps 72 degrees. (Compare that to the average temperature increase required for a building in a northern city in winter or buildings anywhere in the summer.) Furthermore, the earth surrounding an underground structure tends to keep the same temperature for a considerable length of time so that alternative heating and cooling systems are not necessary, because, if the heating system breaks down[17], the building normally will retain adequate heat until the equipment is repaired.

Underground architecture is also very gentle on the environment. Space above ground is conserved, an especially important consideration in urban areas. Unsightly[18] surface buildings can be razed[19] and open areas created where none previously existed.

Contrary to popular fears of living in enclosed space without natural sunlight, experiments indicate that the physical and psychological effects of living and working underground are positive. After 10 years of studying the underground Abo Elementary School[20], a combined school and fall-out shelter[21] in Artesia, New Mexico, a panel of physicians concluded that the school was not detrimental[22] to the physical and mental health of its students, but actually beneficial to some. Nine out of ten of the citizens surveyed concerning Abo believed that other schools should be like Abo.

For dedicated sun-lovers, architects have many techniques for bringing the sun into underground buildings. These include skylights[23], lightwells[24], and open courtyards. In addition, some architects opt for having an open side for their underground dwellings. Rapid advances in illumination technology should also allay[25] fears of dark and gloomy[26] areas.

The Futurist

11 underground rooms or cellars
12 severe snowstorms with violent wind
13 partly frozen rain
14 shining brightly
15 take legal action, make a claim in a court of law
16 very cold and frozen
17 fails to act, becomes useless, stops working
18 displeasing to the sight
19 destroyed utterly, made level with the ground
20 *Br* primary school
21 a place protecting people from the radioactive material resulting from the explosion of an atomic or thermonuclear bomb
22 harmful
23 windows in the roof or ceiling
24 hole in the ground to permit light to descend
25 make less, quieten
26 dark, unlighted

Plant your first tree this spring

M C GOLDMAN

When nature landscaped the earth, her design was **lavish**[1] in trees. Every imaginable tree sprang up in every part of the globe, to serve and protect, to feed and shelter and beautify. Nowadays, greenery is routinely bulldozed as developments, parking lots, shopping centers and acres of **criss-crossing**[2] highways take over the world's architecture.

Yet it need not remain lost, the wonder of trees. Your own yard can **harbor**[3] the delights they bring – the unique **fragrance**[4] of balsam, the **blaze**[5] of maples in autumn, the **crackle**[6] and flavor of a just-picked apple.

Planting a tree on the village green.

And besides the gifts we readily see and taste, there are those you need to **ponder**[7] more deeply: the effective way trees help fight for cleaner air, **filtering**[8] dirt, providing oxygen and cooling the environment like some great free outdoor **air-conditioner**[9]: the way they soften both storms and noise, bringing **shade**[10] and privacy; the way they house birds and wildlife, creating a natural surrounding that's cheerful as well as balanced.

Organic Gardening and Farming

PLANT YOUR FIRST TREE THIS SPRING

1 generous, abundant
2 which cross each other several times (of roads, lines, etc)
3 give lodging or shelter to
4 perfume
5 bright flame
6 small, cracking sounds one after the other
7 consider, think over
8 allow some parts to flow through and stop others
9 machine which artificially cools the air in a building
10 comparative darkness, a place sheltered from the sun

Discussion

1 Do you think Isaac Asimov's predictions for the future are likely to come true? Give your reasons.
2 If you find his predictions believable, describe the action we should take now to make sure of a better future.
3 If you could make four new laws designed to improve or protect the environment, what would they be, and why?
4 How would you feel about living in an underground house?
5 Describe the ideal house you would design and build if you could. What would be the factors you would take into consideration in arriving at your design?
6 Argue for or against the following statements, 'None of us will be around in the year 2100, so we don't care what effect our present actions have on the future.'
'Man has all the resources of the earth at his disposal, and has the right to use them in any way he chooses.'

Word Study

A Semantic Fields

1 Things we throw away or reject

	objects — or substances	of no further use or value	to be, or having already been, thrown away or disposed of	often the result of a process esp industrial
rubbish	+	+	+	+	
refuse	+	+	+	+	
waste		+	+	+	+

Rubbish and **refuse** differ only in that the use of **refuse** is confined to official contexts (eg by authorities responsible for refuse disposal). In general conversation, **rubbish** is almost always used. always used.

EXAMPLES

rubbish   Is this pile of papers all **rubbish** or do you want to sort through it and keep some things?
I don't know what to do with all this **rubbish** because all the dustbins are full.

refuse   **Refuse** disposal has now become the exclusive responsibility of the town council, and householders are therefore asked to place their **refuse** in the plastic sacks provided free.

waste   A great proportion of so-called **waste** is in fact valuable recyclable material.
Waste from nuclear reactors poses a great problem because it continues to be radioactive for so long.

Rubbish is often used figuratively in the sense of [+nonsense].

EXAMPLE

Seldom have I heard a speaker pack so much **rubbish** into a one-hour lecture and actually fool most of his audience into believing he was talking sense.

2 Bringing relief

	calm — or reduce	worry, discomfort or pain	temporarily	without curing the source of the trouble	desire or want
relieve		+	+		
alleviate		+	+	+	+
allay	+	+		+	
assuage		+			+

Alleviate and **assuage** are not common in colloquial speech.
Relieve is common in the passive.
EXAMPLE
We were **relieved** to hear that he had arrived safely in spite of the storms he encountered.

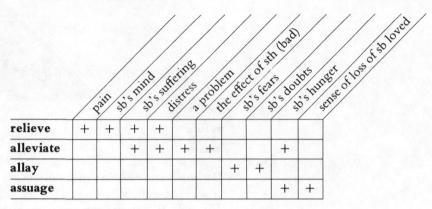

	pain	sb's mind	sb's suffering	distress	a problem	the effect of sth (bad)	sb's fears	sb's doubts	sb's hunger	sense of loss of sb loved
relieve	+	+	+	+						
alleviate			+	+	+	+			+	
allay							+	+		
assuage									+	+

3 Giving or getting protection

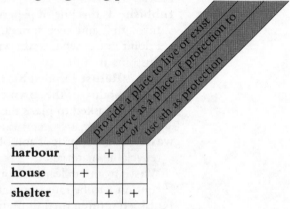

	provide a place to live or exist	serve as a place of protection to	or use sth as protection
harbour		+	
house	+		
shelter		+	+

All three verbs are transitive and **shelter** is also intransitive.
EXAMPLES
harbour   It is a crime to **harbour** someone you know to be in trouble with the law.
Even a minute crack in a piece of china may **harbour** thousands of bacteria.
house   Unfortunately it is impossible to **house** any more students in this residence.
The art gallery is now **housed** in a converted grain store beside the river.
shelter   We **sheltered** in a cave until the rain storm was over.
A row of trees **shelters** the house from the cold east wind.

Figuratively, **harbour** means [+hold in the mind].
EXAMPLE
It is hardly surprising that he **harbours** a lot of resentment for the man who caused him to lose his job.

4 Destroying

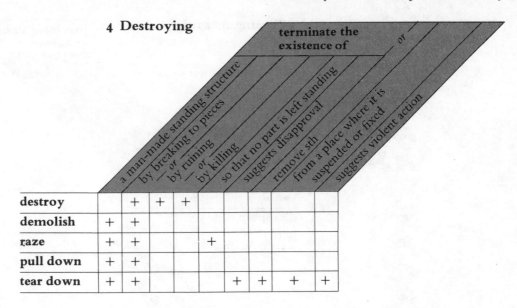

	a man-made standing structure	by breaking to pieces *or*	by ruining *or*	by killing	terminate the existence of — so that no part is left standing	suggests disapproval	remove sth	from a place where it is suspended or fixed *or*	suggests violent action
destroy		+	+	+					
demolish	+	+							
raze	+	+			+				
pull down	+	+							
tear down	+	+				+	+	+	+

Demolish and **pull down** are synonyms, except that only **demolish** may be used figuratively. **Pull down** and **tear down** are less usual in formal writing. **Destroy, demolish** and **raze** often appear in passive constructions.

EXAMPLES

The horse which broke its neck in a fall had to be **destroyed**.

Many beautiful buildings have been **demolished** recently to make way for new development.

Whole villages have been **razed** to the ground.

	the contents of a house	an animal	notices	posters	a painting	a wall	a building	a house	a street	a town	sb's arguments	sb's hopes	sb's ambitions
destroy	+	+	+	+	+					+	+	+	+
demolish					+	+	+	+		+			
raze						+	+	+	+				
pull down					+	+	+	+					
tear down			+	+	+	+	+	+					

5 Passing from sight

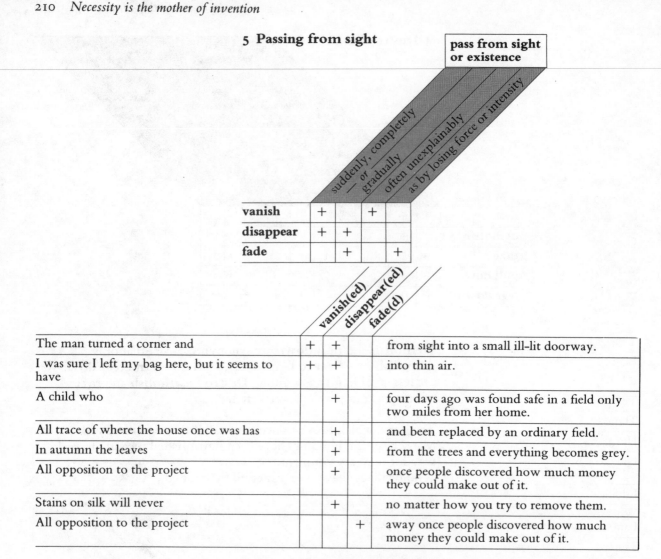

pass from sight or existence

	suddenly, completely — *or* — gradually		often unexplainably	as by losing force or intensity
vanish	+		+	
disappear	+	+		
fade		+		+

	vanish(ed)	disappear(ed)	fade(d)	
The man turned a corner and	+	+		from sight into a small ill-lit doorway.
I was sure I left my bag here, but it seems to have	+	+		into thin air.
A child who		+		four days ago was found safe in a field only two miles from her home.
All trace of where the house once was has		+		and been replaced by an ordinary field.
In autumn the leaves		+		from the trees and everything becomes grey.
All opposition to the project		+		once people discovered how much money they could make out of it.
Stains on silk will never		+		no matter how you try to remove them.
All opposition to the project			+	away once people discovered how much money they could make out of it.

6 Losing strength or freshness

	lose freshness — *or* — lose strength or vitality	*usu* of plants		cause to lose strength	*usu* of lights and colours	become wrinkled	diminish in size	*usu* from lack of moisture	because of exterior limitation of action — *or* — because of unfulfilled desire	cease to stand erect or straight
fade		+	+		+	+				
wilt	+		+					+		
wither		+	+					+		
shrivel					+	+	+			
languish		+							+	+
droop	+	+	+							+

All the verbs are intransitive, and **fade**, **wither** and **droop** are also transitive. When transitive, **wither** has only the figurative sense of [+cause to feel ashamed or confused] and **fade** requires a [+light] or [+colour] object.

Notice that the verbs which do not refer, in their literal sense, to human beings, may be extended to do so while retaining the same meaning.

	fade(d)	wilt(ed)	wither(ed)	shrivel(led)	languish(ed)(ing)	droop(ed)(ing)	
Coloured cotton tends to	+						if exposed to bright sunlight.
Could you	+						the lights down to suggest nightfall?
Cut flowers	+	+				+	very quickly in hot weather.
This heat really does make me		+					
The leaves have all			+				because of lack of water.
These plants have			+				from lack of water.
Peregrine started to protest but I just			+				him with a look and he shut up.
If I don't eat something soon I shall			+				away from lack of food!
The apples are all				+			up and dry.
These plants have				+			up from lack of water.
Her skin was				+			and brown like a walnut.
He					+		in exile from his homeland for 5 long years.
I think she is really					+		for her family and her home.
While you are out enjoying yourselves, I am					+		in my room, trying to complete this book.
The shoulders of the exhausted man						+	as he trudged off to meet his fate.

7 Giving or producing freely

	giving easily and readily	or given easily and readily	or unselfish	large, plentiful	suggests excess	producing abundant moist green foliage	stresses quantity	stresses richness
lavish	+	+		+	+			
generous	+	+	+	+				
profuse				+		+		
luxuriant						+	+	
lush						+		+

When used predicatively, **lavish**, **generous** and **profuse** collocate with the preposition **in**; **generous** can also be followed by **with**.

EXAMPLES

The professor is not known for being **lavish** in his praise of his students.

The company has been very **generous** in financing my research degree in control theory.

It's easy to be **generous** with someone else's money.

He was **profuse** in his use of difficult technical words.

	expenditure	furnishings	gesture	gift	helping of icecream	person	action	behaviour	nature	apologies	thanks	tears	vegetation	growth of vegetation	foliage	ripe fruit	green grass
lavish	+	+	+	+	+												
generous			+	+	+	+	+	+									
profuse	(+)								+	+	+	+					
luxuriant													+	+	+		
lush													+	+	+	+	+

8 Occurring widely

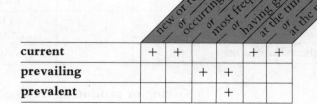

	new or recent	occurring widely	most frequently occurring	having gained wide acceptance at the time specified	at the present time
current	+	+			+	+
prevailing			+	+		
prevalent				+		

EXAMPLES

current I try to keep up with **current** affairs by reading the papers.

In the 19th century it was **current** practice for children to begin work at the age of 9 or 10.

The **current** issue of *Language* has a very good article on lexical analysis.

His **current** preoccupation seems to be finding a girlfriend.

prevailing The **prevailing** wind is from the north.

The **prevailing** current of opinion seems to be against tax reform.

prevalent The idea that stealing from the State is not wrong is very **prevalent** these days.

A very **prevalent** attitude is one of caring only for oneself.

B Synonymous Pairs

1 **smell**
   fragrance | [+always sweet, pleasant]

Note that **smell** may also be used for [+sweet, pleasant].
Fragrance is the more literary term.
EXAMPLES
The garden was fresh with the **fragrance** of spring flowers.
There is no more beautiful **fragrance** than that of the rose.

2 **to think**
   to ponder | [+deeply] [+consider carefully]

Ponder often co-occurs with **over**.
EXAMPLES
It has not been an easy decision to reach, and I **pondered** a long
time before being able to make it.
He sat alone, **pondering** over his recent strange experiences.

3 **advantageous**
   beneficial { [+helping] } [+towards a specific goal]
                                 or [+having a good effect]

Both adjectives can be used attributively and predicatively.
When predicative, they collocate with the preposition **to**.
EXAMPLES
Taking brewer's yeast regularly can be **beneficial** to one's health.
A knowledge of Latin would be **advantageous** to you if you wish
to study medicine.

	move	deal	association	visit	effect	course of treatment
advantageous	+	+	+	+		
beneficial	(+)	+	+	+	+	

4 **valuable**
   precious | [+very expensive] or [+much loved]

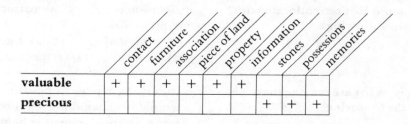

	contact	furniture	association	piece of land	property	information	stones	possessions	memories
valuable	+	+	+	+	+	+			
precious							+	+	+

Exercises

1 Find words to fit the following definitions/descriptions:

1 one who makes and repairs locks
2 underground passages with shelves on the sides used for burying the dead in ancient Rome
3 a small movable lock with a bow-shaped link to be passed through a staple, chain or eye
4 a small animal with thick, dark, velvet-like fur that lives underground most of the time
5 a hut, shed, protection built to keep off wind and rain
6 a structure with revolving sails used to pump water or to grind cereals, actioned by wind
7 a large natural hollow place in the side of a cliff or a hollow in which people used to live in prehistoric times
8 unroofed space with walls and/or buildings round it
9 of a size which prevents a project from being carried out – usually of cost or time
10 that which remains after a part has been removed, destroyed, etc

2 Explain the meaning of each of the following:

1 skyrocketing prices   2 power station   3 rooftop solar heaters
4 level crossing   5 an acre of land   6 criss-crossing highways
7 surface structures   8 power generators   9 shopping centre
10 industrial plant   11 hardware shop   12 ring road
13 condominium   14 vault

3 Fill in the blanks with appropriate words from the list given.

break down   stoke up   rocket   issue   overturn   allay   run out
design   capture   drop

1 His firm stand . . . . . all fears.
2 The Post Office . . . . . a new series of stamps.
3 Who has . . . . . your house?
4 Telephone charges have . . . . . by two cents.
5 Is that big mirror up there supposed to . . . . . solar energy?
6 A bunch of hooligans . . . . . all the cars in the street.
7 John, could you . . . . . the fire?
8 There won't be any cake today, because I've . . . . . of flour.
9 She had been under severe strain and finally . . . . ..
10 The spacecraft . . . . . to the moon.

4 In each case provide a few nouns that can collocate with the following:

1 (a) fading . . .   2 (an) advantageous . . .   3 (a) gigantic . . .
4 (an) offshore . . .   5 (a) balanced . . .   6 (a) current . . .
7 (a) prehistoric . . .   8 (an) inflatable . . .   9 (a) boundless . . .
10 (a) beneficial . . .   11 (a) legendary . . .   12 (a) scarce . . .
13 (a) chilly . . .   14 (a) dedicated . . .

5 What use can one make of the following?

1 a battery   2 a beast of burden   3 an air conditioner
4 a temple   5 a windmill   6 a buoy   7 a spacecraft   8 an oil rig
9 a furnace   10 a navigation light

6 Describe the differences and/or similarities between:

1 shade/shadow   2 storm/blizzard   3 waste/rubbish   4 precious/costly   5 coal/oil/gas   6 highway/motorway   7 wildlife/livestock   8 ponder/think   9 sleet/snow/hail   10 chat/speak to   11 wiring/wire   12 fossil/stone

7 Fill in the following collocational grids:

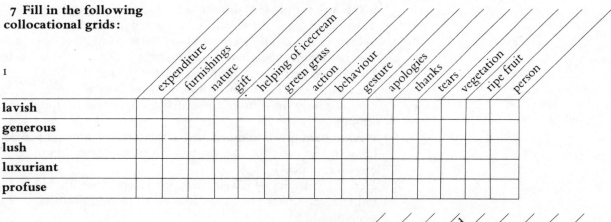

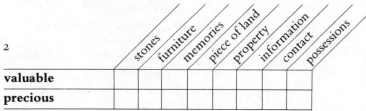

8 What kinds of things can you:

1 overturn?   2 set ablaze?   3 bulldoze?   4 relieve?   5 alleviate?   6 destroy?   7 surround (with a fence)?   8 raze?   9 plug in?   10 win?   11 fade?   12 allay?   13 gather?   14 entrust to sb?

9 Guess the right word.

1 The story is so far . . . . . that no-one will believe it, even though it is in fact the whole truth.

2 The book covers were all f . . . . . from lying in the sun for months on end.

3 Although sun filled the room, the atmosphere was nevertheless g . . . . . .

4 The huge bonfire b . . . . . against the night sky.

5 The f . . . . . we found in the garden convinced us that thousands of years ago this region had been below sea-level.

6 She asked for her wrap, for the late summer's evening had turned c . . . . ., and she didn't want to catch a cold.

7 The r . . . . . left in the test-tubes after evaporation completely baffled the scientists.

8 We were on the point of executing our plans when we realised there was a s . . . . . which made this impossible.

10 What differences and/or similarities are there between the following pairs?

1 alleviate/assuage   2 vanish/disappear   3 wilt/wither   4 ponder/think   5 shrivel/languish   6 languish/droop   7 luxuriant/lush   8 prevailing/prevalent   9 generous/profuse   10 fragrance/smell

11 Choose the word which is most appropriate in each case. Modify its form where necessary.

1 There was nothing we could do to . . . . . her hurt feelings. (relieve, alleviate, allay)
2 I gave the thief a long, ..., searching look. (even, steady, regular, stable)
3 The oldest and most attractive part of the town was . . . . . to make way for modern office blocks. (destroy, raze, demolish)
4 The doctor . . . . . the patient's fears when he told her that an operation was not necessary. (relieve, allay, assuage)
5 The fire that had begun during the night had . . . . . the house to the ground by the next morning. (destroy, raze, demolish)
6 He was a . . . . . little man, whose stomach bore all too conspicuously the signs of too much drinking. (stout, tough, strong)
7 Having been given so much advice by so many different people, he went away to . . . . . on the best course of action. (think, consider, ponder)
8 Her . . . . . display of jewelry was not a sign of wealth, but rather a sign of her pretention to wealth! (lavish, profuse, generous, lush)
9 The fire in the grate had . . . . . down to a few glowing embers. (dwindle, diminish, decrease)
10 The only . . . . . about leaving right now is that it's started to rain. (difficulty, obstacle, snag)

Revision Exercises

R1 Explain the meaning of each of the following:

1 yearly turnover   2 (un)processed produce   3 be on a diet   4 be on the beat   5 dramatic comeback   6 bare one's teeth   7 surplus fruit   8 open a bank account   9 on an empty stomach   10 a mad rush for the door   11 lunch-time customers   12 windshield

R2 Fill in the following componential grid.

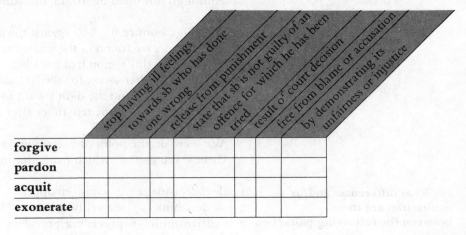

	stop having ill feelings towards sb who has done one wrong	release from punishment	state that sb is not guilty of an offence for which he has been tried	result of court decision	free from blame or accusation by demonstrating its unfairness or injustice
forgive					
pardon					
acquit					
exonerate					

R3 Explain the figurative senses of each of the following words:

1 stagger 2 slide 3 chew 4 scrub (*coll*) 5 deadly 6 gnaw 7 rubbish 8 scour (*coll*) 9 snarl 10 stumble 11 dismal 12 hurl 13 harbour 14 wither

R4 In each case provide a few nouns or nominal expressions which can collocate with the following verbs:

1 assassinate 2 ransack 3 divert 4 suspend 5 loot 6 disrupt 7 slaughter 8 concede 9 exterminate 10 rob 11 deaden 12 donate

R5 Which prepositions can be used with the following verbs?

1 to sip . . . sth 2 to feed . . . sth 3 to hurl sth . . ./. . ./. . . sth/sb 4 to slink . . ./. . ./. . . 5 to be generous . . . doing sth 6 to ponder . . . sth 7 to swig . . . sth 8 to chop . . ./. . . sth 9 to fling sth . . ./. . ./. . . sth/sb 10 to be profuse . . . sth 11 to prowl . . ./. . ./. . . sth 12 to be beneficial . . . sb/sth

R6 What differences and/or similarities are there between the following pairs?

1 ransack/loot 2 mete out/give 3 suspend/exclude 4 embezzle/steal 5 fall/slump 6 exterminate/slaughter 7 dissuade/divert 8 hood/cap 9 thug/criminal 10 probation/parole 11 perennial/annual 12 disparate/different

R7 Which words are derivationally related to the following?

1 demolish 2 cross 3 imagine, imagination 4 suspend 5 anxious 6 green 7 fragrant 8 prohibit 9 deplore 10 add 11 deficient 12 inflate

R8 Guess the right word.

1 The package was too large and b . . . . . to carry.
2 The mincing machine s . . . . . the meat into long, thin strips.
3 Because her grandmother could only swallow light food, the girl g . . . . . an apple for her.
4 The little dog c . . . . . quietly into its basket, for its coat was wet and it had dripped water over the carpet.
5 The c . . . . . she'd put on the window sill were soon eaten by the birds.
6 When the people heard of the new taxes to be imposed, there was a general o . . . . . throughout the country.
7 I didn't c . . . . . what he said.
8 It's impossible to co . . . . . the complete theory if you've not studied the basic essentials.
9 The old manuscript lay h . . . . . behind the bookshelves.
10 The brooch was a poor imitation of the g . . . . . article.
11 The committee as . . . . . its right to veto any new expenditure.
12 Alcohol reduced this great man to the infantile activity of c . . . . . around on hands and knees.
13 In the olden days, e . . . . . people were automatically treated with respect.
14 Seeing that they had little money left, he g . . . . . ly offered to pay for their meal.
15 That little carved wooden box is more p . . . . . to me than all the silver in the house.

R9 Give as many words as you can whose meaning includes the general terms listed.

EXAMPLE: **dirty**: *filthy, grubby, grimy, squalid, foul*
1 strike   2 bite   3 kill   4 talk (informally)   5 soothe/calm
6 drink   7 throw   8 eat   9 fat   10 not fat

R10 What differences and/or similarities are there between the following pairs?

1 stout/portly   2 savoury/pungent   3 slink/sneak   4 mince/dice
5 drink/swig   6 munch/gnaw   7 run away/flee   8 chip/chop
9 lump/crumb   10 trick/hoax

R11 Fill in the following collocational grids:

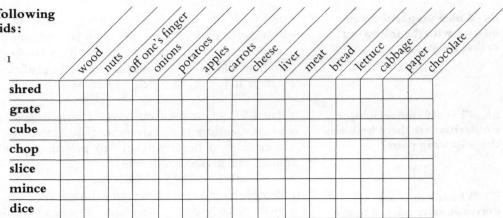

1

	wood	nuts	off one's finger	onions	potatoes	apples	carrots	cheese	liver	meat	bread	lettuce	cabbage	paper	chocolate
shred															
grate															
cube															
chop															
slice															
mince															
dice															

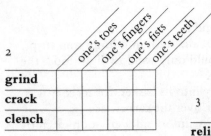

2

	one's toes	one's fingers	one's fists	one's teeth
grind				
crack				
clench				

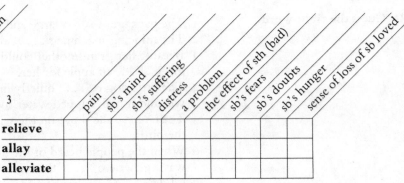

3

	pain	sb's mind	sb's suffering	distress	a problem	the effect of sth (bad)	sb's fears	sb's doubts	sb's hunger	sense of loss of sb loved
relieve										
allay										
alleviate										

R12 Which of the given words have the feature [+violent] included in some of their senses; which have the feature [+sharply], which [+excessive(ly)], and which [+quick or rapid]? Notice that not all of the words are relevant.

1 heave   2 slap   3 blab   4 chatter   5 (to) wolf   6 slide
7 lavish   8 eat   9 sip   10 gobble   11 slip   12 swig   13 toss
14 wriggle   15 babble   16 rob   17 fling   18 smash
19 sprightly   20 nibble   21 swill   22 thrust   23 smack
24 prowl   25 hurl   26 spry   27 agile   28 nimble   29 munch
30 grab

R13 Give the British English equivalents of the following words and expressions:

1 pack (of cigarettes)   2 sidewalk   3 fall (season)   4 quit (eg work)   5 homestead   6 hire (a worker)   7 subways
8 gas(oline)   9 automobile   10 beltway   11 railroad crossing
12 elementary school

R14 Which of these words are likely to be used in colloquial style?

1 assuage 2 shove 3 snuggle 4 thrust 5 pardon 6 freak
7 alleviate 8 pushy 9 yank 10 obese 11 fragrance 12 hunk
(of meat) 13 felon 14 tuck away 15 bloke 16 savoury
17 slay 18 nab 19 emulate 20 wolf down 21 gobble

R15 Produce a logical and coherent story by filling in the blanks with appropriate words from the list and modifying their form where necessary. Not all of the words mentioned are relevant.

blizzard, sleet, waste, hardware, solar energy, heater, flames,
fragrance, ingredients, deficiency, freaks, junk-food, pie, taste,
larder, catacomb, detrimental, unsightly, finely, gloomy, to crackle,
to lick, to gobble, to wolf down, to pinch, to toss, to sneak,
to grate, to dice, to chop up, to allay, to capture, to devise, to slip,
to stoke up, to rattle, to roar away, to rocket, to ponder, to break
down, to break down, to fill, to swig

Mrs Jones was making a cake. Most of the 1 . . . . . were already in
the mixing bowl, and it only remained to 2 . . . . . the nuts, 3 . . . . .
an apple and 4 . . . . . a little orange peel 5 . . . . . over the mixture.
Her son Peter loved sweet things which was why she was making a
cake. She was putting lots of fruit into it to make up for the
vitamin 6 . . . . . he seemed to be suffering from. She 7 . . . . . the
wooden spoon and 8 . . . . . it into the washing-up bowl. Since he'd
been living away at University she was convinced he'd been eating
nothing but 9 . . . . ., which perhaps was all right for some of those
10 . . . . . there, but not for her son!

Her cakes were so good that her family 11 . . . . . them up almost
before they were cool from the oven, and none of them was above
12 . . . . . into the kitchen when she wasn't there to 13 . . . . . a cake
or a 14 . . . . . . But since Peter had gone away he was less choosy
about his food and seemed unnaturally hungry. He would 15 . . . . .
anything she put in front of him. Sometimes, as she lay in bed she'd
hear him 16 . . . . . quietly into the 17 . . . . ., paper would 18 . . . . .,
and she would know that he was hungry again. Something
19 . . . . . to his health must be happening when he was away. A
fine 20 . . . . . was now falling outside, and the wind 21 . . . . . the
window. It reminded Mrs Jones of her son's recent journey home
from University when his car had 22 . . . . . and he had been stuck
in the middle of a driving 23 . . . . . .

The 24 . . . . . that was coming from the oven now 25 . . . . . the
sitting-room where Peter Jones was 26 . . . . . the fire. In a matter of
minutes the fire was 27 . . . . ., and Peter leant back to watch it. He
was studying computer science and was particularly interested in
the 28 . . . . . side of computers. He was also a keen ecologist,
detested modern 29 . . . . ., and as such, was a devout believer in
30 . . . . . . He had himself tried to 31 . . . . . a 32 . . . . . in his room
at University based on this system, but as yet had not succeeded. In
the meantime he wasn't too unhappy to sit in front of the fire and
watch the flickering 33 . . . . .

R16 Solve the crossword puzzle.

Across

1 Well-covered in flesh and of pleasing appearance (5)
3 minor problem (4)
4 very small quantity of sth to be added to a recipe (4)
7 ant quip (anagram), for 'spicy' (7)
8 cut (past) into small cubes (5)
12 G . . . . . some cheese and spread it over the pie. (5)
13 Cats l . . . . . their kittens to clean them. (4)
14 reduce, temporarily, of worry or doubt (5)
16 move, close to the ground, so as not to be noticed (5)
17 beginning of sth bad (5)
19 People love to g . . . . . about each other's misfortunes. (6)
22 very sour taste (4)
23 prevent progress (6)
24 chit (anagram), for 'a skin irritation' (4)
28 look angrily (5)
30 In autumn the apple trees d . . . . . low, weighed down with fruit. (5)
31 sudden loud noise (4)
32 If you have no money, you can always . . . . . a bank. (3)
33 wet snow (5)
34 Your dog has ch . . . . . my bag! (6)

Down

1 think deeply (6)
2 soften the sound of, eg a trumpet (4)
3 wigs (anagram), for 'drink' (4)
4 succeed in discouraging (5)
5 creep away, guiltily (5)
6 soft, not firm (of the muscles) (6)
9 lower the body to avoid being hit (4)
10 so attractive one cannot resist it (12)
11 the noise snakes make (4)
15 once living organism, turned into rock by geological processes (6)
18 rat (anagram) (3)
20 drink in small amounts (3)
21 took the skin off a potato (6)
25 large, uneven piece (4)
26 seize hold of, with the hand (4)
27 T . . . . . the lettuce in a large bowl. (4)
29 Rule (anagram), for 'to tempt' (4)

Index

Words are listed according to Unit (number in **bold** type) followed by the page number.

ACKNOWLEDGEMENTS

The authors and publishers wish to acknowledge, with thanks, the following
illustration sources, and to state that they have attempted to contact all copyright
holders. In any case where they may have failed, they will be pleased to make any
necessary arrangements at the first opportunity.

John Barnard, p. 205. BBC TV Stills Library, p. 158. J. Brownbill, cover, p. 179.
Camera Press (John Whitman), p. 136. J. Allan Cash Ltd, cover, pp. 41, 63, 108 (top),
114, 203, 206. Derek Harrison, pp. 22, 108 (bottom), 182. Keystone Press Agency, p. 46.
London Express News and Features Service, p. 161. National Film Archive/UIP, p. 64.
Novosti Press Agency, Cover, p. 44. Posy Symmonds, p. 133. Malcolm Wells, p. 204.
John Topham Picture Library, p. 87.

The line drawings and cartoons were supplied by

Graham Allen   Robin Christian   Russel Christian   Maria Fernando   Alan Gilham
Tim Marwood   Malcolm Stokes

Design by Milford Hurley Graphic Design, Basingstoke